DISCLAIMER

The authors and www.PeakCapitalTrading.com ("the Company"), including its employees, contractors, shareholders and affiliates, is NOT an investment advisory service, a registered investment advisor or a broker-dealer and does not undertake to advise clients on which securities they should buy or sell for themselves. It must be understood that a very high degree of risk is involved in trading securities. The Company, the authors, the publisher and the affiliates of the Company assume no responsibility or liability for trading and investment results. Statements on the Company's website and in its publications are made as of the date stated and are subject to change without notice. It should not be assumed that the methods, techniques or indicators presented in these products will be profitable nor that they will not result in losses. In addition, the indicators, strategies, rules and all other features of the Company's products (collectively, "the Information") are provided for informational and educational purposes only and should not be construed as investment advice. Examples presented are for educational purposes only. Accordingly, readers should not rely solely on the Information in making any trades or investments. Rather, they should use the Information only as a starting point for doing additional independent research in order to allow them to form their own opinions regarding trading and investments. Investors and traders must always consult with their licensed financial advisors and tax advisors to determine the suitability of any investment.

STOCK MARKET

EXPLAINED

A Beginner's Guide to

INVESTING

and

TRADING

ARDI AAZIZNIA

AMARYLLIS

AMARYLLIS

An imprint of Manjul Publishing House Pvt. Ltd.
• C-16, Sector 3, Noida, Uttar Pradesh 201301, India
Website: www.manjulindia.com
Registered Office:
• 2nd Floor, Usha Preet Complex, 42 Malviya Nagar,
Bhopal 462 003 – India
Distribution Centres
Ahmedabad, Bengaluru, Chennai, Hyderabad,
Kochi, Kolkata, Mumbai, Noida, Pune

Stock Market Explained: A Beginner's Guide to Investing and Trading
by Ardi Aaziznia

This paperback edition first published in India in 2026

ISBN 978-93-5543-654-2

Printed and bound in India by Repro India Limited

CONTENTS

CHAPTER 1

INTRODUCTION

In early 2020, at exactly the same time that I decided to write this book, the worldwide economy went into a very significant recession. As I sit at my computer and type out this introduction, cities, counties, states, provinces, and even entire countries are in lockdown and all non-essential activities and travel are prohibited. Unemployment has reached unprecedented levels and too many people in virtually every country have lost their job or business. The U.S. stock market, as well as stock markets in Europe, and in Asia, and elsewhere have dropped more than 30%. The stock market crash has been among the top news stories on almost every single news channel and social media platform. When I did a search on Google Trends, I found a very interesting correlation between searches for "COVID-19" and for "Stock Market", as shown in Figure 1.1 below.

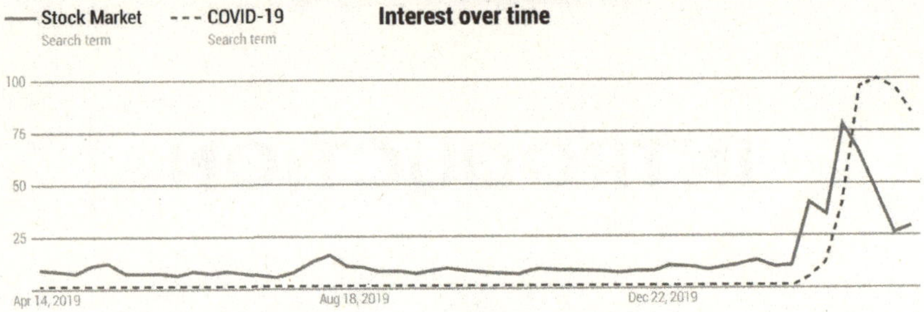

Figure 1.1: "COVID-19" and "Stock Market" keyword Google search trends between April 2019 and April 2020. As you can see, there is a clear correlation. As the stock market drop hit the news cycles, people started searching more and more about the stock market in Google!

I find the most interesting observation in the above figure to be that as the stock market crashed, and its drop made the news, people wanted to learn more about the stock market. This correlation is in fact visible in almost every previous stock market crash, including the 2008 financial crisis and the 2001 dot-com bubble, the latter being when the excessively exaggerated and mostly overvalued prices of the majority of Internet and tech companies burst.

The most recent market volatility of course arises from the COVID-19 pandemic, which has resulted in a horribly painful global recession, as shown by Figure 1.2 below.

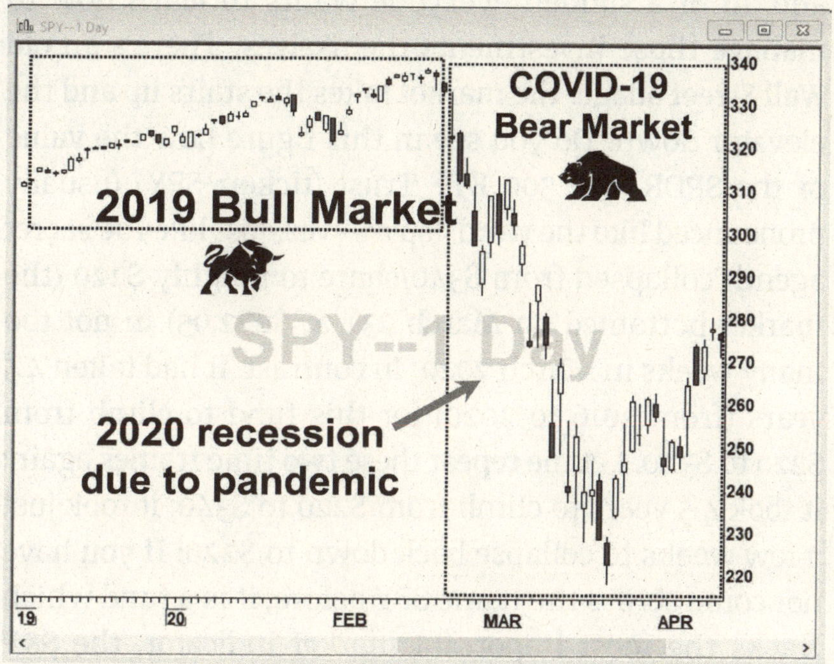

Figure 1.2: Comparison between the bull market of 2019 and the bear market of 2020, as shown by the change in share value of 500 of the largest American companies. These companies are tracked by the S&P 500 and are traded in an exchange-traded fund known as the SPDR S&P 500 ETF Trust (ticker: SPY). For your information, S&P refers to Standard & Poor's, one of the indices which used to track this information.

It is during bear markets that stock markets usually hit the news headlines. Figure 1.2 shows a comparison between the 2019 bull market and the 2020 bear market. As you can see, movements in share value are slow and gradual during bull markets, but bear markets are volatile, and wild, and that's when the general public starts to notice the stock market. That's the moment when everyone becomes concerned about their investments, and all of a sudden everyone wants to learn how to manage those investments themselves. There's an old Wall Street adage: the market takes the stairs up and the elevator down. Do you see in this figure how the value of the SPDR S&P 500 ETF Trust (ticker: SPY) (usually pronounced like the word "spy" - yes, just like the secret agent!) collapsed from $340/share to roughly $220 (the market bottomed on March 23rd at $222.95) in not too many weeks in March 2020. In contrast, it had taken 4.5 years (from 2016 to 2020) for this fund to climb from $220 to $340. Let me repeat these two time frames again: it took 4.5 years to climb from $220 to $340; it took just a few weeks to collapse back down to $220! If you have not come across the name SPY before, it is a fund which tracks the most important market indicator, the S&P 500, which itself is based on the share prices of 500 of the largest companies in the U.S.

I have been working in the finance industry for several years. My role as an investment analyst entails me finding investment opportunities for high-net-worth individuals as well as helping them manage their multi-million-dollar portfolios. Most of the clients I have dealt with through my work are "***investors***" in the stock market. Their money is *invested* in various asset classes in the financial markets, including the stock market, with growth aimed for a period of around 5 to 10 years. (If you are not familiar with the term, stocks, currency, real estate, fixed income investments, cash, and commodities are some of the different "asset classes".) With the start of COVID-19 and the sudden uncertainty in the market, I received numerous calls from my clients, families and friends asking for my professional advice on their investment portfolios. Almost every person I talked to felt helpless, and was looking for some guidance in order to save as much of their money as possible. In some cases, I was dealing with people nearing retirement who had just lost more than 30% of their savings in a matter of weeks. We saw one of the fastest bear markets in history ("bear market" is a term used when the market drops more than 20% in value) and many people lost not just their jobs but also their savings.

Unlike me, who digs into the financial statements of companies and spends hours developing financial models with various computer programs, Andrew, who contributed two chapters to this book, is a seasoned "***trader***" of the stock market, and that is a different category of market participant. Andrew is not an investor. He tracks U.S. and global stock market prices on a much shorter term basis. He's looking at 1-minute, 5-minute and hourly price movements. He is not that interested in learning about balance sheets, sales targets, numbers of employees, or the way a company's management is approaching future growth. As a trader, he is more interested in the price changes of a stock over smaller time frames, and he tries to profit from volatility. Andrew is a technical trader. I will touch base on the terms "technical" and "fundamental" in coming chapters, but please keep in the back of your mind that you can always go and have a look at the glossary at the end of this book whenever you want to learn more about a term I have used but not yet fully explained.

The COVID-19 pandemic has also of course affected traders. Andrew shared with me that these unprecedented times are an excellent opportunity for someone to benefit from the market's volatility, but in order to do so they must first be equipped with the proper tools for trading as well as have the necessary knowledge about the stock market. However, as Andrew is seeing every day, many novice traders who do not know how the market works, nor how to correctly enter the market, and have no carefully thought-out trading plan, are seriously hurting themselves and losing their hard-earned savings. These are the times that you definitely must know what you are doing before you enter the market and place your first trade. Andrew manages a proprietary trading firm in Canada, Peak Capital Trading (*PeakCapitalTrading.com*), and also trades with a group of active traders in an online trading community, Bear Bull Traders (*BearBullTraders.com*). He noticed that as the market became more volatile, and that volatility was making headlines, more and more new traders joined their group, but those new traders experienced a much higher rate of failure than usual. This is because many people who have joined their group for trading are not prepared in the least and they in all honesty should not be trading. I wrote this book, and Andrew contributed two chapters, because we both sincerely want to help those who are interested in learning about the stock market amid this volatility (remember Figure 1.2?).

Writing this book was inspired by all of those telephone calls and conversations I had with my clients, as well as in observing how so many people are now interested in learning "anything and everything" there is to know about the stock market. I thus decided to collaborate with Andrew in writing a simple, easy-to-understand, but also comprehensive book that will serve as an introduction into the world of stock markets, regardless of whether the reader is an investor or trader. Andrew is already a successful author, having published several books about trading. He made a bold move several years back and shifted his career from working as an engineer and scientist to being involved in the financial markets and following his true passion of teaching and mentoring others. Andrew and I both attended the University of British Columbia in Vancouver, Canada. I asked Andrew if he would be interested in sharing with my readers his knowledge and expertise about trading in the stock market. He (thankfully) agreed and here is our finished product. Andrew and I usually run together several times a week, and it was on these runs, rain or shine, that we brainstormed on how best to present all of this information to you.

My goal in writing this book is to not just teach you how to maneuver through the difficult times in the market, but better yet, I want to teach you how to profit from them. If your desire is to trade, I will provide you with techniques you could use during these times of high volatility. If you are an investor, by the time you reach the end of this book you will be familiar with the tactics necessary to make your portfolio resilient and to protect your investment from a recession or market downturn.

Many classic books on investing and trading have survived the proverbial test of time. Two of my favorites are *The Intelligent Investor* by Benjamin Graham (published in 1949) and *Beating the Street* by Peter Lynch (published in 1993). Both of these books, and many more, are very useful reads and a serious trader or investor should have a selection of them on their bookshelf. However, the financial market has changed significantly in the last decades. Trading the stock market used to be reserved for only the Wall Street elites. The average Joe, as well as the average Jane of course, did not have access to the proper tools and platforms for trading, nor any direct access to the markets. Commissions were high, trading or investing was expensive, and while intriguing to many, the markets were also a mystery to most folks. In the last 15 years though, there has been a massive shift in the financial market. The Internet provides access to almost all of the information you could ever need, and there are new brokers such as Robinhood Markets, Inc. which offer commission-free platforms in their apps. The information asymmetry previously in place between Wall Street and Main Street has narrowed to the point where you, sitting in your home, can have access to thousands of equity research reports on the companies which have caught your interest. I'd be remiss if I did not also mention the DIY (do it yourself) attitude of millennials. We are wired to do things for ourselves. They may not all be millennials, but a whole new generation clearly believes they have deciphered the mysteries of Wall Street. Each day, more and more people enter the stock market as traders or investors. There is now a plethora of web-based platforms available, and there are a multitude of free or low-cost online education and training programs, as well as resources such as YouTube, Wikipedia and Investopedia. Nevertheless, it's important to remember that while the stock market is more accessible, it's still not an easy way to make quick money. The stock markets are complicated to understand and require a proper level of education and expertise. Without the proper preparations, the markets remain a very dangerous place for your money.

HOW THIS BOOK IS ORGANIZED

As I mentioned, Andrew is an active trader who has already published and co-authored several best-selling books on trading in the stock market. He suggested that this book should be aimed at people who have an interest in the stock market, but do not necessarily have any formal education or background in it, just like many of our mutual friends. I agreed with Andrew that this book should cover both the "*investing*" and "*trading*" aspects of the stock market, but that I wouldn't overwhelm readers with too many of the details of each element. I will hopefully provide you with sufficient information so that you can decide if being a *day trader*, *swing trader*, or an <u>investor</u> in the stock market is the most appropriate choice for you, and I hope to guide you to the next level as a trader or as an investor, or even both.

Learning about trading and investing is important, regardless of which one suits where you are at in your life right now. In my opinion, the most profitable investors are those who understand technical analysis and the basics of trading. Similarly, the best traders I have met are the ones who have a working knowledge about fundamental analysis. The two concepts truly do go hand in hand and help one another. I therefore recommend you to at least skim over each section of this book, despite whether you identify yourself primarily as a trader or as an investor.

I wrote this book in relatively simple language so that it would be understandable to the largest number of readers possible. I deliberately tried to stay away from using too much jargon. At the same time, I wanted the book to also be beneficial to people who have some background knowledge about trading and/or investing. Therefore, I do introduce more advanced topics such as exchange-traded funds (ETFs), common technical indicators used when trading, and what a company's financial fundamentals are. I'll admit, it turned out to be a bit of a delicate task balancing technical knowledge with simplicity. It is important to emphasize that learning about and then profiting from the world of the stock market is a lifelong pursuit, and if you are a so-called "newbie", by reading this book you are about to embark on what Andrew and I consider to be a fascinating journey (and we hope you will too!). However, by no means is this book designed to turn you into the next hedge fund manager or the greatest trader in the world. Reading one or two books won't be enough for success in any subject, and the stock market is no different. This book is your introductory guide. If, after reading this book, you feel as passionate about the financial markets as we do, we encourage you to continue learning and growing.

I decided to break this book into 5 sections as shown conceptually in Figure 1.3: (1) stock market basics, (2) reading the charts, (3) day trading, (4) swing trading, and (5) investing through the stock market. My goal was to make this book as inclusive as possible. Working in finance, I know very well that people have different expectations with regard to their investing and trading. Some individuals are looking for a consistent cash flow right now, and some have their future retirement in mind and thus take a longer term view. This book is written for both audiences. Since I have less familiarity with day trading and Andrew is a well-established trader, I asked him to provide some commentary on the fundamentals of day trading, strategies he uses for trading, as well as what it takes for someone to be successful in day trading. You'll find that material in Chapters 5 and 6 of this book.

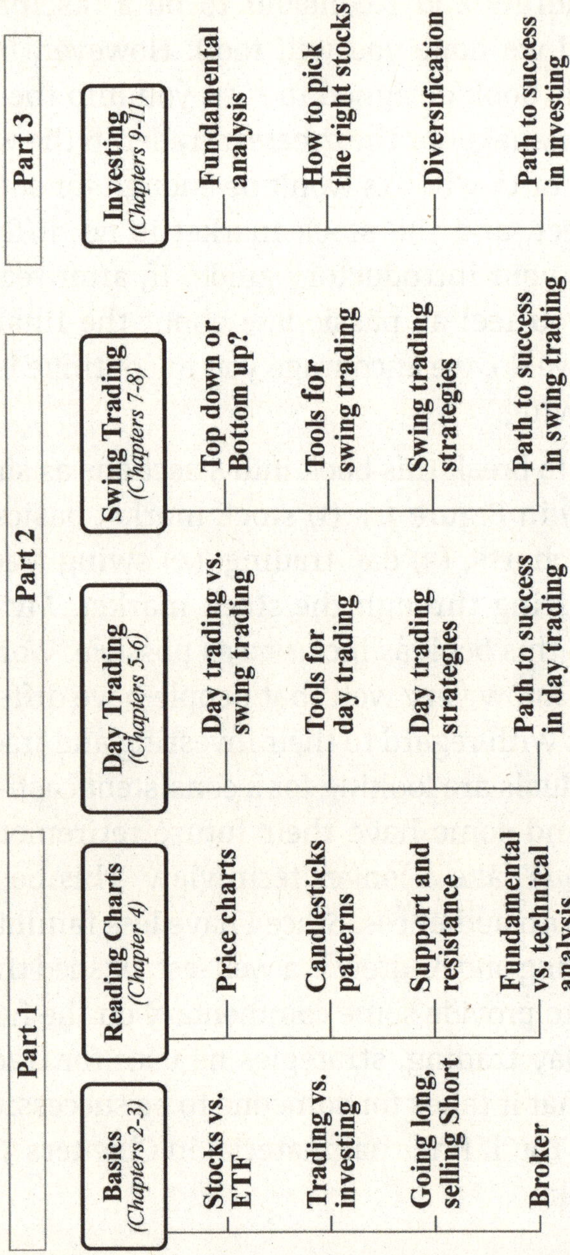

Figure 1.3: How this book is organized. Chapters 1-4 and 7-11 are written by me. Chapters 5 and 6 on day trading are written by Andrew Aziz.

Part 1 of this book includes Chapters 2 and 3, which are dedicated to the important basics one needs to learn before entering the stock market. This book is a great introduction for the reader who has no or minimal experience in the stock market and is looking for a practical step-by-step guide to prepare them in order to be either an investor or trader. The stock market can be overwhelming. You wouldn't believe how much finance-related "lingo" there is to learn plus, for most people, trying to make sense of all of the charts and numbers can be a daunting task. All of this results in many individuals leaving their investments with banks. Regrettably, many banks do not feel any sort of obligation to educate their clients and they at times may sell them financial products that often perform far worse than the stock market does. Therefore, it is important for new generations of savvy traders and investors to learn more about the market and not to always take the word of bankers at face value.

Chapter 2 describes the two main methods of generating wealth - trading and investing - which are then discussed in considerable detail in future chapters. The most important element in Chapter 2, and even in the whole book, is to learn the differences between trading and investing. Both Andrew and I have found that distinguishing between these two activities can cause substantial confusion for many newcomers to the stock market.

Do you want to be an investor, a trader, or both?

There is nothing wrong with being only a trader. There is also nothing wrong with being only an investor. On the other hand, many people do some of both or at least are interested in learning about both. Andrew, for example, has several longer term investment portfolios. He is also a well-known day trader, trading in shorter time frames with other accounts. I can't emphasize enough how important it is to understand this distinction. In my opinion, the most important lesson you want to take away from this book is the ability to define yourself in the stock market. Are you an investor? Are you a trader? Are you both? And how you define yourself, and the goals and expectations you have, will hugely impact the next steps you will take after reading this book. For example, traders need a different type of broker, platform, and approach than investors do. Many banks and brokers who offer investment services are actually not suitable for active traders. And many brokers who offer trading services are not suitable for investors. In Chapter 2, I will help you decide which part of the stock market you would like to benefit from: trading or investing.

In Chapters 2 and 3, I explain what stocks, indices, mutual funds and exchange-traded funds (ETFs) are, and I break down and simplify some of the common language used in the world of finance. I discuss the differences between various stock exchanges as well as the differences between the three types of brokerage firms. I will teach you what it means to go long or to sell short a stock and how you can profit from each method.

In Chapter 4, I will teach you some of the basics of technical analysis. I explain different charts, including those which use bars or candlesticks, and I describe how to correctly interpret charts and candlesticks when trading or investing. I also introduce some of the well-known candlestick patterns such as *Head and Shoulders* and *Cup and Handle*. I then break down support and resistance levels, and their importance in both trading and investing. Think of Chapter 4 as the alphabet of the stock market. In order to trade or invest, you first need to know the ABCs. Therefore, if you are totally new to the world of the stock market, please pay close attention to this chapter.

Part 2 of this book is focused on trading in the stock market. In Chapter 5, Andrew explains what day trading is and he discusses two well-known strategies used by traders. Information on additional resources is also included for those readers who are interested in learning more. In Chapter 6, Andrew outlines what the various "essentials" are in order to become a successful day trader along with some of the main "to dos" and "not to dos" every new day trader must know before entering into the market. Throughout these chapters, Andrew shares anecdotes from both his own day trading experiences as well as those of traders he works with.

In Chapters 7 and 8, the swing trading section of this book, I detail the more common strategies and technical indicators used by swing traders, and I discuss the top-down and bottom-up approaches to identifying Stocks in Play. I provide examples from trades, amply illustrated with price action charts, to help you better understand the various strategies and technical indicators being described. Further, I share some of the common mistakes novice traders make which every new swing trader should be aware of.

The third and last part of the book, which includes Chapters 9 through 11, is focused on investing in the stock market. In this section, I discuss some of the strategies commonly used in the asset management industry. You will learn about growth and value stocks and I provide key guidance on how to identify each one. I will teach you how to read the income statement, balance sheet, and cash flow statement of companies and what to look for before investing in any stock. Examples from actual trades are utilized throughout and free resources are referenced to help you in your journey as an investor. I will teach you key techniques necessary to create a well-diversified portfolio and, using a portfolio that I manage as an example, I demonstrate how I use the techniques taught in this book to manage my client's money. Similar to the day trading and swing trading sections, I also include some comments on the "to dos" and "not to dos" that every investor needs to understand.

As I mentioned just a few pages previously, this book is meant to be understandable to the person who has little or no experience with the stock market but has the intellectual curiosity to learn. As the book advances, I slowly and carefully introduce various technical terms so you can easily follow along. I have included at the back of this book a handy and helpful glossary of the most common terms you will come across in the world of finance. If, as you are reading this book, there is a term or phrase that you don't recall the meaning of, please go and have a look at its definition in the glossary. Andrew and I have used easy to understand language to explain the "lingo" of Wall Street.

Finally, if by the end of this book you feel confident that you would like to start trading or investing, please send me an email at ardi@peakcapitaltrading.com. In return, I will send you a supplementary presentation, as well as including you in our biweekly newsletter mailing list, which was previously available only to our traders. This newsletter is an especially useful collection of information that my research team at Peak Capital Trading and I regularly compile to highlight macro trends, investing and trading opportunities, and major events that might impact your portfolio. We dig deep into 13-F filings of the best-performing fund managers and review 10-k forms of many companies to provide trends and opportunities that you might otherwise miss. If terms like 10-k and 13-F sound overwhelming, please don't worry. You will learn about them in the upcoming chapters.

Buckle up and enjoy the ride!

CHAPTER 2

THE STOCK MARKET: A MONEY MACHINE OR THE VALLEY OF DEATH

WHAT ARE STOCKS?

I'm sure you've heard of the term, the "*American Dream*". The premise of the expression is simple: if you work hard in America, you can make it in America. Owning a business is one of the fastest ways to make the "American Dream" a reality, whether it is operating a restaurant or becoming a doctor.

Buying stock is the same concept. When you buy a share of a company, you become a business owner. Like every owner, you get to share in the profits, suffer in the losses, and (theoretically at least) have a say in the important decisions the company makes. And just like owning any business, there are risks and rewards associated with the decisions you and the other shareholders make.

Let's break this concept down with an example. If you buy a share of Apple Inc. (ticker: AAPL), you own part of Apple's business. At the time that I am writing this part of the book, Apple is trading at $242 per share. So, for $242, you can own a piece of America's favorite tech company. You get a share of the profits through dividends (more on this later), you get to benefit if there's an appreciation in the value of its shares (e.g., the value of your share rises from $242 to $243 (or hopefully even higher), which is called a capital gain in the world of finance), and you get to have your say in Apple's direction by voting at shareholder meetings.

There are two types of equities or shares: private and public. Private equities are shares that are not available to the public for purchase. As an example, Shopify Inc. (ticker: SHOP) was established in 2004, but from then until 2015 only a few venture capitalists were able to invest in the company. It was not until 2015, when it was dual listed on both the Toronto and New York Stock Exchanges, that "ordinary" people could be part of the Shopify success. Airbnb, Inc. is another very large company that almost everyone has heard of, if not used, but this San Francisco-based company remains private, although prior to the COVID-19 pandemic they were considering going public at some point in 2020.

Public equities are shares that are available to institutional and retail investors (retail investors are individuals like you, the reader of this book, while institutional investors are the Wall Street investment banks and other so-called "big guns"). An initial public offering, also known as an IPO, occurs when a company issues its shares to the public for the first time.

An IPO is an excellent option for a company that needs to quickly raise capital, generally in order to expand and/or continue their operations. Going public gives a company access to a larger pool of money than they would usually acquire as a private equity. Two examples of familiar companies which took this route to raise capital are Tesla Inc. (ticker: TSLA) and Uber Technologies Inc. (ticker: UBER). Nonetheless, going public comes with certain disadvantages too, one being that it can be quite expensive to follow all of the stringent regulations and reporting standards set by various national securities and exchange commissions.

WHY INVEST IN THE STOCK MARKET?

If you listen to the news daily, the chances are good that you frequently hear about "the market". The news you hear may be positive, such as the market hitting all-time highs or Apple Inc. (ticker: AAPL) becoming the first trillion-dollar company. It may also be negative, such as the coronavirus wiping $9 trillion out of the global financial markets in just a few days. Despite being regularly discussed on TV shows, on radio programs, as well as online, "the market", the mysterious market, is still a foreign concept to many. One reason may be that more than 50% of Americans do not own any stocks, not directly, and not even indirectly through their retirement accounts. People are definitely interested in learning more about the financial markets, but they do not know how to go about starting their studies (whether on an informal or formal basis). After all, the 2008 crash left many folks cynical of the system, thinking that they can never "beat Wall Street".

The truth is that investing or trading in the market can be an extremely complex undertaking. In the case of hedge funds and large wealth management funds, there are algorithms, regression analysis and hedging strategies (more on these in later chapters) that are used to ensure there is limited exposure to market downturns while also ensuring potentially unlimited upsides. Notwithstanding the complexity inherent in investing or trading, the idea behind the stock market and the ownership of shares of companies is a very simple one. As I've stated before, the goal of this book is not to make you a hedge fund manager (although nothing is impossible and I believe this book is a great start). My goal is to teach you the fundamentals necessary to get going. The stock market is the greatest opportunity "machine" in existence today. It truly can level the playing field for every single working class man and woman.

Let's take the S&P 500 as an example, which includes 500 of the largest companies that are listed in the U.S. As they state on their website, "[it] is widely regarded as the best single gauge of large-cap U.S. equities. There is over USD 9.9 trillion indexed or benchmarked to the index ..." If you read through a list of these 500 companies, I guarantee you would recognize most of their names. Since the inception of its current format in 1957 through to 2018, the S&P 500 had an average annual return of 7.96% (this is the average annual return, there have been years where the return has been considerably less and other years where the return has been considerably more). Comparing an average annual return of 7.96% with a traditional savings account (a 1 to 2% return if you are lucky) or a 30-year Treasury bond (a lower than 1.5% return), is a fairly easy way to demonstrate the importance of stocks and owning equities, in addition to the value of having at least a rudimentary understanding of the financial markets. A similar type of comparison is set out visually in Figure 2.1 below.

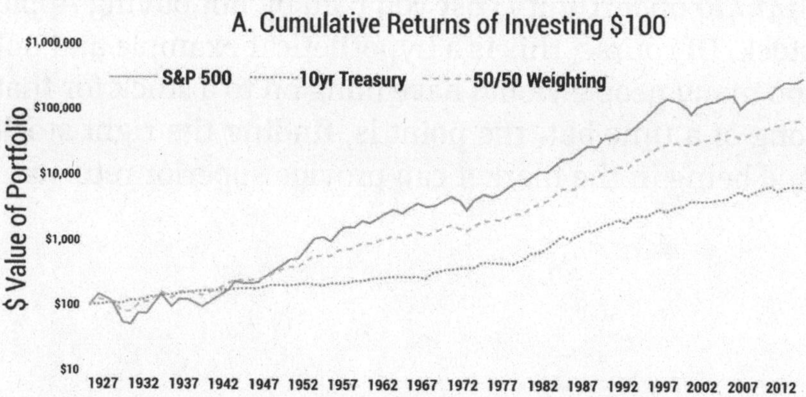

Figure 2.1: The return on investing $100 in an exchange-traded fund known as the SPDR S&P 500 ETF Trust (ticker: SPY) (which tracks the share value of 500 of the largest American companies (as rated by the S&P 500)) vs. investing $100 in the U.S. Treasury bond market vs. investing $100 in a balanced portfolio comprised of 50% stocks and 50% bonds. As you can see, adding stocks to your portfolio can magnify your return in comparison to traditionally safer investments.

Figure 2.2 below compares a hypothetical $300 investment in the stock of Apple Inc. (ticker: AAPL) in 2001 vs. depositing your money in a high-interest savings account with an annual interest rate of 5%. Why $300 you ask? Well, because around the same time (October 2001 to be exact), Apple released its legendary iPod for $299. Let's say you decided not to buy the iPod but instead invested your money. $300 invested in Apple in 2001 would have been worth more than $142,000 in the spring of 2020. This does not include the over $5,000 dividend you would have received in the same time period and which you could have reinvested. On the other hand, your $300 deposited in a high-interest savings account would have been worth $590 in the spring of 2020. That is a whopping $141,410 opportunity cost you paid by not buying Apple stock. Of course, this is a hypothetical example and not too many people would have hung on to a stock for that long of a time but, the point is, finding the right stock and being in the market can provide superior returns.

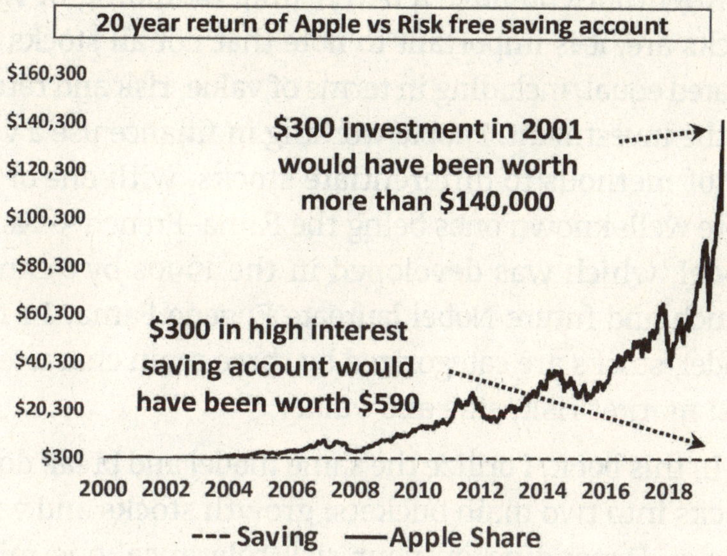

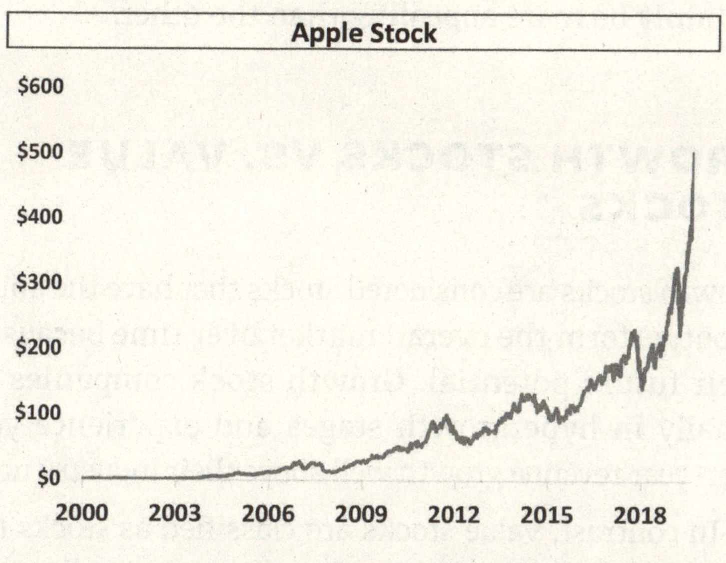

Figure 2.2: A hypothetical $300 investment in the stock of Apple Inc. (ticker: AAPL) in the beginning of 2001 would have increased to over $140,000 by April 2020. This is despite 3 major crashes: the dot-com bubble of 2001, the financial crisis of 2008, and the pandemic of 2020. By comparison, the same $300 investment in a high-interest savings account would have only been worth $590 in 2020.

Now that you have a better understanding of what stocks are, it is important to note that not all stocks are created equal, including in terms of value, risk and return on the investment. People working in finance use a variety of methods to differentiate stocks, with one of the more well-known ones being the Fama-French 3-Factor Model, which was developed in the 1990s by Kenneth French and future Nobel laureate Eugene Fama. In this model, stocks are categorized by three main characteristics: market risk, size and value.

In this book, I utilize the same model and break down stocks into two main buckets: growth stocks and value stocks. Depending on your risk tolerance, one might certainly be more appealing than the other.

GROWTH STOCKS VS. VALUE STOCKS

Growth stocks are considered stocks that have the ability to outperform the overall market over time because of their future potential. Growth stock companies are usually in hypergrowth stages and experience year-over-year revenue growth well above their industry norm.

In contrast, value stocks are classified as stocks that are currently trading below what they are actually worth and are, therefore, expected to provide a superior return. Value stock companies are at more mature stages in their life cycle and are growing at about the same rate as the U.S. GDP.

Figure 2.3 below summarizes some of the key differences between growth stocks and value stocks. Figure 2.4 below provides a visual representation of the performance of a well-known growth stock vs. a well-known value stock from 2016 to 2019.

Value Stock	Growth Stock
Shorter time horizon	Longer time horizon, Often not profitable yet
Pays regular dividend	No dividend
Grows at speed of national economy (GDP)	Grows much faster than national economy
Excellent for people near retirement	Excellent for younger people with 10-15 years time horizon

Figure 2.3: Value stocks are ideal for people near retirement or those who are looking for steady cash flow. In contrast, growth stocks could provide a far greater return on investment in the long run but can also be much riskier.

Let's again use Shopify Inc. (ticker: SHOP) as an example. (Why you ask? Well, my bias is that I am a proud Canadian, and Shopify is a Canadian tech powerhouse!) In the past five years, Shopify has been growing at 50 to 60% year-over-year. To put this into perspective, most companies on average grow in the low- to mid-single digits every year. The shares of Shopify are definitely growth stock. Shopify also at this time is not paying any dividends and is instead reinvesting its money.

Most growth stocks may be losing money per share, but an avid investor will still buy these shares because of the growth potential. They can be found in many different sectors, with some notable ones being the shares of Uber Technologies Inc. (ticker: UBER), Netflix Inc. (ticker: NFLX), Facebook, Inc. (ticker: FB), and Amazon.com Inc. (ticker: AMZN). As you know from the news, all of these companies are expanding operations and growing fast. Each could easily be considered the future of their industry (transportation, entertainment, communications and commerce, respectively). In addition, they pay no dividends (yet) and they all have huge upside potential. It is important to note that while growth stocks do have a huge upside potential due to their high growth nature, they are also the most sensitive to economic slowdowns, and once analysts believe they have reached their potential, they will quickly lose their growth stock status.

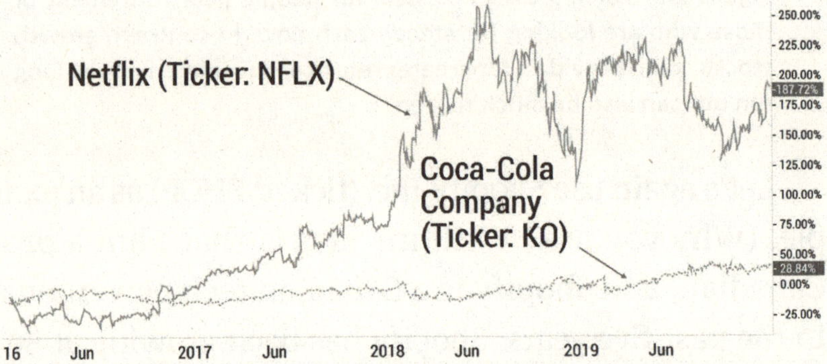

Figure 2.4: Performance of the shares of Netflix Inc. (ticker: NFLX), a growth stock, vs. the shares of The Coca-Cola Company (ticker: KO), a value stock, from 2016 to 2019. Coca-Cola pays dividends and offers its investors a steady cash flow, however Netflix outperforms Coca-Cola in terms of capital gains.

On the other hand, the shares of larger, more well-established companies that are at the maturity stage of their life cycle are often categorized as value stocks. These companies have steady cash flow from their activities and pay reasonably high dividends. In most cases, these companies are conglomerates, owning multiple brands under their umbrella. In contrast to growth stock companies, recessions and economic slowdowns provide opportunities for value stock companies to consolidate the market and buy up other businesses.

Chevron Corporation (ticker: CVX) is a good example. It is a well-established global energy conglomerate with operations in upstream, midstream and downstream production. Chevron's dividend yield (explained in Chapter 9) is about 6% (more than 4 times a Treasury yield) and the company is in its mature stage. No investor expects Chevron, or for that matter the oil industry in general, to grow exponentially any longer; therefore, investors expect to be compensated by a steady income in the form of a dividend. In addition, now that oil prices are at an all-time low (around $30/barrel as of writing this chapter, in comparison to a high of $60 in 2019), Chevron has the opportunity to consolidate the market by buying up some of the smaller players who are struggling.

Some other value stock company examples are Exxon Mobil Corporation (ticker: XOM), Johnson & Johnson (ticker: JNJ), AT&T Inc. (ticker: T), JPMorgan Chase & Co. (ticker: JPM), and General Electric Company (ticker: GE). Each of these companies is in its mature stage and each is able to guarantee a steady cash flow.

STOCK EXCHANGES: A BRIEF REVIEW

Stocks are usually bought and sold on what are called "stock exchanges". A stock exchange is simply a place where buyers and sellers meet to either exchange their shares for money or their money for shares. In the past, the stock exchange was strictly a building, and in order to make a transaction you had to telephone or personally attend. But now, most exchanges are electronic as well as brick and mortar, and all trades can be made online.

One of the exchanges' key functions is providing liquidity in the market. During the 2020 coronavirus pandemic, although exchanges were empty in New York City and elsewhere due to social distancing rules and lockdowns, they remained open virtually to provide investors with access to the liquidity they need. (As an aside, successful traders need liquidity, there must be both a sufficient volume of stock being traded in a particular company and a sufficient number of orders being sent to the exchanges for filling to ensure you can easily get in and out of a trade. You want plenty of buyers and plenty of sellers all eyeing the same stock.)

The two most well-known exchanges in the U.S. are the New York Stock Exchange (NYSE) and the Nasdaq. The NYSE is the largest exchange in the world and is recognized for its high quality (blue chip) stocks like The Coca-Cola Company (ticker: KO) and McDonald's Corporation (ticker: MCD). As you can no doubt imagine, there are a number of requirements to be met before a company is approved for listing on the NYSE, one being that their shares must always trade at a price above $4. It is considered a badge of honor to be listed on a prestigious exchange such as the NYSE.

The Nasdaq is the world's leading electronic exchange and is best known for its tech stocks such as Netflix Inc. (ticker: NFLX) and Apple Inc. (ticker: AAPL). Similar to the NYSE, companies listed on the Nasdaq must follow certain U.S. Securities and Exchange Commission (SEC) regulations. These include the filing of quarterly and annual reports, which in return help an unsophisticated investor make more solid investment decisions.

One of the main differences between the NYSE and the Nasdaq is that while the NYSE has a trading floor with traders and dealers present, the Nasdaq operates exclusively online and all transactions are electronic in nature. Although the NYSE has a physical space (you may very well have seen news coverage of the ringing of the opening or closing bell by a celebrity or other prominent individual), traders can also trade stocks listed on the NYSE electronically. As of April 2020, the Nasdaq is home to 3800 companies and the NYSE is listing 2400 companies.

There are of course also other exchanges in the market, some of which are called "over-the-counter" exchanges (or OTC exchanges, for short). These exchanges usually feature smaller companies which are either not eligible to be listed on the Nasdaq or the NYSE, or for some reason have been delisted from those larger and more credible exchanges. One of the better known OTC exchanges is the Over-the-Counter Bulletin Board or OTCBB. The OTCBB is an electronic community of market makers (a broker-dealer that offers shares for sale or purchase on the exchange). Companies that fall off of the Nasdaq often end up listing in the OTCBB.

If you are new to investing, my advice is to stay away from the over-the-counter exchanges, as these exchanges are much less regulated and not as closely scrutinized by the SEC. There are no minimum sales or liquidity thresholds, and companies trading in the OTC markets are not required to release quarterly information (through the filing of an SEC Form 10-Q). This lack of transparency and liquidity can lead to unbearable damages for you as an investor. It is worth noting though that some strong and viable companies have deliberately switched to the OTC markets to avoid the administrative burden and costly fees that accompany regulatory oversight.

Two of the other well-known exchanges in the United States are the NYSE American (formerly known as the American Stock Exchange, or AMEX), where most exchange-traded funds (ETFs) are listed and traded, and the Chicago Mercantile Exchange (CME), where primarily futures, options and commodities are traded. If you are not familiar with the term, "commodities" being traded can include products such as oil, lumber, wheat, currencies or interest rates. I read not too long ago that the original name of the CME in the late 1800s was the Chicago Butter and Egg Board, which suggests a definite focus on the commodities produced by farmers.

INDICES

Indices are basketfuls of stocks that can be weighted based on various factors including their price or market capital (the size of the company). The previously mentioned S&P 500 index, for example, is an index following the share value of 500 of the largest U.S. companies. Another example is the Dow Jones Industrial Average index (DJIA), or simply the Dow, which is a stock market index that measures the stock performance of 30 large companies listed on stock exchanges in the United States. Dating back to 1896, the Dow was initially designed to show the strength of the heavy industrial sector of the U.S. economy. The "Industrial" portion of the name is however largely historical, as many of the modern 30 components have little or nothing to do with heavy industry. As the American economy expanded, new companies emerged, they grew, and subsequently replaced the traditional industrial and resource-based companies that were originally listed. The replacement of General Electric Company (ticker: GE) by the pharmaceutical company, Walgreens Boots Alliance Inc. (ticker: WBA), is one of the most recent changes. General Electric had "qualified" for the first list established in 1896, was delisted, relisted, delisted again, but had then earned a continuous position on the index from 1907 through to 2018. When you hear on the news that the "Dow" is up 500 points, this is the index being referred to. Figure 2.5 below lists the 30 companies indexed on the Dow as of April 2020. As you can see, non-industrial companies such as Nike Inc. (ticker: NKE), Apple Inc. (ticker: AAPL), and The Walt Disney Company (ticker: DIS) are included, but giants like GE are missing. As an aside, the reasons for that specific revision to the list were decreases in the value of General Electric's shares as well as questions about the overall future of the company.

30 Companies Comprising the Dow		
Microsoft	Home Depot	Nike
Apple	Walt Disney	IBM
Visa	Coca-Cola	Raytheon Technologies
JP Morgan Chase	Verizon	American Express
Johnson & Johnson	Merck & Co	3M
Walmart	Pfizer	Goldman Sachs
Procter & Gamble	Chevron	Caterpillar
Intel	Cisco Systems	Walgreens
UnitedHealth	Boeing	Dow
Exxon Mobil	McDonald's	Travelers

Figure 2.5: The 30 companies that comprise the Dow Jones Industrial Average index as of April 2020. As you can see, many of the companies represent the Information Technology Sector, showing the shift in the U.S. economy from an industrial and resource-based focus to a service focus.

One useful purpose for indices is that they can be used to measure the performance of mutual funds and exchange-traded funds (ETFs). For instance, many companies which offer mutual funds will compare their returns to those of the S&P 500, and that helps consumers to decide if it would be more advantageous to invest their money in a particular mutual fund or in an index fund.

ETFS VS. MUTUAL FUNDS

ETFs

An exchange-traded fund is a collection of securities that often tracks an underlying index although they can also be invested in any number of industries or sectors. ETFs are listed on exchanges and their shares trade throughout the day just like ordinary stock. Two well-known ETFs that follow indices are the SPDR S&P 500 ETF Trust (ticker: SPY), which (obviously) tracks the S&P 500 index, and Invesco QQQ Trust, Series 1 (ticker: QQQ), which follows the Nasdaq-100 index, which itself tracks 100 of the largest non-financial companies traded on the Nasdaq. It includes many familiar names such as Apple Inc. (ticker: AAPL), Facebook, Inc. (ticker: FB) and Netflix Inc. (ticker: NFLX).

As an example, by purchasing one share of SPY, you will own small, allocated percentages of every stock listed on the S&P 500 index. This means you will own a tiny fraction of a share of Apple Inc. (ticker: AAPL), Alphabet Inc. Class A and Class C (tickers: GOOGL and GOOG, respectively), Berkshire Hathaway Inc. Class B (ticker: BRK.B), and the stocks of 497 other companies, all for the cost of one share of SPY.

ETFs can contain many types of investments, including stocks, commodities and/or bonds. ETFs offer low expense ratios (the cost to operate and manage the fund) and fewer broker commissions than if you were to buy the stocks individually. Since there are multiple assets within an ETF, they can also be a popular choice for diversifying your portfolio. In Chapter 11, I share three of my favorite low-cost ETFs and why they may be an excellent choice based on your risk profile and investment goals.

One of the world's most astute investors, Warren Buffett, has long recognized the value of ETFs. For example, in his Chairman's Letter accompanying the 1993 Berkshire Hathaway Inc. annual report, he wrote, "*By periodically investing in an index fund ... the know-nothing investor can actually out-perform most investment professionals.*"

Mutual Funds

A mutual fund is another way to invest in stocks, bonds, gold, or other assets. The main difference between mutual funds and ETFs is the fact that mutual funds are managed by banks or professional money managers who apportion their funds' assets and attempt to produce capital gains which beat the market index. Because of this, mutual funds have higher expense ratios than ETFs do.

Although I hold certain low-cost mutual funds in my portfolio, my overall view is that they cannot consistently beat the market once all expenses are taken into account. I know there are cases where fund managers such as Peter Lynch crush the performance of the stock market, but for every successful market-beating manager, many more managers underperform. While some may question this argument, considerable research is available to support my conclusion.

One analysis, conducted by Morningstar in 2015, found that fewer than 22% of large-cap stock funds beat the market over the 10-year period from 2005 to the end of 2014.

TRADING VS. INVESTING: WHICH ONE IS RIGHT FOR YOU?

There are two main approaches when it comes to the market. As an individual, you are either a trader (and for most people that often results in being a swing trader or a day trader) or you are an investor. Fundamentally, both have a common goal: to make money. However, there are many differences between the two. This book will explain each approach in detail, but in the end, it is up to you, the reader, to decide if trading or investing is best for you.

When you are trading a stock, you don't really care about the company's fundamentals (which means such aspects of the company as the product or service they sell, their earnings, or what is contained in their financial statements). You do not care whether the stocks you are trading have been issued by a solid company with growing sales, or by a dying business on the verge of bankruptcy. Your aim is to get in the trade, get out of the trade, and be profitable. In addition, the timeline for trading is usually much shorter than it is for investing.

Day traders are in trades for as brief as a few seconds, and then exit as soon as they hit their profit target (for each trade you set up, you should have a specific profit target that your strategy is based upon). Swing traders, on the other hand, might stay in a position for days or even weeks. Your job in both swing trading and day trading is to look for chart patterns and technical indicators so that you may profit from powerful moves on the long side (you buy stock in anticipation of it increasing in price) or short side (you borrow shares from your broker, sell them, and hope that the price goes lower so you can buy them back at the lower price, return the shares to your broker, and keep the profit for yourself).

In comparison, investing has a longer time horizon than trading. You want to focus on stocks that are undervalued with price targets that might take a few years to reach. In investing, you do care about business fundamentals and valuation. You should spend time looking at a company's income statement, balance sheet, cash flow statement and risk levels (and more!) versus the overall market. You also need to look at hedging strategies and how to most effectively minimize your downside (all of which I will discuss later in this book).

Buy and Hold Investing

If you are a buy and hold investor, you care little to none about price swings in a stock. Your main goal is to understand the fundamentals of the business you are considering investing in. You will buy stocks that in your estimate are undervalued and/or have an amazing upside and future. You will use different measurements and tactics to understand a company's business model, their solvency and liquidity, and you will then make an educated long-term investment. Unlike when trading, in a buy and hold investment strategy you do not rely as much on price action charts and technical indicators.

The timeline in investing is far longer than in trading. The minimum horizon until the stock you invested in hits your price target will generally be around two years. In fact, buy and hold investors tend to have a portfolio turnover rate (the rate at which their entire portfolio is bought and sold in a year) below 30 percent.

Day Trading

Even just 15 or 20 years ago, day trading was almost exclusively an activity for the pros on Wall Street, as only they had access to trading tools, platforms and brokers, but with the recent advances in technology and the Internet, many of these tools are now available for people at a very reasonable price.

A day trader (usually) trades a large volume of stocks in both short and long trades in order to profit from intraday (the same day) stock market price fluctuation. The stock market is normally very volatile in the first 2 hours of the market Open (9:30 to 11:30 a.m. New York time). Your job is to look for stocks that are making quick moves to the upside or to the downside in a relatively predictable manner and then, once found, you are going to trade them in one day. You will not keep any position overnight. If you buy stock in Apple Inc. (ticker: AAPL) today, for instance, you will not hold your position overnight and sell it tomorrow. If you hold onto any stock overnight, it is no longer day trading, it's called swing trading. Figure 2.6 below is an example of a day in the life of Apple's shares. You can see how the volume of shares being traded, their price, and their volatility changes as the trading day unfolds.

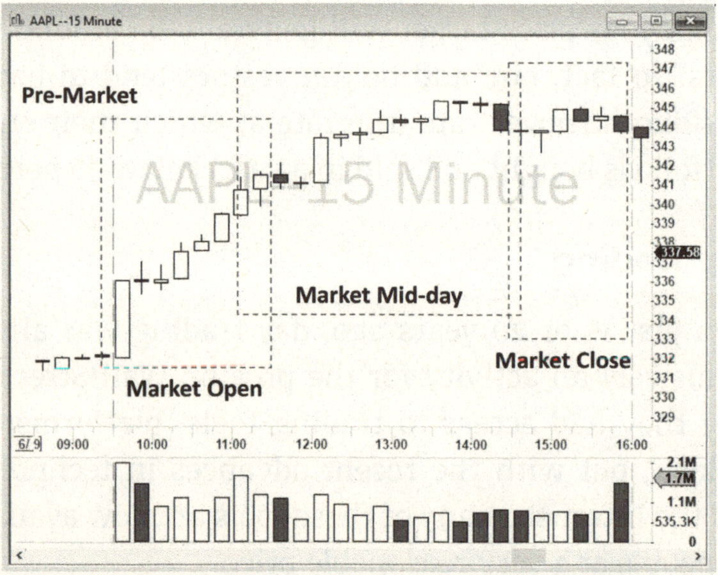

Figure 2.6: A chart showing the volume being traded, the price and the volatility of shares of Apple Inc. (ticker: AAPL) over a single trading day. Note that the volume of shares being traded is high during the Open, it decreases during the Mid-day, and then increases again during the Close. Volume is usually very low in the pre- and post-market. In case you are not familiar with a standard trading chart, volume is shown in the bottom section. You can see that at about 9:30 a.m., the volume of shares being traded was some 2.1 million. Price is shown in the top section of the chart. I will discuss candlesticks (the red and white "boxes" in the top section of this chart) later in this book. They are what track the price of the stock, with the numbers on the right-hand side being the price (for example, at 4:00 p.m., Apple is priced at around $344.00/share).

Day trading requires the right tools, software and education, in addition to an abundance of patience and practice. In order to learn how to trade with real money, you will have to dedicate countless hours to studying trading styles, observing experienced traders, and practicing (and practicing some more) in a simulator. An average successful day trader with a $100,000 account can make between $500 and $1,000 every day.

Swing Trading

Swing trading is the "art and science" of profiting from the short-term price movement of stocks (generally periods of a few days to a few weeks — one or two months, max). It is a trading technique used by everyone from retail investors (you'll recall that these are individuals like you, the reader of this book, people who may have anywhere from a few thousand to several hundred thousand dollars in their account) all the way up to hedge fund managers and institutional traders.

In swing trading, you use technical analysis to identify specific patterns in charts which you can then use to accurately predict the future price movement of a stock. In the pages to come, I will discuss how to trade some of the well-known chart patterns such as "Head and Shoulders" and "Cup and Handle". I will also discuss some of the strategies I use to identify appropriate stocks for swing trading.

A significant difference between swing trading and day trading is the time commitment. A day trader needs to be available for at least the first two hours that the market is open (9:30 to 11:30 a.m. ET). You also require software that provides direct access to the market in real time. For swing trading on the other hand, you could identify a pattern and enter a trade, and then wait a few weeks before you sell your shares for a profit. The end-of-day data that is available on the Internet for free is sufficient for your purposes. While this might give the illusion that swing trading is a more relaxed or laid-back process, it still requires making a meaningful effort to understand the technical analysis, and that of course does take a commitment of time.

None of the trading or investing methods described in this book, including those for swing trading, are going to lead to overnight wealth. Anyone who tells you to the contrary is either lying to you or has made an incredibly risky trade and been lucky with the result. I could go and put $1,000 on a roulette wheel, double my money, and call it a career (that gives me less than a 50% chance to win by the way, so I hope I don't inspire you to (dare I say) give it a spin). Although there is a fine line between calculated risk taking and gambling, trading and investing should never be compared to gambling, and if you have the expectation that they are similar, you should not be reading this book.

As a novice swing trader, you can anticipate your own returns to complement the expected market return. It is important to remember that this "expected market return" projection is not based on historical returns. It is based on what the experts predict the market will make and it will vary depending on different economic outlook forecasts. In 2020, for example, when most analysts see the U.S. GDP shrinking 6 to 10%, the expected market return is around 5%.

As a stellar swing trader, you can expect your returns to be around 20% annually. If you are expecting more returns, then you should look into day trading or possibly purchase a crystal ball!

HOW DO YOU MAKE MONEY IN THE MARKET?

The answer to this very common question is influenced by whether you are planning to invest in the market or trade in the market.

As an investor/shareholder, your money-making chances are tied to company management. Management can create value for their shareholders in three main ways: share price growth, dividend payments and stock buybacks. It is paramount to understand these value creation methodologies, as they in turn will help you pick the best stocks.

Firstly, you want to ensure that the stock has been growing in the past few years. This is called price appreciation or capital gain. After all, some of the value created from owning a stock comes from growth in the value of the company. Figure 2.7 below compares the price of the stock of Apple Inc. (ticker: AAPL) with that of Capri Holdings Limited (ticker: CPRI) (the parent company of Michael Kors, Versace and Jimmy Choo) for the period of 2012 to 2019. As you can see, one company has been on an upward trajectory and the other not so much. While sometimes great investment opportunities come from stocks that are underpriced, you do want to pay close attention to the trend your target company has been on.

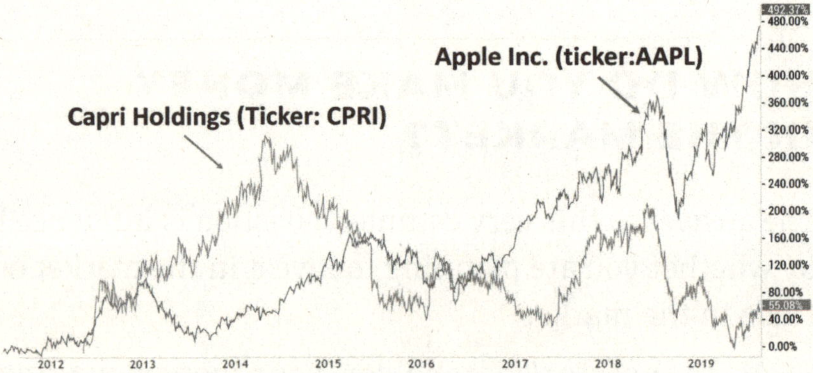

Figure 2.7: The price of stock of Capri Holdings Limited (ticker: CPRI) vs. Apple Inc. (ticker: AAPL) for the period of 2012 to 2019. Although Capri has offered higher dividends, Apple has been able to provide investors with more capital gains due to the value of its stocks growing in this time frame. The growth opportunity of a stock should be an important factor in stock selection.

Secondly, you want to confirm whether or not the company is paying dividends. Some investors pay close attention to this. Kevin O'Leary, founder of O'Leary Funds Inc. and an investor on ABC's hit TV show, *Shark Tank*, occasionally quotes the advice his mother gave him when he was young, "*Never buy a stock that doesn't pay a dividend.*" The logic behind O'Leary's thinking, and his mother's, and many other investors is simple. O'Leary puts it this way, "*70 percent of the time all the return comes from dividend. Yahoo never paid a dividend. It's never made money for anyone except all the CEO's.*" There are many companies that do not pay dividends and grow in value, but in many cases they will lose all of their value before making you (the investor) any money.

And lastly, the third way management and CEOs can create value for their shareholders is through stock buybacks. When management buys its own shares back, it sends a signal to Wall Street and the rest of the markets that its stock is undervalued. Almost always after a buyback, the stock of the company moves up.

If you are a trader on the other hand, your faith is placed in a company's charts and your own technical analysis, and not in the company's management. A trader makes money through speculation and by understanding chart patterns that have a proven track record. In Chapter 4, I detail different strategies that many traders use to successfully speculate and profit in the market.

The amount of return a trader can make depends on their approach, effort, time dedicated to trading, and how much money they have available in their account. A good day trader can expect a 0.5–1% daily return, which with 20 trading days a month can potentially lead up to a return of over 200% each year. At first glance, this is an astonishing return, and seems to be too good to be true because the average Wall Street hedge fund manager only tries to achieve a 10-15% per year return. This type of return is attainable for people trading from their home offices though because it is possible for us to day trade with smaller accounts in the neighborhood of $5,000 to $100,000. If a trader has millions of dollars in their account, they really can't day trade. They are in a similar position to many hedge fund managers who are responsible for billions of dollars of assets. The market is essentially not liquid enough for the type of huge buys and sells required. A multimillion-dollar or multibillion-dollar account needs to be properly broken down between trading and various other investment scenarios. I had a client who wanted to put $5 million aside for day trading. I recommended that he deposit about $4.9 million into long-term investments, and only allocate $100,000 for active trading. A $100,000 account, for a good day trader, can generate $500-$1,000/day of profit, which is a very attractive return.

As referenced not too many paragraphs ago, a seasoned swing trader who carefully tracks each of the trades they enter and uses a well-practiced solid strategy can expect a 20% return per year.

TRADER OR INVESTOR? WHICH IS BETTER?

In my personal opinion, trading and investing are both inherently challenging and demand considerable research and study before the novice will gain the necessary understanding of the market. There are definitely key differences between the two though, which depending upon your preferences would make one more appealing than the other.

Firstly, is the consistent cash flow. If you are looking to produce a regular income which permits you to pay your mortgage or have some extra cash on hand for spending every month, then you should pursue trading rather than investing. Based upon how large your account is and how much time you have to devote to trading, you could potentially earn a predictable monthly income equivalent to what you might receive from a part-time or full-time employment position. In contrast, dividends are the most consistent cash flow you could expect to receive from investing in stocks and, for those companies that do pay dividends, they are often only paid out quarterly.

The second reason to select one method over the other is time and energy. If you choose swing trading, you should expect to put a minimum of one hour each day into reviewing what is transpiring in the markets. You need to track your positions closely and make sure you can execute your trades in a timely manner. If you choose day trading, as stated previously in this chapter, you must be available for at least the first two hours that the markets are open (9:30 to 11:30 a.m. ET). In contrast, if you choose investing, you could go days without checking in. Of course, you really should be monitoring your investments often, but if you have created a well-diversified portfolio, daily movement should not cause you worry.

The third reason you may find you prefer one method more than the other is risk tolerance. In swing or day trading, oftentimes you will short a stock (which means bet against it - as I noted earlier, you borrow shares from your broker, sell them, and hope that the price goes lower so you can buy them back at the lower price, return the shares to your broker, and keep the profit for yourself). While shorting can provide amazing opportunities (you probably have seen the 2015 movie, *The Big Short*, if not, mark where you are in this book and go watch it now!), it also results in immeasurable risk exposure. There are no restrictions on how high a stock can go up in value, but in the worst case scenario its value can in fact literally drop to zero. The potential losses in a short position are therefore unlimited. All in all, if you have a higher tolerance toward risk, then trading is probably a better option for you.

I must reiterate what I wrote before. Trading and investing require studying and research. And lots of it. I'll add to this caveat that they both also require practice. Much practice. If you are the type of person who is solely looking for a rush of adrenaline and you want to treat the market as a get-rich-quick scheme, you will have a better chance of making that happen at a casino. In order for someone to understand and appreciate the markets, the methods I explain in this book will require many hours each week of what the professionals refer to as "due diligence".

By now, you should have an overview of the market, and know the differences between trading and investing. As I explained in Chapter 1, this book has been divided into two main parts: one on trading and one on investing. If you sense you want to invest your money, you could just skip over to Chapters 9 through 11. I recommend you read every chapter regardless of whether trading or investing resonates best with you. In the chapters focused on trading, you will learn about price action charts and certain technical analysis skills that you can use as an investor. In the investing section, I write about fundamental analysis and how you can use it to your advantage even if you are a trader. In my experience, the successful traders are the ones who, in addition to their technical skills, have the ability to interpret a company's fundamentals.

CHAPTER 3

HOW TO ENTER THE WORLD OF THE STOCK MARKET

"The secret of getting ahead is getting started."

—Mark Twain

In this chapter, I am going to discuss brokerage firms as well as review a fairly recent development in brokerage account commissions. I break down the cost structures of the three types of brokers and provide information on their respective pros and cons. I also explain the two different types of accounts you could open with a broker (cash or margin), and I expound on some terms you will likely come across in trading and investing (volume, float, market cap, buying long, selling short).

BROKERAGE OPTIONS: THE GOOD, THE BAD AND THE UGLY

As you've been reading along, an obvious question that may have arisen in your mind is: How do I actually buy stocks?

As an individual trader or investor, you cannot trade directly on a stock exchange. For that, you will need a "broker" or "brokerage account". A broker is simply an intermediary who gives people access to a stock exchange. They're very similar to real estate agents who facilitate real estate deals and receive a fee for their service. They are necessary evils; nobody wants to pay them the commission, but they offer essential services. In the past you had to telephone a brokerage firm to execute a trade, but now everything is processed electronically and all you do is log on to their website (or online platform or mobile app). You can electronically transfer money from your bank account to your brokerage account and, in reverse, electronically withdraw your money (your profits!) back to your bank account.

There are three types of brokers. **Full-service brokers** are suitable for investors or swing traders, and **discount brokers** are suitable for active traders (they're also frequently referred to as direct-access brokers). A new type of broker is also entering into this mix. They're called **commission-free brokers** and the pioneer in this field was Robinhood Markets, Inc., which was established in 2013. As the term suggests, commission-free brokers permit traders to trade "more or less" free of charge. I will discuss these three types of brokers here and then later, in the day trading chapters, Andrew will provide further commentary on brokers and their services.

Full-Service Brokers

You're no doubt familiar with the names of conventional brokers such as The Charles Schwab Corporation, Fidelity Inc., Ally Invest, and Merrill (officially Merrill Lynch, Pierce, Fenner & Smith Incorporated). While these brokers generally have retail spaces where you can meet in person with advisors, they often do not offer super-fast execution of trades as their services tend to place a greater emphasis on research and fundamental analysis functions for investors over speed execution for active traders. At times called full-service brokers, they provide research and advice, retirement planning, tax tips, and much more. They typically direct customer trade orders to market makers (a broker-dealer that offers shares for sale or purchase on the exchange) and other liquidity providers through pre-negotiated order flow arrangements. This multi-step procedure takes time - from a few seconds to several minutes. Full-service brokers are usually perfect for investors and retail swing traders (retail swing traders are people like you, the readers of this book, who trade from a home office and not for a company), but due to slow speed execution, they are not a good choice for day traders who need fast execution of their trades (entry and exit are often only a few seconds apart).

Discount Brokers

Their title is self-explanatory. Discount brokers offer fewer services to their clients than full-service brokers do but, on the other hand, they focus on trade execution. Discount brokers are often called direct-access brokers, as they allow you to bypass a broker and trade with an exchange or market maker directly via electronic communication networks (ECNs). This allows you to see who is offering or bidding for the shares you are interested in. Direct-access trading system transactions are executed in a fraction of a second and their confirmations are instantly displayed on your computer screen. With most direct-access firms, you need to download their software so that your computer can stream the data faster than if you were retrieving it through a website.

In the U.S., three well-known direct-access brokers are Lightspeed Trading, Interactive Brokers and E*TRADE. You most likely have never heard of these companies as they are designed more for active traders than normal investors. Some full-service brokers who you know and have worked with may also operate a direct-access brokerage service. Likewise, some direct-access brokers now also offer a full range of services for a different fee structure. It is best to check their website and contact their customer service representatives.

Direct-access brokers are a must for day traders but are not necessary for swing traders who usually analyze price action in a slower time frame and do not need a super-fast trade execution. There are disadvantages to using direct-access brokers, including volume requirements (some firms bill inactivity fees if a minimum monthly trading volume has not been met) and technical knowledge (you must practice in a broker's simulator platform to ensure you are very comfortable at using their platform, routing your orders, and entering and exiting trades). New and inexperienced traders may find it challenging to become conversant with the process. It is important to remember that when direct-access trading, you are only one click away from making a dangerous mistake and blowing up your account, while if you are on the telephone with an agent in a full-service brokerage, they may catch your mistake or advise you before executing your order.

Do make sure that whichever broker you select provides you with a charting and trading platform. The charting platform needs to include real-time charting, quotes and order entry capability. Trading platforms are either web-based, or downloadable to your PC or Mac, and sometimes include a mobile phone app. Different brokers use different platforms.

Robinhood and Other Commission-Free Brokers

In April 2013, Robinhood Markets, Inc. was founded by Vladimir Tenev and Baiju Bhatt, who had previously built high frequency trading platforms for financial institutions in New York City. The company's name comes from its mission to "provide *everyone* with access to the financial markets, not just the wealthy". Tenev noted in an interview that, "We realized institutions were paying fractions of a penny for trading and transactions," but that individual investors were typically being charged fees of $5 to $10 per trade, as well as being required to have account minimums of $500 to $5,000. They were right. Brokerage fees were very expensive up to that point and there was a demand from the Main Street people (such as you and I) to have access to better and more affordable tools in comparison with Wall Street. Robinhood is headquartered in Silicon Valley and similar to the philosophy of many other tech giants, they decided to reduce their costs by operating entirely online, without fees, and with no storefront offices. This is a very important and disruptive approach by Silicon Valley. The world's largest taxi firm, Uber Technologies Inc. (ticker: UBER), owns no cars. The world's most popular media company, Facebook, Inc. (ticker: FB), creates no content. The world's most valuable retailer, Alibaba Group Holding Ltd. - ADR (ticker: BABA), based in China, carries no inventory. And the world's largest accommodation provider, Airbnb, Inc., owns no property. Disruptive indeed.

The Robinhood app officially launched in March 2015 and, according to one study, 80% of the firm's customers belong to the "millennial" demographic (people born in the 1980s through mid-1990s), with the average customer being 26 years old. By March 2020, Robinhood had over 10 million user accounts. To put that in context, giant brokerage firms TD Ameritrade and The Charles Schwab Corporation (who are planning to merge) have 24 million users combined.

Robinhood can be a good option for swing traders and investors, but I do not recommend it for active day trading. Robinhood makes most of its money from the interest earned on customers' cash balances, the lending capability which arises from the stocks that its users keep in their accounts, as well as from selling their order flow to high frequency traders (this is the type of trading the computer programmers on Wall Street work away at, creating algorithms and secret formulas to try to manipulate the market).

Figure 3.1 below summarizes the three different types of brokers I have discussed in this section of the book.

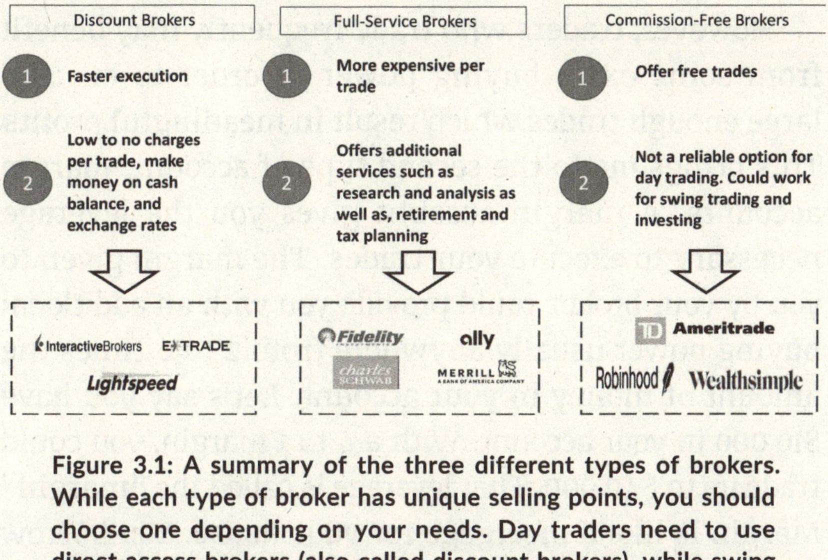

Figure 3.1: A summary of the three different types of brokers. While each type of broker has unique selling points, you should choose one depending on your needs. Day traders need to use direct-access brokers (also called discount brokers), while swing traders and investors can use either full-service or commission-free brokers.

UNDERSTANDING DIFFERENT ACCOUNTS: CASH AND MARGIN

There are two main types of accounts which you can open with your broker: cash or margin.

A cash account is simple – you trade with what you have. If you have $10,000 in your cash account, this is your buying power. Cash accounts are the best type of account for investors who plan to grow their account in the long term and do not plan to trade too many times. They are used only for buying and selling positions, you cannot "sell short" in these accounts. Examples of cash accounts are government-registered and tax-deferred accounts such as IRAs and 401(k)s in the United States, and TFSAs and RRSPs in Canada.

However, traders who trade frequently may benefit from some extra buying power in order to execute large enough trades which result in meaningful profits. This brings me to the second type of account, margin accounts. A margin account gives you the leverage necessary to execute your trades. The margin given to you by your broker could provide you with an additional buying power usually anywhere from 2 to 6 times the amount of money in your account. Let's say you have $10,000 in your account. With a 4 to 1 margin, you could trade up to $40,000. That leverage is called the "margin". Margin is like a mortgage for your house. You borrow a significant amount of money and buy a residence. Banks will give you a mortgage, but they won't take any responsibility or risk on it. For example, imagine that you put

$100,000 down and borrowed $900,000 on a mortgage from your bank to buy a $1,000,000 house (10:1 leverage). If the price of your house goes up to $1,200,000, you still owe the bank the original $900,000 plus their interest. So the extra $200,000 is your own profit that actually came from margin leverage. You couldn't have bought that house without mortgage leveraging. Now assume that the price of the house drops to $900,000. You still owe the bank $900,000 plus their interest, so the drop has hit your main $100,000 and you have lost all of your original down payment of $100,000. That is the other side of leveraging. Therefore, you need to be responsible about when and how much you make use of your account margin.

When a broker notices that you are using leverage and losing money, they might issue a "*margin call*" to you. A margin call is a serious warning and traders must avoid getting them. It means that your loss is now equal to the original money you had in your account. You must add more money or else your broker will freeze your account. If you are interested in reading more about margin, leverage or margin calls, check your broker's website and/or do some research on the Internet.

Investors should use cash accounts and swing traders or day traders should have a margin account. You can also of course have both types of accounts. For example, I have a cash account for my long-term investments and I have two margin accounts with two different brokers, one for swing trading and one for day trading.

Remember, you're allowed to trade on margin, but you need to be responsible about it. It is easy to buy on margin, but it is also very easy to lose on margin. If you lose on margin, your broker takes the loss from your main money account. Therefore, margin is a double-edged sword. It provides you with an opportunity to buy more, but it also exposes you to more risk. There is nothing wrong with buying on margin, but you do have to be responsible.

VOLUME

Trading volume, or volume of trade, is the total quantity of shares traded on any given day for a specified security (such as stocks, bonds, options contracts, futures contracts and all sorts of commodities). As an example, the daily trading volume of Amazon.com Inc. (ticker: AMZN) is somewhere in the neighborhood of 5 to 10 million shares. This trading volume is distributed between pre-market trading (before 9:30 a.m. ET), during market hours (which means when the stock market is open (9:30 a.m. to 4 p.m. ET)), and in after-hours trading (after 4 to around 8 p.m. ET). Figure 3.2 below shows Amazon's daily trading volume from December 2019 into February 2020. As explained in the caption to Figure 2.6, the bottom section of the chart is where trading volume is recorded (using bars). You can see below that one day in late January 2020, Amazon's trading volume for this time frame peaked at some 15.6 million shares.

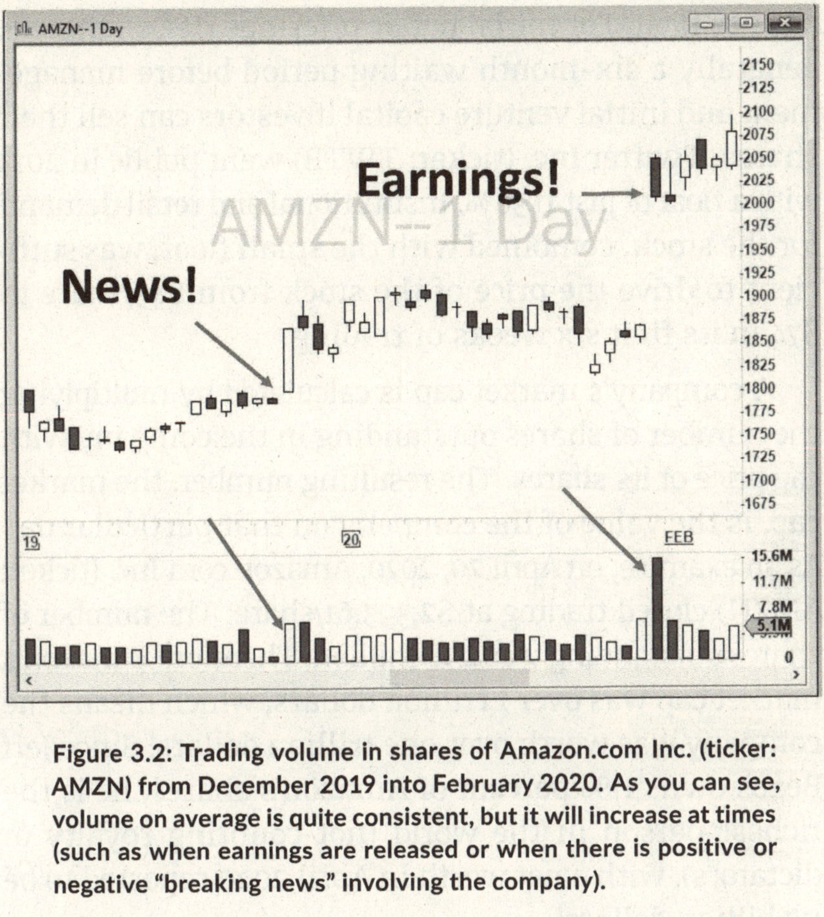

Figure 3.2: Trading volume in shares of Amazon.com Inc. (ticker: AMZN) from December 2019 into February 2020. As you can see, volume on average is quite consistent, but it will increase at times (such as when earnings are released or when there is positive or negative "breaking news" involving the company).

FLOAT AND MARKET CAP

The float is the number of shares available for trading. Float is calculated by subtracting what are called closely held shares—those owned by insiders, employees, the company's employee stock ownership plan, or other major long-term shareholders—from the total shares outstanding (all of the shares of the company). At the right price, of course, the closely held shares may also start to float. For initial public offerings (IPOs), there is generally a six-month waiting period before management and initial venture capital investors can sell their shares. Twitter Inc. (ticker: TWTR) went public in 2013 with a float of just 11.38%. Institutional and retail demand for the stock, combined with the small float, was sufficient to drive the price of the stock from $45/share to $74 in its first six weeks of trading.

A company's market cap is calculated by multiplying the number of shares outstanding in the company with the price of its shares. The resulting number, the market cap, is the value of the company on that particular day. As an example, on April 20, 2020, Amazon.com Inc. (ticker: AMZN) closed trading at $2,393.61/share. The number of shares outstanding was 498 million. Therefore, Amazon's market cap was over 1 trillion dollars, which means the company was worth over one trillion dollars! Since Jeff Bezos owns 11% percent of Amazon's shares, he is the richest person in the world (not counting royalty or dictators), with a net worth in April 2020 reported to be 113 billion dollars!

As the share price grows, so does the market capitalization. If the company issues more shares, the market cap also grows. Market cap is an important factor because it demonstrates whether or not the company is considered mega, large, medium or small cap. The stock of small cap companies can be manipulated far easier with large trading volumes and are thus considered much riskier. As of March 2020, the largest company in the world by market cap is Microsoft Corporation (ticker: MSFT). Apple Inc. (ticker: AAPL) is the second largest. To provide an example of how a company's market cap can change, on October 3, 2018, Apple had a market cap of $1.103 trillion. Today (April 20, 2020), its market cap is $840 billion.

Figure 3.3 below details the market capitalization, trading volume and other financial data for four different companies.

Company	Ticker	Number of share outstanding	Price/share as of April 17th	Average daily trading volume	Market Capitalization	Category
	AAPL	4.37 B	$282.80	39.2M	$1.24T	Mega Cap
	NKE	1.24B	$89.91	9.3M	$111.49B	Large Cap
AMERICAN FINANCIAL GROUP, INC	AFG	89.8M	$71.36	1M<	$6.4B	Med Cap
PIZZA PAPA JOHNS	PZZA	32.28M	$65.13	1M<	$2.1B	Small Cap

Figure 3.3: The market cap, trading volume and other financial data for four different companies as of April 2020. As you can see, companies with bigger market capitalization also have higher daily trading volumes.

BUYING LONG, SELLING SHORT

Traders buy stocks in the hope that their price will go higher. This is called *buying long*, or simply *long*. When you hear me or another trader say, "*I am long 100 shares AAPL,*" it means that we have bought 100 shares of Apple Inc. (ticker: AAPL) and would like to sell them at a higher price for a profit. Going long is good when the price is expected to go higher. The chart in Figure 3.4 below is an example of going long on Apple in a swing trade.

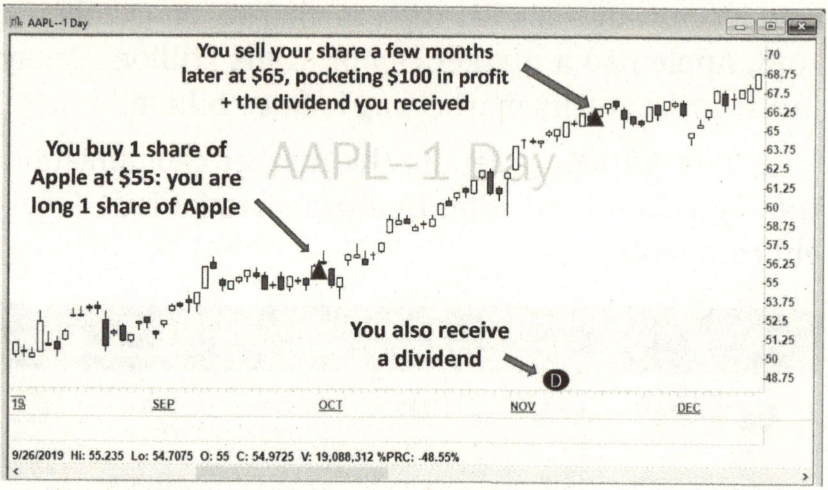

Figure 3.4: An example of going long on Apple Inc. (ticker: AAPL) in a swing trade. In addition to a capital gain, you also receive a dividend.

But what if prices are dropping? In that case, you can *sell short* and still make a profit. As I've noted previously, traders can borrow shares from their broker and sell them, hoping that the price will go lower and that they can then buy those shares back at the lower price and make a profit. This is called *selling short*, or simply *short*. When people say, "*I am short Apple,*" it means they have sold short stocks of Apple and they hope that the price of Apple will drop. Let's pretend that when the price was going lower, you borrowed 100 shares of Apple from your broker. You accordingly owe 100 shares to your broker (it probably shows as –100 shares in your account), which means you must return 100 shares of Apple to your broker. Your broker doesn't want your money; they want their shares back. So, if the price has gone lower, you can buy them cheaper than when you earlier sold them, return the shares to your broker, and make a profit for yourself. Let's imagine that you sold the 100 shares of Apple that you borrowed from your broker for $100 per share. Apple's price then drops to $90, so you buy back those 100 shares at $90 and return the 100 shares to your broker. You have made $10 per share or $1,000. What if the price of Apple goes up to $110? In that case, you still have to buy 100 shares to return to your broker because you owe your broker shares and not money. Therefore, you have to buy 100 shares at $110 in order to return 100 shares to your broker, and you will have lost $1,000.

The chart in Figure 3.5 below is an example of going short on Boeing Co. (ticker: BA) in a swing trade.

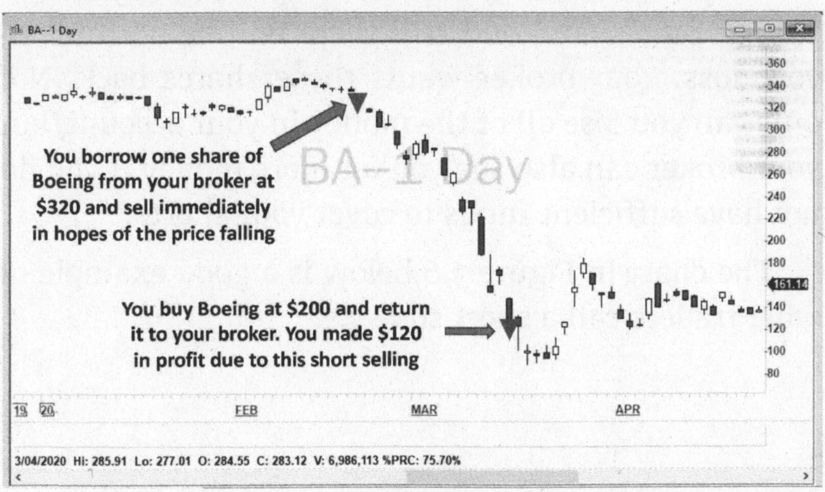

Figure 3.5: An example of a short seller taking profit on Boeing Co. (ticker: BA) in a swing trade. While short selling can increase your return potential, you need to understand that the risks are also higher. Theoretically, stocks can increase infinitely in price, making it very risky if you are holding a short position in them.

Short sellers profit when the price of the stock they borrowed and sold drops. Short selling is important because stock prices usually drop much more quickly than they go up. Fear is a more powerful feeling than greed. Short sellers, if they trade right, can thus make astonishing profits while other traders panic and start to sell off.

However, like anything in the market that has great potential, short selling has its risks too. When buying stock in a company for $7/share, the worst case scenario is that the company goes bankrupt and you lose your $7/share. There is a limit to your loss. But if you short sell that company at $7/share and then the price, instead of going down, starts going higher and higher, there won't be any limit to your loss. The price may go to $10, $20, or $100/share, and still there will be no limit to your loss. Your broker wants those shares back. Not only can you lose all of the money in your account, but your broker can also sue you for more money if you do not have sufficient funds to cover your shorts.

The chart in Figure 3.6 below is a good example of what traders call a short squeeze.

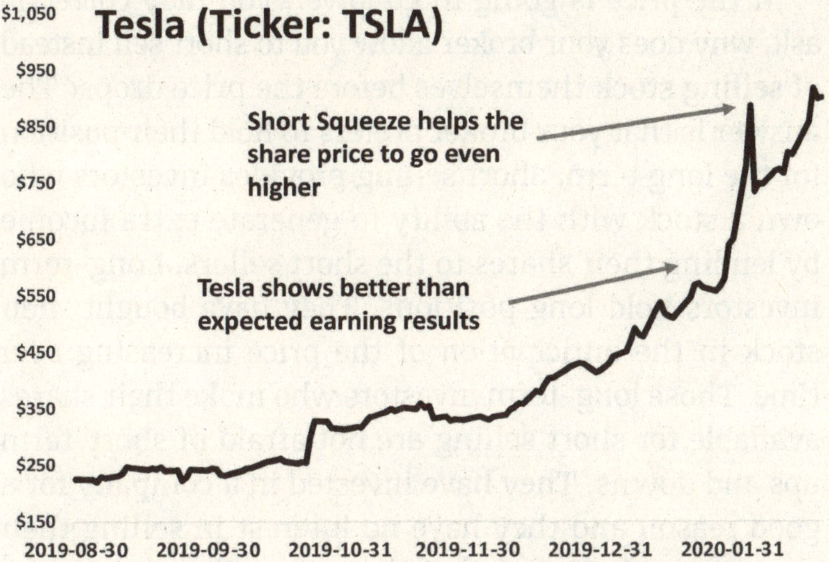

Figure 3.6: A chart showing the price of the stock of Tesla Inc. (ticker: TSLA) increasing due to a great earnings report. As the price of the stock increased, those traders who were short panicked and scrambled to return their borrowed shares to their brokers. Their purchases of Tesla's shares in order to cover their shorts caused the price to reach even higher levels. This is called a short squeeze.

Why does the government allow traders to benefit when the market is dropping? Although some believe that short selling should be banned, it is indeed a legal activity, and for good reason. It provides the markets with more information. Short sellers often complete extensive and legitimate due diligence to discover facts and flaws that support their suspicion that the target company is overvalued. If there were no short sellers, the price of stocks could unreasonably increase higher and higher. Short sellers are balancing the market and adjusting prices to their reasonable value. Their actions are conducive to the health of the market.

If the price is going to go lower, you may correctly ask, why does your broker allow you to short sell instead of selling stock themselves before the price drops? The answer is that your broker prefers to hold their position for the long term. Short selling provides investors who own a stock with the ability to generate extra income by lending their shares to the short sellers. Long-term investors hold long positions. They have bought their stock in the anticipation of the price increasing over time. Those long-term investors who make their shares available for short selling are not afraid of short-term ups and downs. They have invested in a company for a good reason and they have no interest in selling their shares in a short period of time. They therefore prefer to lend their shares to traders who wish to make a profit from short-term fluctuations of the market. In exchange for lending their shares, they will charge interest. Therefore, by short selling, you will need to pay some interest to your broker as the cost of borrowing those shares. If you short sell only during the same day, you usually will not need to pay any interest. Swing traders who sell short usually have to pay daily interest on their short stocks.

Short selling is often a dangerous practice in trading. Some traders are long-biased. They only buy stocks in the hope of selling them higher. Many hedge funds, for example, are structured for only selling long. With that said, I don't have any bias. I will short sell when I think the setup is ready, and I will buy whenever it fits my strategy. Having said that, I am more careful when I short stocks.

CHAPTER 4

CANDLESTICK CHARTING AND UNDERSTANDING PRICE MOVEMENT

FUNDAMENTAL ANALYSIS / TECHNICAL ANALYSIS

When it comes to selecting a stock, two methods are used to identify a potentially good buy: fundamental analysis and technical analysis. To put it simply, fundamental analysis will tell you what to buy, and technical analysis will tell you when to buy.

Fundamental analysis is necessary for people who are looking to **invest** in the stock market. In Chapter 9, I explain in detail techniques that are used in fundamental analysis. Essentially, it involves taking the time to understand a company's internal financial health by in part reviewing its income statement, balance sheet and cash flow statement, in addition to calculating various financial ratios (knowing basic math is definitely a prerequisite!). Equally important, you must also investigate what the economic outlook is for the company (and industry or sector) you are potentially investing your money in.

In contrast, technical analysis is all about reading price action and charts. You spend hours looking for patterns and indicators in order to identify when is the best time to enter a particular stock and to predict how that stock is going to move in the near future. Figure 4.1 below summarizes some of the key elements of fundamental analysis and technical analysis.

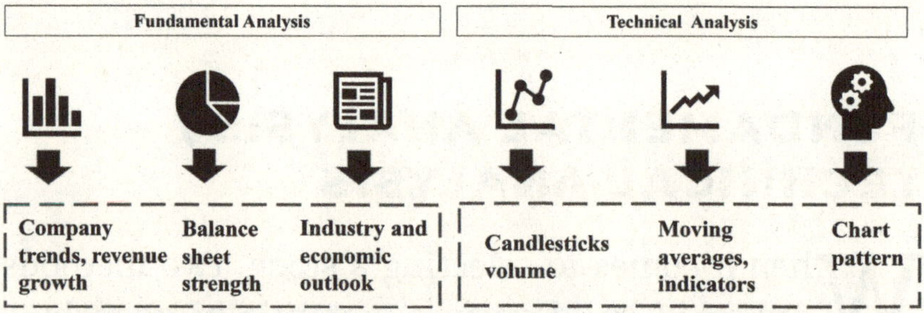

Figure 4.1: Some of the key elements of fundamental analysis and technical analysis. Fundamental analysis looks at the health of the company and the economy, while technical analysis focuses solely on the company's price charts.

The art of reading and charting the price of a stock is called technical analysis (and trust me, it truly is an art). For any stock being considered, you need to know what its current price on the market is, and how that compares to previous days, weeks, months and/or years. (Day traders also need to be able to track a stock's price in intervals of minutes and seconds.) Technical analysis can be as simple as a line or bar or candlestick on your charts, or it can involve utilizing sophisticated mathematical indicators. In this book, I skip over many of these complicated technical indicators. They have some value, but most of the time, complex analysis does not necessarily provide a better signal or indication. One of my professors was a major advocate of KISS (*Keep it Simple, Stupid*), and I've found that principle works very well for the trading and investing that I do.

As I just mentioned, there are several ways of charting the price of the stock including by line chart, bar chart, or candlestick. You probably are most familiar with the line chart. This is the chart you see on Yahoo Finance, the iPhone Stocks app, and almost all news channels when they are reporting on the price of a stock. You need to master the skill of reading at least one type of chart, and the most important one is the candlestick chart. Candlestick charts convey significantly more essential information about a stock than a simple line chart can ever do. For any time period, candlestick charts give you the opening price, the high price, the low price, and the closing price. A successful trader or investor must learn how to extract information from price movements by monitoring what is happening in real time during the trading day and by studying past data. And all of those figures allow you to make various assumptions as you weigh entering into a specific trade or investment. Figure 4.2 below is a visual presentation of the three main types of charts.

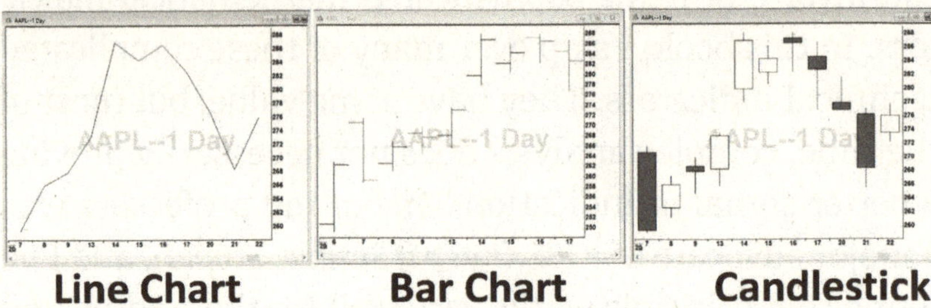

Figure 4.2: The three main types of charts. Swing and day trading rely heavily on candlestick charts while line charts can be used successfully when investing.

It is known that in the 17th century the Japanese began using technical analysis and some early versions of candlesticks to trade rice. Much of the credit goes to a legendary rice trader named Homma from the town of Sakata, Japan. While these early versions of technical analysis and candlestick charts were different from today's version, many of the guiding principles are actually very similar. Candlestick charting, as we know it today, first appeared sometime after 1850. It is likely that Homma's original ideas were modified and refined over many years of trading, eventually resulting in the system of candlestick charting that we now use.

In order to create a candlestick chart, you must have a data set that contains the (1) opening price, (2) highest price in the chosen time frame, (3) lowest price in that period, and (4) closing price values for each time period you want to display.

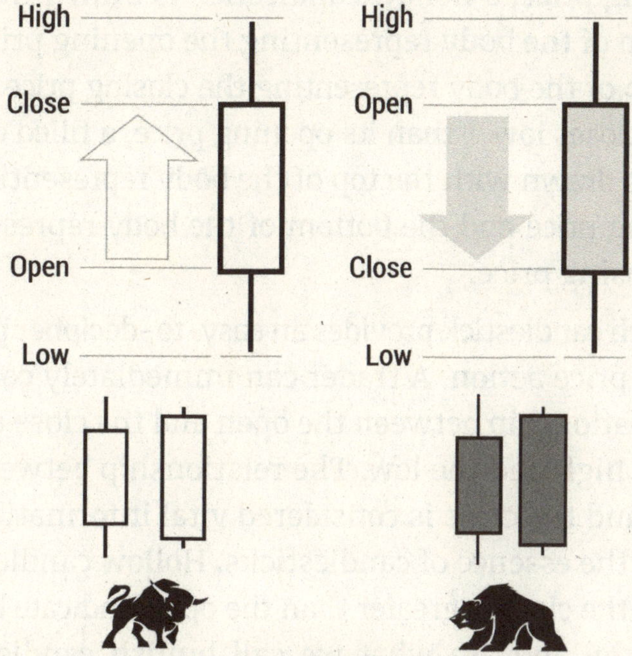

Figure 4.3: Candlestick examples.

The time frame can be daily, 1-hour, 5-minute, 1-minute, or any other period you prefer. The hollow portion of the candlestick (usually white or green in color depending upon your charting format) or the filled portion of the candlestick (usually red or black in color) is called "the body" and represents the range between the opening price and the closing price. The long thin lines above and below the body represent the high/low price range and are called "shadows" (also referred to as "wicks" and "tails"). The high is marked by the top of the upper shadow and the low by the bottom of the lower shadow. Two examples are shown above in Figure 4.3. If the stock closes higher than its opening price, a hollow candlestick is drawn with the bottom of the body representing the opening price and the top of the body representing the closing price. If the stock closes lower than its opening price, a filled candlestick is drawn with the top of the body representing the opening price and the bottom of the body representing the closing price.

Each candlestick provides an easy-to-decipher picture of the price action. A trader can immediately compare the relationship between the open and the close as well as the high and the low. The relationship between the open and the close is considered vital information and forms the essence of candlesticks. Hollow candlesticks, where the close is greater than the open, indicate buying pressure, and are what we call bullish candlesticks. Filled candlesticks, where the close is less than the open, indicate selling pressure, and are what we call bearish candlesticks. If you are not familiar with these terms, the bears and the bulls are explained in the following section.

CANDLESTICK CHARTING AND MASS PSYCHOLOGY

At every moment in the market, there are three types of traders: the buyers, the sellers, and the undecided. Buyers obviously want to pay as little as possible, while sellers want to sell for the highest price possible. Buyers (bulls) and sellers (bears) are under pressure by undecided traders waiting in the background, who could suddenly appear and make the deals the others are considering. If buyers wait too long to decide on a transaction, someone else could beat them to it and drive up the price. Sellers who wait too long for a higher price might be thwarted by other traders who sell at lower asks and drive down the price (an "ask" or an "offer" is what a seller asks as a sale price for their stock). The presence of undecided traders puts pressure on buyers and sellers to deal with each other.

Buyers are buying because they expect that prices will go up. Buying by bulls pushes the market up, or as I like to phrase it, "The buyers are in control." I call them "aggressive buyers". The result is that buyers are willing to pay higher and higher prices and to bid on top of each other. They realize that they will end up paying higher prices if they don't act now. Undecided traders accelerate price increases by creating a feeling of urgency amongst buyers, who then buy quickly and cause prices to go higher.

Sellers are selling because they expect that prices will go down. Selling by bears pushes the price down, or as I like to express it, "The sellers are in control." I call them "aggressive sellers". The result is that sellers are willing to accept lower and lower prices. They are afraid that they may not be able to sell any higher and may have to end up selling at even lower prices if they miss selling now. Undecided traders make prices decrease faster by creating a sense of urgency amongst sellers. They rush to sell and push the prices lower.

The goal of a successful trader is to figure out if the sellers will end up in control or if the buyers will end up in control, and then at the appropriate time, quickly and tactically, make a calculated bet on the winning group. Your job is to analyze the balance of power between buyers and sellers and then bet on the winners. Fortunately, candlestick charts reflect this fight and mass psychology in action. A successful trader is a social psychologist sitting in front of a computer running charting software. Trading is the study of mass psychology.

Candlesticks will tell you a great deal about the general trend of a stock and the power of buyers or sellers in the market. Candles are always born neutral. After birth, they can grow to become either bearish, bullish or, on rare occasions, neither. When a candle is born, traders do not know what it will become. They may speculate but they do not truly know what a candle is until it dies (closes). After a candle is born, the battle begins. The bulls and the bears fight it out, and the candle displays who is winning. If buyers are in control, you will see the candle move up and form a bullish candle. If sellers are in control of the price, you will see the candle move down and become a bearish candle. You may be thinking that this is all very obvious, but many traders don't see candles as a fight between buyers and sellers. That little candle is an excellent indicator that tells you who is currently winning the battle, the bulls (buyers) or the bears (sellers).

BULLISH AND BEARISH CANDLESTICKS

Hollow candles with large bodies toward the upside, as you will see on the left-hand side of Figure 4.3 above, are very bullish. It means that the buyers are in control of the price action, and it is likely that they'll keep pushing the price higher. The candle not only tells you the price, it tells you that the bulls are winning and that they have power.

Bearish candles, on the other hand, are any candles that show a bearish body. So what does the bearish candle tell you? It tells you that the sellers are in control of the price action in the market and that buying, or a "long" position, would not be a great idea.

Filled candles that have a big filled body, such as on the right-hand side of Figure 4.3 above, mean that the open was at a high and the close was at a low. This is a good indicator of a bearishness in the market. If you want to go long, you definitely don't want to go long after seeing a series of big bearish candlesticks. You don't want to stand in the way of bears. If the price gets really extended and the candlesticks become smaller and smaller, then it might be time to take a reversal if you want to go long.

By learning how to read candlesticks, you will begin to generate an opinion on the general attitude for a stock. Again, this is called the "price action". Understanding who is in control of the price is an extremely important skill in day trading. As I just mentioned, a successful trader is a social psychologist armed with a computer and trading software. Day trading is the study of mass psychology during the day.

If bulls are much stronger, you should buy and hold. If bears are much stronger, you should sell and sell short. If both camps are about equal in strength, wise traders stand aside. They let the bulls and the bears fight with each other and then enter trades only when they are reasonably certain which side is likely to win. You never want to be on the wrong side of the trade. It is important therefore to learn how to read candlesticks and how to constantly interpret the price action while you are trading.

INDECISION CANDLESTICKS

Dojis: Simple, Shooting Star, Hammer

Dojis are an important candlestick pattern and come in different shapes and forms, but are all characterized by having either no body or a very small body. Figure 4.4 below provides some examples of Dojis. Dojis are often called indecision candles. In these candlesticks, the powers of the buyers and the sellers are almost equal. Although no one is in control of the price, the fight continues on. Usually, the volume is lower in these candlesticks as traders are waiting to see who wins the fight between the sellers and the buyers. Trends in price can change immediately after indecision candles and they therefore are important to recognize in the price action.

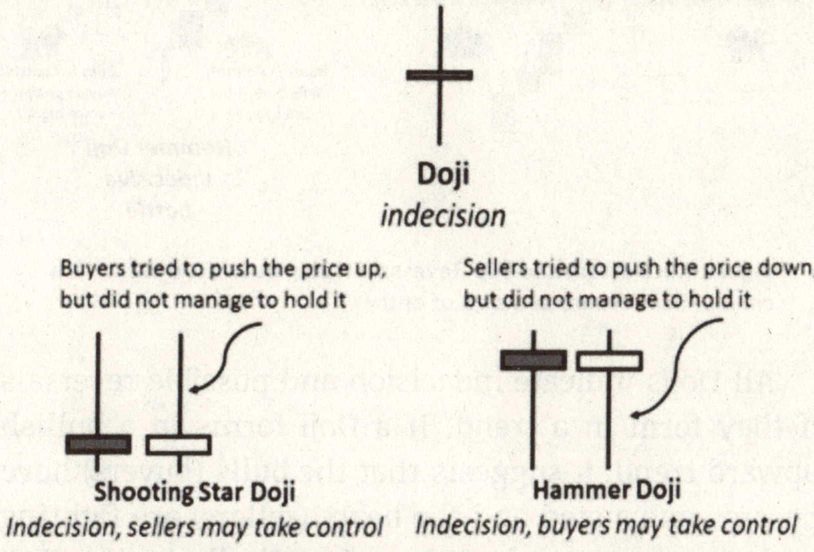

Figure 4.4: Buying and selling pressure definition on Dojis.

Simple Dojis are candles that have similarly-sized high wicks and low wicks. At other times, Dojis will have unequal top and bottom wicks. If the top wick is longer, it means that the buyers tried unsuccessfully to push the price higher. These types of Dojis, such as the shooting star, are still indecision candlesticks, but they may indicate that the buyers are losing power and that the sellers are about to take over.

If the bottom wick is longer, as in hammer Dojis, it means that the sellers were unsuccessful in trying to push the price lower. This may indicate an impending takeover of price action by the bulls.

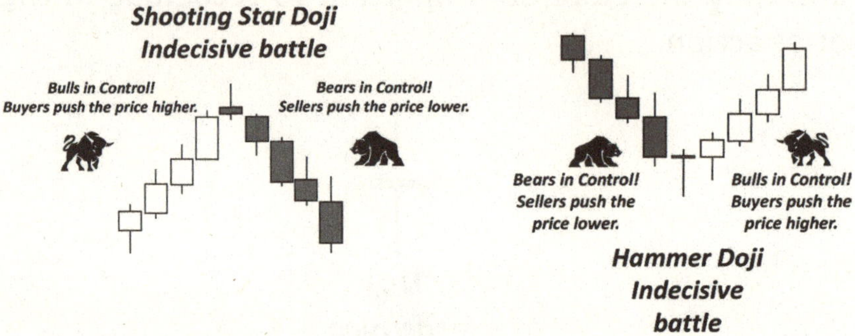

Figure 4.5: Bottom and Top Reversal Strategies with an indecision candlestick formed as a sign of entry.

All Dojis indicate indecision and possible reversals if they form in a trend. If a Doji forms in a bullish upward trend, it suggests that the bulls (buyers) have become exhausted and the bears (sellers) are fighting back to take control of the price. Similarly, if a Doji forms in a bearish downward trend, it suggests that the bears have become exhausted and the bulls are fighting back to take control of the price. You will see examples of these in the above Figure 4.5.

After learning to recognize these candlesticks, it is important that you do not get too excited too quickly. Candles are not perfect. If you take a trade every time you see a Doji formed in a trend, you will end up with significant losses. Always remember that these candles only indicate indecision and not a definite reversal.

CANDLESTICK PATTERNS

In analyzing the price of a stock, rising and falling candlesticks often form in recognizable patterns. These patterns can at times be very powerful and when you see one of them on your chart, you can fairly accurately predict the future direction of the price of the stock (in other words, you can predict with some certainty what is going to happen in a battle between buyers and sellers). As a trader, you need to be familiar with some of the most common and important candlestick patterns.

With that said, chart patterns can be very convoluted and ambiguous. Traders love to identify complicated patterns and make trading decisions based on them. There are hundreds of imaginatively-named candlestick patterns that you will find with an online search including Abandoned Baby, Dark Cloud Cover, Downside Tasuki Gap, Dragonfly, Morning Star, Evening Star, Falling Three Methods, Harami, Stick Sandwich, Three Black Crows, Three White Soldiers, and many more. Believe me, I did not make any of these names up. These candlestick patterns are really out there. As intriguing as their names might be, many of them, in my opinion, are useless and confusing. They're exceptionally arbitrary and fanciful.

Cup and Handle, as well as Head and Shoulders, are two chart patterns that have been well studied and proven to be quite reliable, and they are what the next section will discuss. If you are interested in learning more about candlestick patterns than what is referenced here, there are many excellent resources available. I personally am fond of Steve Nison's book, *Japanese Candlestick Charting Techniques.* Although Andrew and I may differ occasionally on the chart patterns we prefer, we both are in favor of keeping our chart analysis simple and clean. Conducting more (and even more!) sophisticated analysis is not necessarily beneficial, but it is a trap that many new investors and traders fall into.

In Chapter 5, Andrew will detail two strategies you could use when day trading in the market. However, before you can consider trading any strategy whatsoever (or investing in the market for that matter), it is integral that you understand how to read price action charts in addition to how to go about making decisions based on the information that you glean from them.

Cup and Handle Pattern

To illustrate this pattern, let's take a look at the SPDR S&P 500 ETF Trust (ticker: SPY). You'll recall this is an exchange-traded fund (ETF) that tracks the S&P 500, which itself is an index that tracks the share value of 500 of the largest companies in the U.S. Starting near the end of February 2020, the global economy entered into a "massive" recession due to the pandemic. As I set out in the opening pages of this book, SPY dropped from $340/share in February 2020 to almost $220 by the fourth week of March 2020. Anyone with even a modest interest in the markets took a deep breath and waited to see what would happen next.

Figure 4.6: An example of a Cup and Handle Pattern on the daily chart of the SPDR S&P 500 ETF Trust (ticker: SPY). Sellers pushed the price down to the $220/share level, while buyers recovered the price twice, forming a Cup and Handle Pattern on the chart.

In late March 2020, the market recovered some of its losses and by early April 2020, the price of SPY went back up to $260/share.

Figure 4.6 above is an example of a Cup and Handle Pattern on SPY. I have marked the pattern for you on the chart. You can see in this instance that although sellers (the bears) brought the price down, buyers (the bulls) were able to push the price back up, to complete the cup part of the pattern. Sellers later took control again and pushed the price down, but they could not take it back down to the bottom of the cup part of the pattern (around $220). Buyers were then able to push the price up again (to $260 per share). This signaled a definite bullish pattern (all Cup and Handle Patterns are bullish). I knew the buyers were now stronger than the sellers, and that it was a good time to invest in the market. I therefore decided to invest a big portion of the trust that I manage.

As you can see in Figure 4.7 below, the following week was strong and SPY gained over 5%. Not a bad profit, if I dare say so myself!

Figure 4.7: Continuing the example of a Cup and Handle Pattern on the daily chart of the SPDR S&P 500 ETF Trust (ticker: SPY). The inability of sellers to push the price back down to the $220/ share level showed a lack of conviction amongst sellers. Buyers were then able to take control, causing the price to go up.

A similar example is from SPY in December 2019. You can see in Figure 4.8 below that sellers took control in late November 2019 and were able to push the price down to $308/share. Buyers then recovered the price to $314. The inability of sellers to bring the price down to where it had been was a signal that buyers were in control, and that led to the price of SPY jumping to $320.

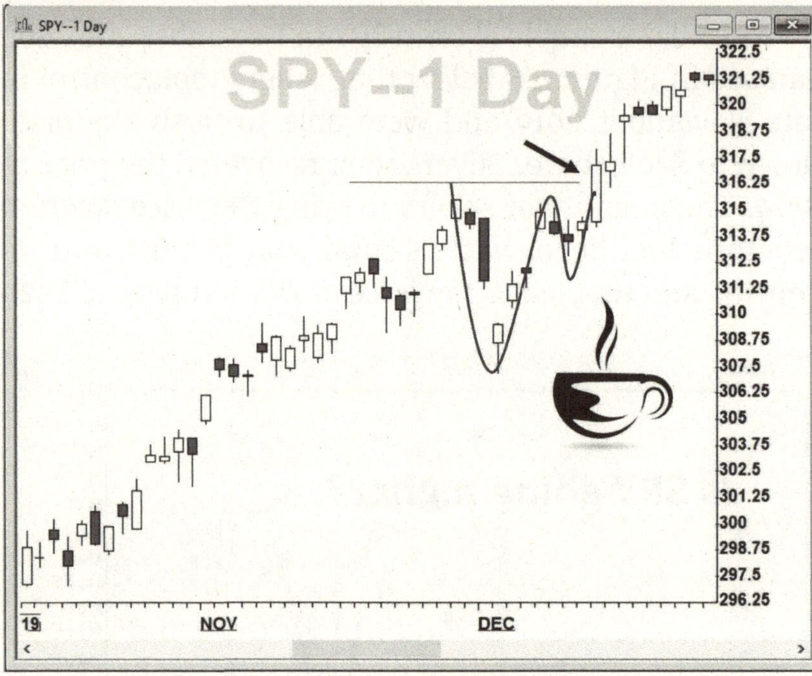

Figure 4.8: Example of a Cup and Handle Pattern on the daily chart of the SPDR S&P 500 ETF Trust (ticker: SPY) in December 2019. Similar to the previous example, sellers took control of the price and pushed it down to the $308/share level. Buyers recovered the price to $314. Sellers were then unable to bring the price back down to where it had been, and that led to the pattern of a handle forming on the chart. With buyers in control, the price was pushed up to the $320 level.

The Cup and Handle Pattern can also appear in a reversed form on your charts, indicating that sellers (or short sellers) are in control of the price action (all Reverse Cup and Handle Patterns are bearish). Figure 4.9 below shows a Reverse Cup and Handle Pattern on Facebook, Inc. (ticker: FB). In January 2020, buyers were able to get the price of Facebook up to the $220/share level. After sellers took control and pushed the price down, buyers were not able to take the price back to the earlier $220 level, thus signaling that sellers were stronger than buyers.

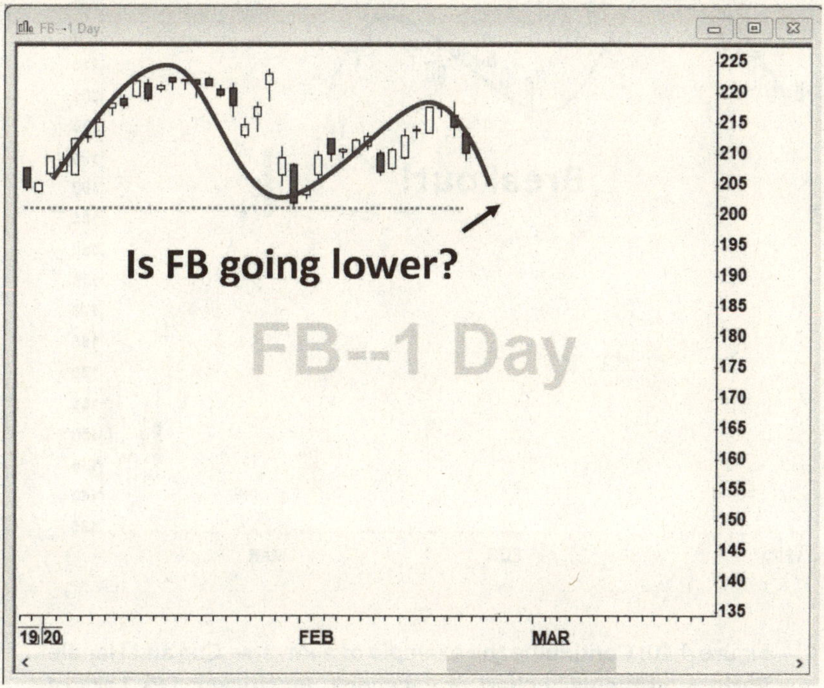

Figure 4.9: Example of a Reverse Cup and Handle Pattern on the daily chart of Facebook, Inc. (ticker: FB). In January 2020, buyers were able to push the price of Facebook up to the $220/share level. After sellers took control and succeeded in lowering the share price, buyers were unable to take the price back up to the $220 level, and thus the pattern of a reversed handle was formed on the chart. This demonstrates a lack of conviction amongst buyers.

As you can see below in Figure 4.10, sellers were indeed stronger than buyers, and by March 2020 they had forced the price of Facebook down to $140/share.

Figure 4.10: Continuing the example of a Reverse Cup and Handle Pattern on the daily chart of Facebook, Inc. (ticker: FB). Lack of conviction amongst buyers caused sellers to take control. By March 2020, sellers had pushed the price of Facebook down to the $140/share level.

Head and Shoulders Pattern

The Head and Shoulders Pattern is a bearish distribution pattern which marks the end of an uptrend. This is certainly one of the more reliable patterns, but don't just take my word for it. Even the very credible Federal Reserve Bank of New York has published a paper (in 1995) acknowledging its predictive ability in generating profits. The Head and Shoulders Pattern is composed of three hills, with the right and left hills (the shoulders) being approximately the same size, and the middle hill (the head) being the largest of the three.

Figure 4.11 below is an example of how I was able to identify this pattern on the daily chart of Home Depot Inc. (ticker: HD) and then trade accordingly. Buyers were initially able to rally the price up to $202/share and then later to $207. Sellers were able to bring the price down to $200 and complete what presents as the pattern of a head on Home Depot's chart. Finally, buyers attempted to once again raise the price up significantly, but instead they were only able to push it to around the $202 level (the level which had earlier created the image of a left shoulder on the price chart). This last move by buyers resulted in the image of a right shoulder on the daily chart, and that completed the Head and Shoulders Pattern. Can you see what looks like the image of a head and two shoulders on the chart below? Most often, a lack of conviction amongst buyers usually leads into a selling off, which is then followed by lower prices. (Do note that the designation of left shoulder and right shoulder is based on your perspective as the trader or investor looking at the price chart in front of you. The shoulder on your left, for example, is known as the left shoulder.)

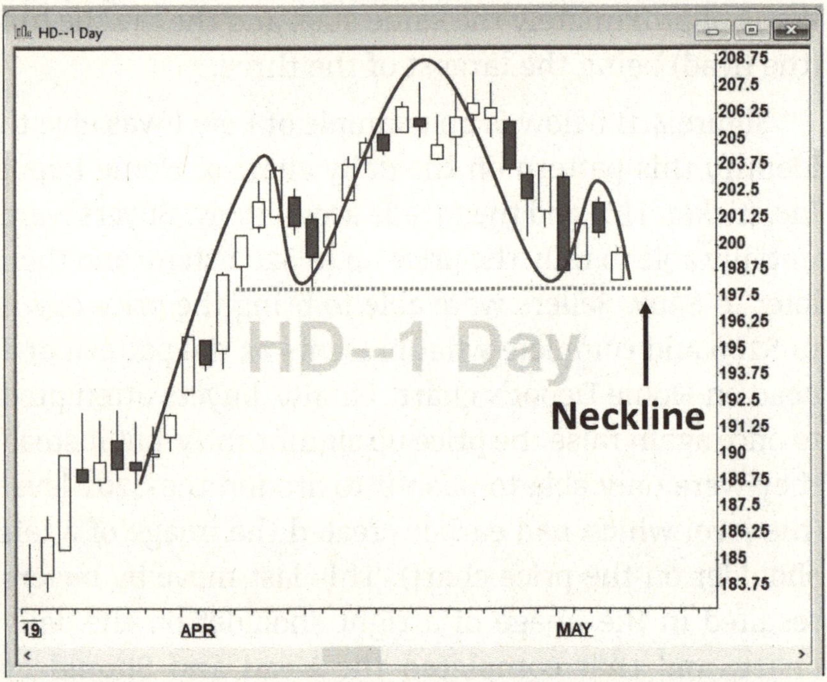

Figure 4.11: Example of the Head and Shoulders Pattern on the daily chart of Home Depot Inc. (ticker: HD). Buyers were initially able to move the price up to the $202/share level, and then up to the $207 level. Sellers were able to bring the price down to $200 but then buyers were not able to push the price back to the $207 level. These price movements created an image on the price chart of a left shoulder, a head, and then a right shoulder. The inability of buyers to move the price back up to the $207 range signals weakness amongst buyers.

As predicted, HD sold off and sellers were able to push the price down to $187/share in the last part of May 2019. Much of this price movement is shown in Figure 4.12 below. The Head and Shoulders Pattern can be used to predict the minimum a stock's price will fall after the creation of the image of a right shoulder on a price chart. This price drop is calculated by taking the difference in price between where the top of the image of the head reached on the chart (in this case, $207) and where the image of the right shoulder's neckline placed on the chart ($200). For this example, you could have safely estimated that the value of HD's stock would go down at least $7 ($207–$200) once the sellers took control.

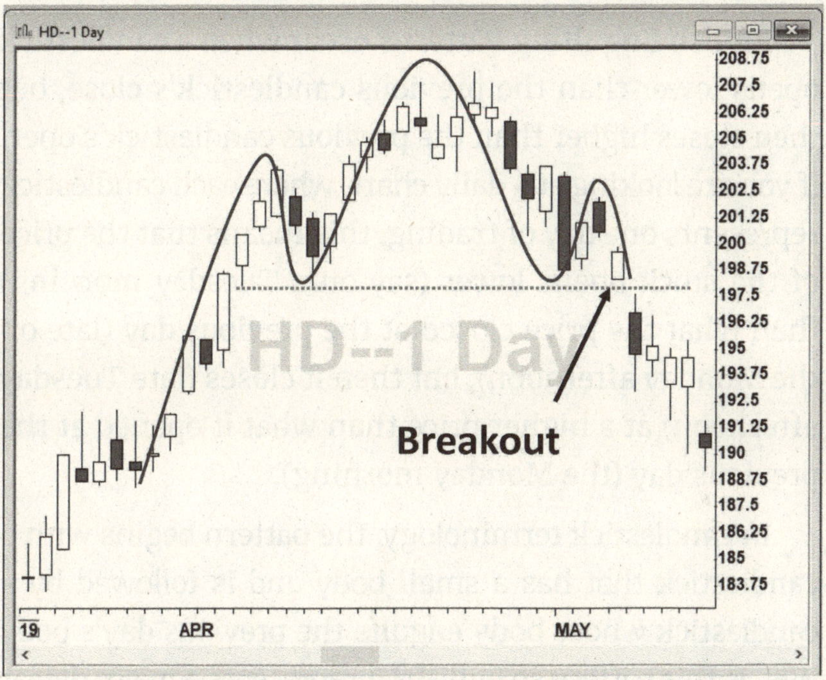

Figure 4.12: An example of using the Head and Shoulders Pattern to predict how far the price of a stock will drop after the appearance of the image of a right shoulder on a price chart. In this instance, following the creation of the right shoulder, sellers took control and pushed the price down to $187/share. Oftentimes, you can expect the stock's value to fall at least as far as the difference in price between where the pattern of the right shoulder's neckline placed and where the top of the pattern of the head reached. In this case, the neckline is at the $200 level and the head is at the $207 level. You could therefore expect the price of the stock to fall at least $7.

Engulfing Candlesticks

One of my favorite patterns to look for on price action charts is the Engulfing Pattern. This pattern can be bullish or bearish, involves two candlesticks (not one), and can act as a great indicator of the direction a stock's price is heading.

Bullish Engulfing Patterns occur when a candlestick opens lower than the previous candlestick's close, but then closes higher than the previous candlestick's open. If you are looking at a daily chart, where each candlestick represents one day of trading, this means that the price of the stock opens lower (say on a Tuesday morning) than what the price closed at the previous day (late on the Monday afternoon), but then it closes (late Tuesday afternoon) at a higher price than what it opened at the previous day (the Monday morning).

In candlestick terminology, the pattern begins with a candlestick that has a small body and is followed by a candlestick whose body engulfs the previous day's body. Why is this pattern so bullish? It represents a major defeat, so to speak, for bears (the sellers). When the second candlestick opens, sellers are already pushing prices below the prior day's close. Since the prices for shares are dropping, buyers step in and begin purchasing en masse. Not only are they able to reverse the direction from the open but they also manage to push prices higher than where sellers began the previous day. Think of a Bullish Engulfing Pattern as a surprise victory in a battle where an infantry division loses not only the gains it made in the previous day but also much more.

Over the years, I've found Bullish Engulfing Patterns to be accurate and reliable for both day and swing trading as long as proper risk control measures are in place.

Figure 4.13 below is an example of two Bullish Engulfing Patterns on the May 2018 price chart of Facebook, Inc. (ticker: FB).

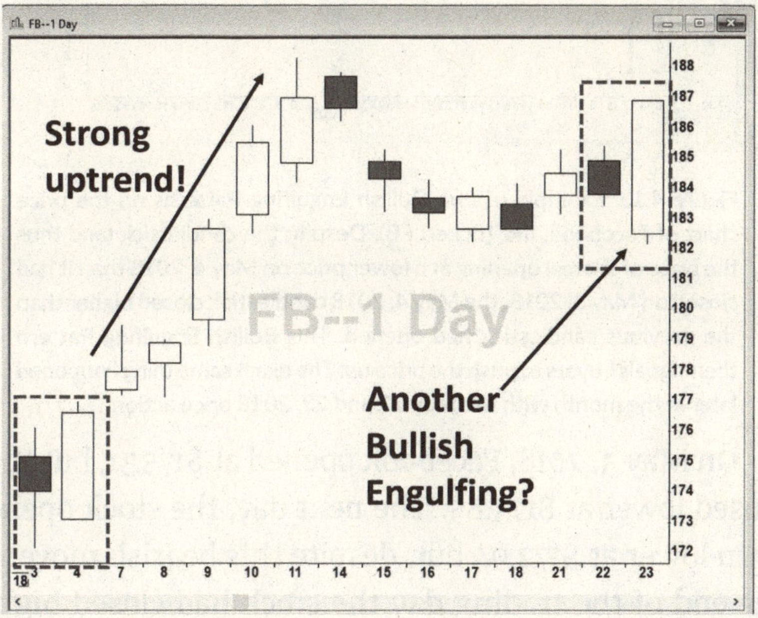

Figure 4.13: Example of two Bullish Engulfing Patterns on the price chart of Facebook, Inc. (ticker: FB). Despite the candlestick (and thus the price of shares) opening at a lower price on May 4, 2018 than it had closed on May 3, 2018, the May 4, 2018 candlestick closed higher than the previous candlestick had opened. This Bullish Engulfing Pattern then signals buyers to push the price up. The exact same thing happened later in the month with the May 22 and 23, 2018 price action.

On May 3, 2018, Facebook opened at $175.31, but then closed lower at $173.85. The next day, the stock opened even lower at $172.94 but, despite this bearish move, by the end of the trading day the stock had closed higher (at $176.58) than the previous day's open. This showed that sellers were exhausted and the stock was in an upward momentum. The same Bullish Engulfing Pattern showed itself again on May 22 and 23, 2018. The stock opened at $184.76, but then closed lower at $183.67. The next day, the stock opened even lower at $182.40 but was able to close higher (at $186.94) than the previous day's open. Again, this Bullish Engulfing Pattern signals the buyers to push the price even higher.

Figure 4.14 below is an example of a Bearish Engulfing Pattern on a daily price chart of The Kroger Company (ticker: KR). On February 24, 2020, KR opened at $29.89/share and closed higher at $30.24. The next day, despite opening higher than the previous day's close (at $30.50), sellers were able to close the price lower than the previous day's open (at $29.64). This confirmed the Bearish Engulfing Pattern, signaling that sellers now have control over the price action.

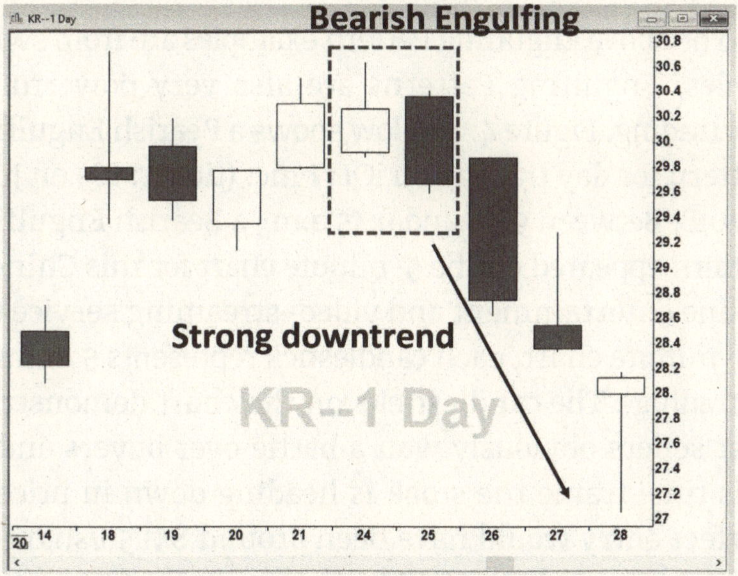

Figure 4.14: Example of a Bearish Engulfing Pattern on the price chart of The Kroger Company (ticker: KR). The candlestick (and thus the price of shares) opened higher on February 25, 2020 than it had closed the previous trading day, but the candlestick closed lower on February 25, 2020 than the previous day's candlestick had opened, showing weakness amongst buyers. Sellers had taken over control of the stock's price, and pushed it down further the next day.

As this week in February 2020 progressed, you can see that Kroger's stock dropped further, down to $27/share, which created a great opportunity for making profits.

Bearish Engulfing Patterns occur at the end of uptrends and mark important reversals. They also involve two candlesticks, each representing whatever time frame your price chart is based on. The first candlestick consists of a small body. The second candlestick opens higher than the previous candlestick's close, but closes lower than the previous candlestick's open, thus engulfing the first candlestick.

The above Engulfing Pattern examples are from swing trades. Engulfing Patterns are also very powerful in day trading. Figure 4.15 below shows a Bearish Engulfing Pattern for day trading on iQIYI Inc. (ticker: IQ) on June 4, 2018. Between 9:40 and 9:45 a.m., a Bearish Engulfing Pattern appeared on the 5-minute chart for this Chinese online entertainment and video-streaming service (on a 5-minute chart, each candlestick represents 5 minutes of trading). The candlesticks on the chart demonstrate that sellers obviously won a battle over buyers and in this time frame the stock is heading down in price. A perfect entry would have been around $31.50/share for a short to cover below $28 for an over $2 profit per share. A 1,000 share trade could have profited over $2,000 in 10 minutes or so!

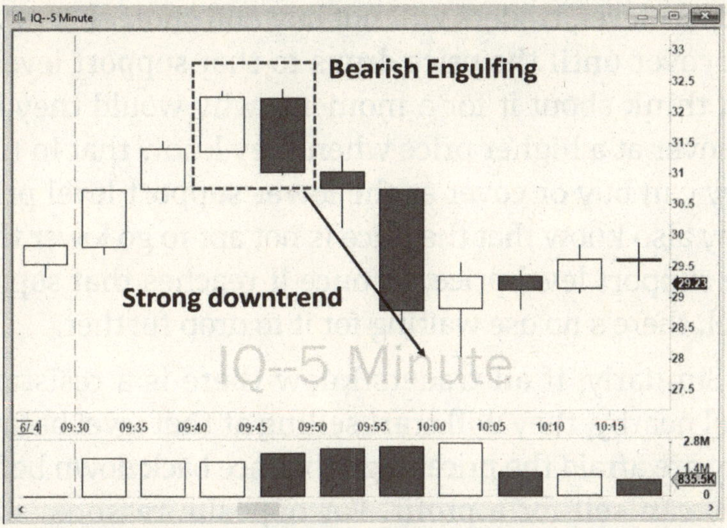

Figure 4.15: Example of a Bearish Engulfing Pattern on the 5-minute price chart of iQIYI Inc. (ticker: IQ) on June 4, 2018. As you can see, a 5-minute candlestick opened higher than the previous candlestick had closed, but closed lower than the previous candlestick had opened, signaling that sellers were in control. The stock then sold off over the next 10 minutes.

SUPPORT AND RESISTANCE LEVELS AND TREND LINES

A *support* is a price level where buyers entered the trade (or short sellers covered their shorts) with enough force to keep prices from going any lower.

A *resistance* is a price level where sellers entered the market (or old buyers dumped their shares) with enough force to keep prices from going any higher.

Support and resistance levels are very important reference points because so many traders recognize them and believe in their significance. It's herd mentality 101. If enough traders believe in the significance of a support level, traders will not buy and short sellers will not cover until the price drops to that support level. If you think about it for a moment, why would they buy or cover at a higher price when they know that in time they can buy or cover at the lower support level price? They also know that the price is not apt to go lower than the support level price, so once it reaches that support level, there's no use waiting for it to drop further.

Similarly, if all traders know there is a resistance level nearby, they will start selling at that level because they are afraid the price might bounce back down before they can sell for a profit. For opposite reasons, short sellers will also start selling at the resistance level, but they do so in anticipation of the price falling.

It is at these levels that the balance of power between buyers and sellers will usually shift. For example, if buyers are aggressively bidding with higher and higher prices, therefore causing prices to rise, and all of a sudden there are many traders who are willing to aggressively sell for lower and lower prices, thereby causing an immediate price reversal, the price level at which the price reversed is now a resistance level. It really doesn't matter why the balance of power shifted from buyers to sellers. There could be all sorts of reasons behind what caused the price to reverse. What is really important is that traders will remember that the market reversed at that particular price level. As a result, moving forward, that price will have a degree of significance in the minds of traders.

If the market reversed very strongly the last time that prices approached this level, there will be a good number of traders who will think it will probably reverse again and they may very well act based on this belief.

As part of a successful trading plan, you need to be able to identify meaningful and important support and resistance price levels on your charts. There are many ways to find these levels and there are many types of support and resistance.

Horizontal support and resistance levels, such as shown below in Figure 4.16, are among the most important levels. This is because the market remembers price levels, which is why horizontal support and resistance lines on previous price levels make sense.

Another type of support and resistance are diagonal trend lines, as shown below in Figure 4.17.

Figure 4.16: From August 2019 to December 2019, shares in Amazon.com Inc. (ticker: AMZN) traded between a support level (their price could not go lower than) and a resistance level (their price could not go higher than). As soon as the price of the stock broke the resistance level, the price was able to move higher. The resistance level then became the support level for the stock.

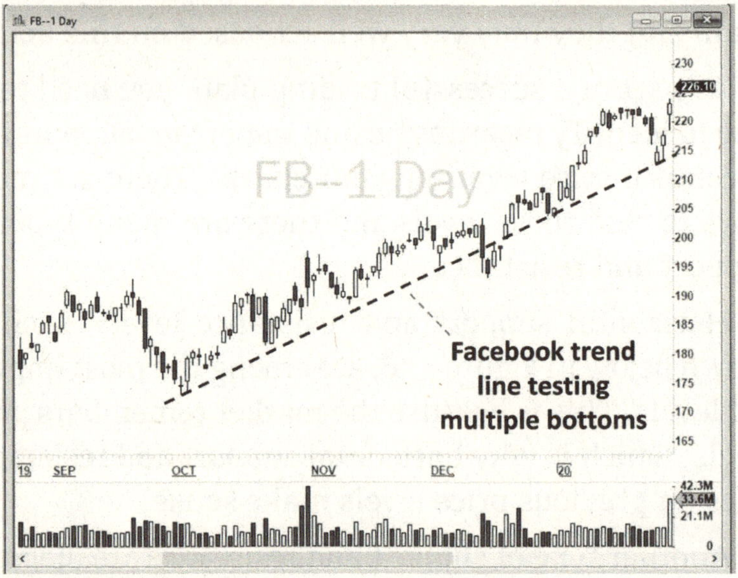

Figure 4.17: The share price of Facebook, Inc. (ticker: FB) in an upward trend testing multiple bottoms. The upward trend will not be challenged unless Facebook breaks the support level.

In my opinion, trend lines can be deceptive, and I personally avoid them. Many traders may disagree with me here, and they will stress the importance of trend lines, triangles, Rising and Falling Wedge Patterns, channels, and such. I must emphasize that what I have written about in this book is my method of trading, and while it works very well for me, it might not work for everyone. There is no wrong or right way to trade, and it is important that each trader find their own style of trading. More than anything else, trading is perhaps most similar to being a professional athlete. Professional athletes each have their own training schedule and process, and no two athletes train in exactly the same fashion.

One professional coach might implement a certain training regimen, while the coach of another team might utilize a completely different system. Both may be correct and produce good results depending on the performance of the athletes on the day of competition. Similarly, you can learn many trading styles, and they all can be right, but the overall results of your trading depend on your daily execution of what you have learned.

In this book, I will teach you how to determine support and resistance on candlestick charts. Once support and resistance are identified, they can be very helpful in the execution of your trading plan during the market hours (I provide some thoughts in Chapter 8 on what should be included in a trading plan).

You may have heard that old support becomes resistance and old resistance becomes support. An excellent example of this was set out in the above Figure 4.16. When the price of stock of Amazon.com Inc. (ticker: AMZN) broke the resistance level, the resistance level then became the support level for the stock.

This market insight is valid but do remember that when you identify one of these levels on your chart, depending upon which direction the price is approaching it, the level can act as either a support or a resistance.

You may recall I earlier wrote that technical analysis (reading and charting the price of a stock) is an art. Finding support and resistance levels is definitely part of that, shall I say, artistic endeavor. Some traders use mathematical equations such as pivot points and Fibonacci levels (although beyond the scope of this book, considerable information about these aspects of technical analysis can be found online). I personally use three important price levels:

1. All-time high and all-time low
2. 52-week high and 52-week low
3. Extreme price levels on a daily chart (a chart where each candlestick represents the changes in price of a stock over one specific trading day)

Figure 4.18 below is a chart tracking the price of stock of Amazon.com Inc. (ticker: AMZN) from January 2016 to the spring of 2020. At the time of writing (spring 2020), due to unprecedented demand following the lock-downs related to COVID-19, Amazon is experiencing staggering growth, and that is being reflected in the all-time highs the price of its stock is making (which can be viewed as a resistance level). If Amazon blows past the earnings expectations of analysts, their stock will likely test the resistance level again and may very likely make a new all-time high.

Figure 4.18: Shares of Amazon.com Inc. (ticker: AMZN) were making all-time highs in the spring of 2020 due to an unprecedented level of demand for Amazon's services and products as well as the agility of its business model in the midst of the pandemic and economic slowdown.

Figure 4.19 below is the other side of the spectrum. Aurora Cannabis Inc. (ticker: ACB) has experienced quite a few consecutive bad earnings seasons and its stock is trading near all-time low levels (at the time of writing). One of my friends owns a portion of his retirement in this stock (I will talk about that more in Chapter 11). If the company misses its earnings again, it will probably test the all-time low support level again, and the price of its shares might go even further down.

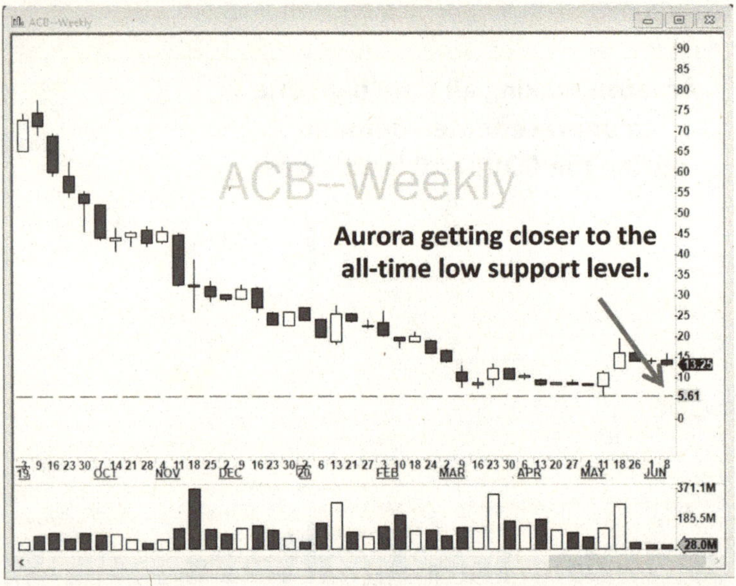

Figure 4.19: Shares of Aurora Cannabis Inc. (ticker: ACB) were making near all-time lows in the spring of 2020. The stock had been missing earnings projections for multiple quarters, and that sent the stock in a downward frenzy.

Often on a daily chart you can see significant price reversals for multiple days at price levels that have been shown in the past to be critical. A large wick to the upside or downside on a daily chart will immediately catch my attention (please see Figure 4.21 below where I have marked with an arrow (the bottom arrow that is all by itself) an example from January 5, 2017 for the company then named Michael Kors Holdings Ltd. (ticker: KORS)). I usually try to identify that level with a line that touches the maximum number of reversals or wicks. The more of a line that is touching extreme price lines, the more that the line is a better support and resistance and has more value. Sometimes it is not clear which line is the optimum line, and in those situations all you can do is just draw the best that you can.

The price must have a clear bounce from that level. If you are not certain if the price has bounced in that level, then it is probably not a support and resistance level. Important support and resistance levels on daily charts stand out. They shout at you: "grab me by the face".

For day trading, it is better to draw support and resistance lines across the extreme prices or wicks on daily levels rather than across areas where the bulk of the candlesticks stopped. This is the complete opposite of swing trading. For swing trading, you need to draw support and resistance lines across the edges of congested areas where the bulk of the candlesticks stopped rather than across the extreme prices. Swing traders often ignore those wicks on daily charts. This is because the close price is more important for swing trading than the extreme wicks in daily candlesticks are. The close price of a stock on a daily chart is the price that the market makers (a broker-dealer that offers shares for sale or purchase on the exchange) and professional traders have agreed on. Previous extreme high and low wicks have been made by day traders, so you should look at those. To better illustrate these above points, let's take a look at Figure 4.20 below, a daily chart for Tesla Inc. (ticker: TSLA) without support and resistance lines and another daily chart which includes those lines.

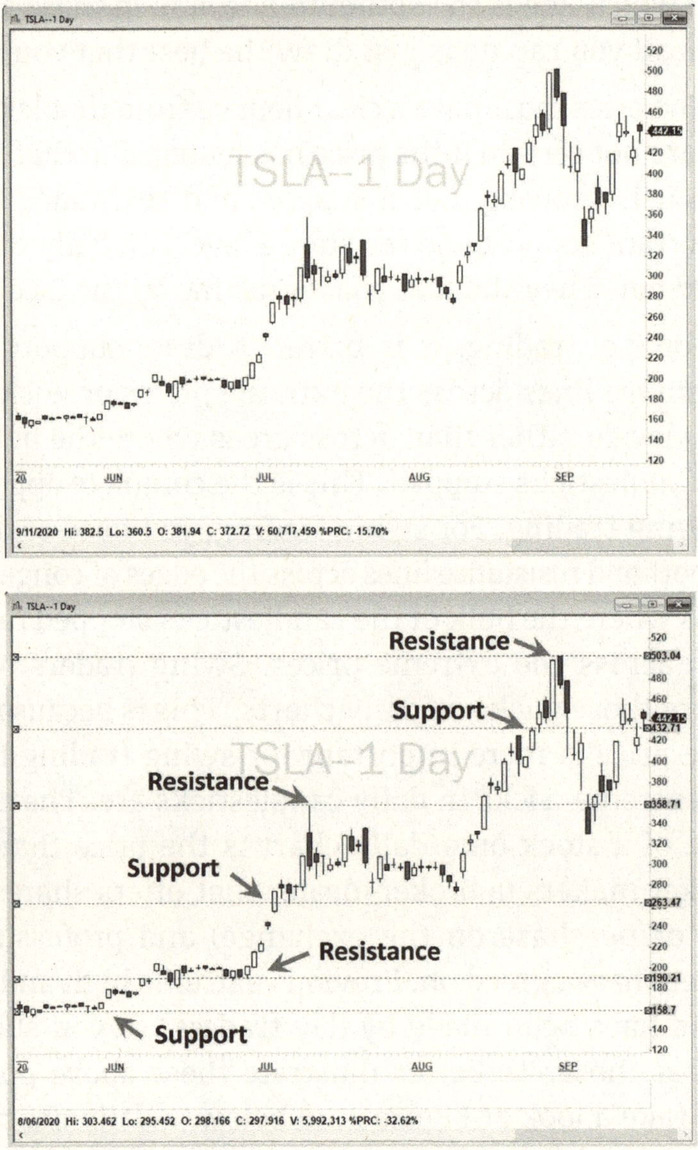

Figure 4.20: Daily chart of Tesla Inc. (ticker: TSLA), firstly without and then with support and resistance lines plotted.

You will see that I marked areas that the price bounced back on the daily chart.

Another example is shown in Figure 4.21 below, where two levels are noted, and I marked the areas that caught my attention in order to draw those specific levels. Please note that there are more levels that can be plotted on this chart, I just highlighted these two levels as an example.

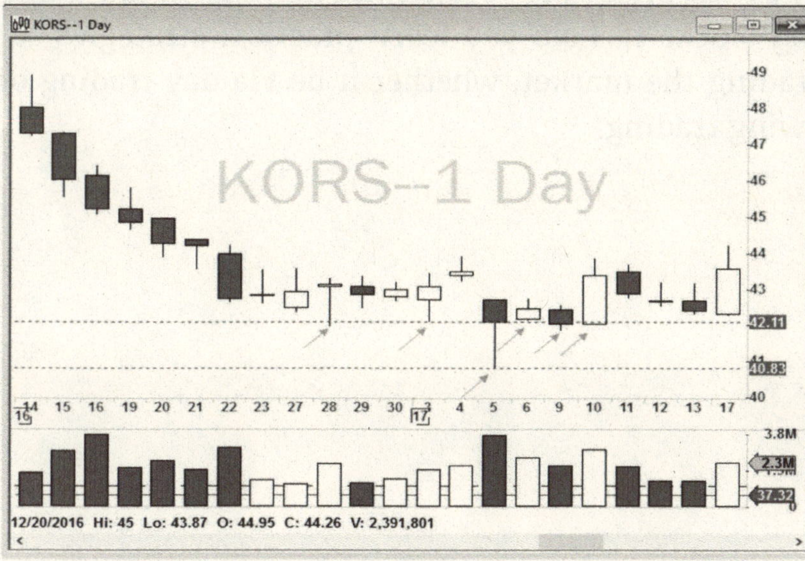

Figure 4.21: Daily chart of the company then named Michael Kors Holdings Ltd. (ticker: KORS), with two support and resistance lines marked.

Support and resistance lines on daily charts are not always easy to find. If I cannot see anything clearly, I don't have to draw anything. There is a good chance that other traders will also not see those lines clearly and therefore there is no point in forcing myself to draw support and resistance lines that are more or less meaningless.

I have discussed candlesticks, Dojis, price action patterns and support and resistance in this chapter. As I referenced in the first chapter, think of this information as the alphabet of technical analysis. You cannot expect to write a poem in any language before knowing that language's alphabet. In the chapters to come, Andrew and I use all of this background material as the building blocks to help you learn practical strategies for trading the market, whether it be via day trading or swing trading.

CHAPTER 5

DAY TRADING IN THE STOCK MARKET

By Andrew Aziz (with edits by Ardi Aaziznia)

About the Author of Chapters 5 and 6

Andrew Aziz (Ph.D., P.Eng.) is a Canadian trader, Forbes Business Council member, investor and author living in Vancouver, British Columbia. After earning a Ph.D. in Chemical Engineering, Andrew exchanged the world of science and research for his true calling and passion - teaching, trading, and mentoring. Andrew is the founder and CEO of Peak Capital Trading (*PeakCapitalTrading.com*), a Vancouver-based proprietary trading firm, as well as the founder and principal of Bear Bull Traders (*BearBullTraders.com*), the leading international community of serious traders dedicated to making trading better for everyone. Andrew is the author of several trading books including *How to Day Trade for a Living* and *Advanced Techniques in Day Trading*. He has ranked as one of Amazon's top 100 best-selling authors in the "Business and Finance" category and his books in finance and stock market trading have been published in 8 different languages (English, Chinese, Portuguese, Vietnamese, Spanish, French, Russian, and Japanese). An entrepreneur since childhood, Andrew actively invests in FinTech companies related to the development of AI for trading. When not busy watching the markets go and up down, Andrew enjoys trail running, climbing, skiing, and high-altitude mountaineering.

In this chapter, I (Andrew) will review many of the basics of day trading in the stock market and hopefully answer your questions about what day trading is and how it works. This chapter will also introduce some of the main tools and strategies that you will use as a day trader. Of course, tools are of no value unless you know how to properly use them. This section will be your guide in gaining an understanding of how to use these tools.

In my opinion, the most important lesson that you can take away from reading these two chapters is that **you will not get rich quickly by day trading (or swing trading) in the stock market**. Trading is not the same as gambling or playing the lottery. This is the most important misconception that people have about trading and I hope you will come to a similar conclusion. Both day and swing trading appear deceptively easy, especially in hindsight, when you are looking at charts after the fact. That is why trading unfortunately attracts some of the most impulsive and gambling-prone people out there.

Brokers do not normally release customer statistics to the public but, in Massachusetts, a state court did order the release of the records of financial brokers. Those records indicated that after six months of trading, **only 16%** of day traders actually made money. It is very easy to be one of those 84% of traders who are losing money. Thus:

The golden rule of trading: Trading is not a strategy to get rich quickly.

Stay away from anyone who thinks the stock market is a get-rich-quick scheme. In light of the 2020 COVID-19 pandemic and social distancing guidelines, Figure 5.1 below shows two particularly important social distancing directives. One protects your health; the other protects your wealth! Stay away from anyone who think stocks are designed to help you get rich overnight!

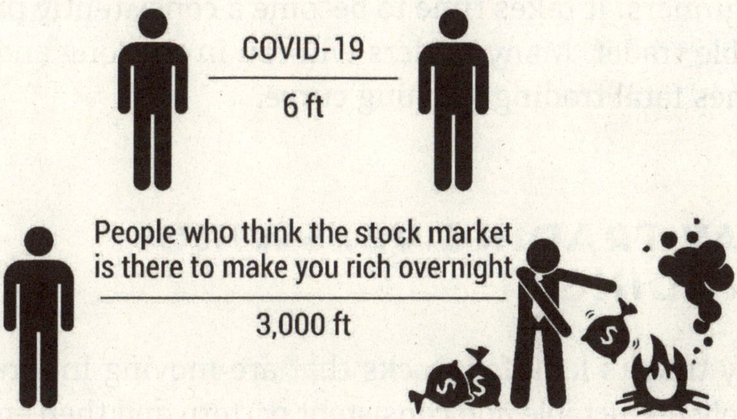

Figure 5.1: Images of a social distancing guideline related to COVID-19 (to protect your health), and a social distancing guideline related to those who want to make you rich overnight via the stock market (to protect your wealth). (For my non-American friends, 6 feet is about 1.8 meters, and 3,000 feet is about 900 meters.)

A very common misbelief that people have about trading is that it is **easy**: "*buy low, sell high*" or "*buy the dip, sell the rally*". Again, trading looks deceptively easy, but it is not. If it were that simple, everyone would be a successful trader. If you want to get rich quickly and easily in the stock market, perhaps by trading some penny stocks (if you are not familiar with the term "penny stocks", Ardi provides information on them in upcoming chapters), you should stop reading this book right now and spend the savings that you put aside for trading on a nice family vacation. It would be much more satisfying to spend your money that way, rather than losing it in the stock market. Having mentioned all of these points, trading can be a profitable profession. But keep in mind that it is a highly demanding endeavor and most definitely not a casual activity for beginners. It takes time to become a consistently profitable trader. Many traders will fail in the long and at times fatal trading learning curve.

DAY TRADING VS. SWING TRADING

Day traders look for stocks that are moving in a relatively predictable and consistent pattern and then enter and exit them (do a trade) in the same day. As a day trader, you will not keep any position overnight. If you buy stock in Apple (ticker: AAPL) today, for instance, you will not hold your position overnight and sell it tomorrow. If you hold onto any stock overnight, it is no longer day trading, it's called swing trading. Swing trading is a form of trading in which you hold stocks over a period of time, generally from one day to a few weeks. It is a completely different style of trading, and you shouldn't use the strategies and tools that you learn for day trading to do swing trading.

If we assume day trading is a business, swing trading is also a business, but a completely different kind of one.

The differences between swing trading and day trading are similar to the differences in owning a restaurant and owning a food delivery company. They both involve food, but they are very different: they operate with different time frames, regulations, market segments and revenue models. You should not confuse day trading with other styles of trading just because the trading involves stocks. Day traders always close their positions before the market closes.

Like many traders, I do both day trading and swing trading. However, I am aware that I am running two different businesses and I have gone through separate educational and training programs for these two kinds of trading. One of the key differences between day trading and swing trading is the approach to stock picking. I do not swing trade and day trade the same stocks. Swing traders usually look for stocks in solid companies that they know won't lose their entire value overnight. For day trading, however, you can trade anything, including companies that will soon go bankrupt, because you don't care what happens after the market closes. In fact, many of the companies that you will day trade are too risky to hold overnight because they might lose much of their value in that short of a period of time.

In my first book on trading, *How to Day Trade for a Living*, I introduced a series of rules for traders to follow. My third rule was (and still is a rule I follow!): "Day traders do not hold positions overnight. If necessary, you must sell with a loss to make sure you do not hold onto any stock overnight."

Several traders over the years have emailed me about this rule, and wondered why I advise them to close their position at the end of the day, even with a loss. Of course, I do not want you to lose money, but I often see traders suddenly change their plan at the end of the day because they do not want to accept a small loss. They should get out of a losing trade, but they instead suddenly decide to stay in the trade and hold it overnight, in the "hope" that perhaps a stock will come back the next day. I myself have turned some of my day trades into swing trades, and I paid a heavy price for that. Often, many of the stocks you day trade will lose even more of their value overnight. As a day trader, you must stick to your daily plans. You should never change a day trade that was supposed to close at the end of the day into a swing trade. It's a common human inclination to accept profits quickly but to also want to wait until losing trades return to even.

As Ardi has discussed earlier, it is also very important to remember that "trading" is different from "investing". Friends will often ask me about trading, but when I sit down with them and listen to their expectations, I realize that most of them want to invest their money, they are not looking for a new or additional career as a day or swing trader. They actually want to invest their money themselves rather than settle for the gains that typical mutual funds offer. They are not looking to become a trader. They don't realize the differences and are incorrectly using the words investing and trading interchangeably. Most of them have some money saved in their savings or retirement accounts and would like to grow that investment at a faster rate than what mutual funds or other managed investment services offer. I explain to them the differences between a trader and an investor, to ensure they are clear about a trading career. Of course, most of them are not ready to become a trader. Make sure you know if you want to be a trader or an investor. They are different.

TRADING SYSTEMS: DISCRETIONARY VS. MECHANICAL

Regardless of whether you want to be a swing trader or a day trader, it's critical that you understand the two different systems of trading.

Discretionary traders evaluate potential trades based on their trading plan (Ardi provides some thoughts in Chapter 8 on what should be included in a trading plan). They use fundamental analysis and/or technical analysis to determine whether each trade meets their requirements. Although the discretionary trader's rules are written down, they may also pass on or take trades based on experience or "gut". The discretionary trader doesn't follow a program such as, "If A, then B." Instead, they synthesize all available information, weigh the various options out, and then make a call.

Mechanical traders are much different on the other hand. They map out trading strategies that a computer can execute. The mechanical system can be based on technical inputs (like price, indicators, and so on) or fundamental ones (such as earnings surprises, sales growth rates, and other corporate events). The strategies are programmed into a computer software program that tests them on historical market data. The mechanical trader analyzes those results to determine whether the strategy is worth pursuing — if it produces higher profits than the overall market, for example. Of course, the two systems both have advantages and disadvantages.

Discretionary trading allows for a fresh look at each situation and the ability to pass on trades when external data that may not be easily captured in a computer program indicates decreased chances of success. However, because the discretionary trader must make a decision on each buy or sell, they are more prone to failing to follow the well-thought-out trading plan they had earlier prepared or, believe it or not (and it truly does happen), they fall in love and become emotionally attached to a particular trade, and just can't bring themself to break up with it.

Mechanical trading largely takes the human out of the equation. A computer program, barring some kind of catastrophe, executes the trades as programmed. The only input on the trader's part is the amount of capital devoted to each position, the entry signals, and the exit rules.

After those factors are determined, the mechanical trader can step back and watch the computer work its magic. But mechanical trading systems also have their drawbacks. Can a system be designed to capture all contingencies or possibilities that may arise? Of course not. And when losses occur, the mechanical trader must determine whether the setback is a temporary part of the system or whether it represents a fundamental failure of the strategy.

This book is geared heavily toward discretionary traders. Although hard data on the proportion of traders who are discretionary or mechanical is difficult to come by, based on my experience, discretionary trading is the more common approach. After all, some things, such as recognizing chart patterns, can't be easily programmed into a computer. And most traders feel more in control when they evaluate each trade instead of relying on a computer to execute transactions. I myself am an absolute discretionary trader as are the majority of traders I know and have worked with. Although I create a trading plan for each of my day trades, I do not execute them like a machine. As I referenced not too many paragraphs ago, my experience and my "gut" feelings are also part of my approach.

HOW DAY TRADING WORKS

In this chapter, I will review many of the basics of day trading and hopefully answer your questions about what day trading is and how it works. This chapter will also introduce some of the main tools and strategies that you will use as a day trader. Of course, tools are of no value unless you know how to properly use them. This book will be your initial guide in learning how to use these tools, but know this, you will not become a day trader by just reading this chapter or this book. There are many elements in day trading that Ardi (and I in my two chapters) had to only very quickly touch on or omit entirely for the sake of keeping this book a manageable length. If you really want to know more about day trading, I would like to suggest two of my other books: *How to Day Trade for a Living* and *Advanced Techniques in Day Trading.* They're both available in various formats on Amazon. With that said, please do not be offended by this unsolicited advertisement for my previous books. By no means do I want you to go and purchase these for my own benefit. I have to be honest with you though, you will need much more education and training than this book offers before you are ready to enter into the jungle of the financial markets, where some of the sharpest minds in the world are waiting to take your money. In short, there are many excellent books and credible online resources available about day trading. I encourage you to take advantage of everything you are able to.

When you look at the price of a stock on a daily or weekly chart, since each candlestick represents, respectively, the price action for one day or one week of trading, you see the price movement over a longer time frame, but in reality the price can fluctuate significantly during even one trading day. For example, let's look at Figure 5.2 below, the 5-minute chart for Virgin Galactic Holdings

Inc. (ticker: SPCE). This is a spaceflight company within the Virgin Group (Richard Branson and team) developing commercial spacecraft. (Don't forget that tracking the share price on a 5-minute chart means that each candlestick represents 5 minutes of price action.) You can see that the price opened at $32 per share at the beginning of the trading day, and then closed at $30. However, when you look at the range of the price during this day, you can see the price spanned from $29 to over $38 in just one trading day! That is an over 30% move up and down for a stock that opened at $32 and closed at $30! If you are an investor or swing trader, you do not see any benefit from this movement. You had SPCE at $32, and at the end of the day when you check your account, your SPCE shares are now worth $30. But if you are a day trader, you could possibly buy and sell SPCE many times during the day and benefit from its price movement. For example, you could buy at $30 and sell at $36, then buy again at $33 and sell at over $37. Or you could short stock at $38, and for a very decent profit, cover your short at $30. You could do this over and over and over again, and profit from this price volatility and fluctuation during the day.

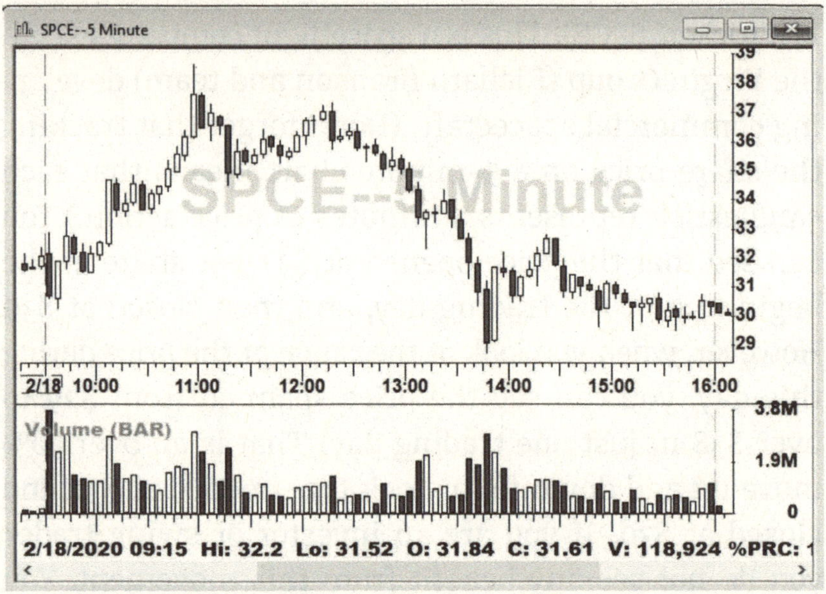

Figure 5.2: 5-minute chart of Virgin Galactic Holdings Inc. (ticker: SPCE) showing intraday (the same day) price movements. There is significant potential for day traders to benefit from the price volatility.

Of course, the above example is somewhat hypothetical. In this section, I just wanted to demonstrate the opportunities that are out there for day traders in comparison to swing traders or long-term investors.

Tools Required for Day Trading

Amongst all of the different forms of trading or investing, day traders need access to the most advanced tools. Why? Because they are entering and exiting trades in the most volatile times of the trading day. They need to be fast, real fast, and they need to execute their orders in seconds. Most day traders hold their positions for a matter of seconds, maybe minutes, and rarely do they wait hours. They cannot trade from a mobile app such as the Robinhood Markets, Inc. one (you'll recall Ardi wrote about these commission-free brokers in Chapter 3). These types of simple apps are designed mostly for providing an overview of the markets, not for trading in them.

Day traders need to use a different set of brokers. Ardi previously explained the differences between direct-access brokers (also known as discount brokers), full-service brokers and commission-free brokers. As their name implies, direct-access brokers are designed to service active traders who require direct access to exchanges such as the Nasdaq and the NYSE and who need to have their orders filled as fast as possible. A trader in Hong Kong who wants to make a trade in the U.S. market cannot pick up the telephone, dial a number, wait on hold, and eventually request a day trade from their broker. No, they need to have access to high-speed Internet, have the ability to press "buy" on their own trading platform, and be confident that a second later their order is filled and they are now long (meaning, they bought stock in the hope that it will increase in price). If the price does quickly rise, they can then press "sell", and sell for the profit!

Every second is important for day traders, as the volatility of the market is both very beneficial and very dangerous. If you are long a position, and the price starts to drop fast, you need to get out before you take a heavy loss. Day trading is the most sophisticated form of trading or investing and it requires the most advanced tools. But as mentioned earlier in this book, developments in technology, online platforms, and changes in the financial market have made many of these tools easily available and affordable for people who are trading from their home office. Today, active traders can receive fast transactions along with other services such as streaming quotes and market data, interactive charts, Level 2 Nasdaq quotes (the real-time Nasdaq TotalView Level 2 data feed) and other real-time features that once were only accessible to Wall Street professionals. In addition, direct-access brokers have in recent years cut down their costs significantly and increased efficiency, which provides traders a significantly lower commission than traditional full-service brokers are able to offer.

Robinhood and other Commission-Free Brokers for Day Trading?

Commission-free brokers such as Robinhood Markets, Inc. and TradeZero (which does not permit residents of the United States to hold accounts) are suitable for swing trading and investing, but not for day trading. Sometimes when something is free, it is free for a reason! Although Robinhood has steadily improved its app and website platforms since its launch, as of writing (April 2020), it is still not a reliable brokerage service for day trading. The opportunity cost or loss because your broker cannot execute your order fast enough or your platform crashes can be much more expensive than the commissions that you must pay to a good and reliable broker. This has in fact been experienced several times thus far in 2020 by Robinhood's clients. In March 2020, during the unprecedented volatility of the stock market due to the COVID-19 pandemic, the Robinhood app crashed multiple times, blocking users from accessing their accounts, causing them severe losses and opportunity costs. Immediately, a frustrated Robinhood user filed a potential class-action lawsuit in federal court in Tampa, Florida that accuses the company of failing to meet contractual obligations, violating its warranty, and negligence.

It is very important to note that although I do not recommend Robinhood for day trading, I credit the company with revolutionizing the stodgy trading industry. Robinhood has forced established players to either abolish or significantly reduce their commissions and it has even sparked the potential blockbuster merger of The Charles Schwab Corporation and TD Ameritrade.

While many other brokers have indeed introduced commission-free programs to attract new clients, my research has shown that most of these commission-free programs are not suitable for active day traders, as unlike swing traders and investors, day traders require fast execution of trades. For example, Interactive Brokers, one of the long-standing brokers, has introduced two types of accounts: **IBKR Lite** (commission free with access to an app and web-based platforms) and **IBKR Pro** (discounted commissions (not free) with access to direct-access platforms).

Day traders should choose IBKR Pro or a similar service that offers fast execution of trades. I myself use

Interactive Brokers Canada Inc. As you investigate which broker might be best for you, please take a moment to read some commentary about various brokers on my website (BearBullTraders.com).

Trading Platform

An electronic online trading platform is a computer software program that is used to place orders for day trading. The trading platform is different from the direct-access brokers themselves, however, I see often that traders confuse the two as one. Your trading platform sends and places your order at the exchange, so your direct-access broker can then clear the order for you. Usually, direct-access brokers offer their own proprietary trading platform to their clients. The quality, charting capability, speed of the software, and many other features vary significantly, which also of course affects their pricing. Many brokers provide their platform for a monthly fee, but they may waive that fee if you make sufficient commissions for them. Interactive Brokers, for example, offers a trading platform called Trader Workstation (TWS), but it also allows you to use the DAS Trader platform. Lightspeed Trading has its own platform called Lightspeed Trader. TD Ameritrade's own software is called *thinkorswim*.

Stock Selection for Day Trading

Stocks in Play

"You are only as good as the stocks that you trade" is an often-repeated saying in the day trading community. You can be the best trader in the world, but if your stocks do not move or have enough volume, then you cannot make money consistently. Trading a stock that doesn't move is a trading day wasted. You don't just look though for stocks that simply move. You also want to be able to determine that they will move in a certain direction. It is possible that a stock that moves $5/share intraday (the same day) may never offer you excellent risk/reward opportunities. Some stocks move too much intraday without foreshadowing their direction.

I often gets emails from traders saying that they struggle with finding the right stocks to day trade. Many of them understand how day trading works and have a proper education and the right gear for day trading, but when it comes to actually finding stocks to trade in real time, they are (and I don't want to sound mean) clueless. I certainly experienced this as a new trader myself. If you learn and practice the strategies later explained, but you cannot make money consistently, it is possible that you are trading the wrong stock. Again, you are only as good as the stocks that you trade. You need to find the stocks that are in play by day traders or, as I call them, the *Stocks in Play.*

There is more than one way to select Stocks in Play and make money trading them, and there is definitely more than one correct way. This part of the book details how I and many of the traders in our trading community find Stocks in Play. Of course, this is not the only method. While I avoid trading exchange-traded funds (ETFs), others, like my friend Brian Pezim, the author of the best-selling book, *How to Swing Trade*, regularly trade ETFs. Others have developed proprietary filters to find stocks. Still others concentrate on trading the markets as a whole with index futures. Often, professional traders at the trading desks of the big banks strictly trade in a sector like gold or oil or tech. But remember, as a retail trader, you have limited amounts of capital, so you must be efficient with selecting your Stocks in Play. As a day trader, you must be very efficient with your time and buying power.

A Stock in Play is a stock that offers excellent risk/reward setup opportunities – opportunities where your downside is 5 cents/share and your upside is 25 cents, or your downside is 20 cents and your upside is one dollar. That is a 1:5 risk to reward. You can regularly read a Stock in Play that is about to trade higher or lower from its present price. Stocks in Play move, and their moves are predictable and frequent and catchable. A good intraday stock offers numerous and excellent risk/reward opportunities.

Every day, there are new stocks that are in play. Trading Stocks in Play allows you to be the most efficient with your buying power. They often offer much better risk/reward opportunities intraday and allow you to execute your ideas and trading rules with more consistency. Trading the right Stocks in Play can help you to combat the algorithmic programs of Wall Street.

What are Stocks in Play? They are often:

- A stock with fresh news
- A stock that is up or down more than 2% in price before the market Open (before 9:30 a.m. ET)
- A stock that has an unusual pre-market trading activity
- A stock that develops important intraday levels from which you can trade off

You need to keep in mind that retail trading does not work on all stocks. It only works on the stocks that have *high relative volume.* Some stocks like Facebook, Inc. (ticker: FB) will on average trade millions and millions and millions of shares each day, while other stocks on average might trade only 500,000 shares each day. Does this mean you should trade FB only? No. High volume will be relative from one stock to another. You don't look just for high total volume. There are some stocks that regularly trade with high volume. What you need to look for is what is above average for that specific stock. Thirty million shares of FB traded in one day might very well not be higher than usual, and you should not trade FB unless it has a very unusual trading volume. I have marked on Figure 5.3 below the days in the summer of 2020 that FB had high relative volume. Those are the only days in that time frame you should have considered trading FB. If trading volume is not higher than normal, it means that the trading is being dominated by institutional traders and high frequency trading computers (the algorithms and secret formulas Wall Street uses to try to manipulate the market). Stay away!

Figure 5.3: Daily chart of Facebook, Inc. (ticker: FB) for the summer of 2020. The days that FB had a high relative volume are marked. Those days were suitable for day trading FB.

Another example is seen in Figure 5.4 below, the daily chart of Virgin Galactic Holdings Inc. (ticker: SPCE) for the winter of 2020. I have placed a box around those days that had high relative activity. Interestingly enough, when you take a close look at the chart, you realize that on those days the price of the stock also gapped up or down. If you wanted to day trade SPCE, you should have traded it only on those days. The other days were just normal, high frequency, algorithmic trading and, of course, retail traders should stay away from stocks that are trading normally.

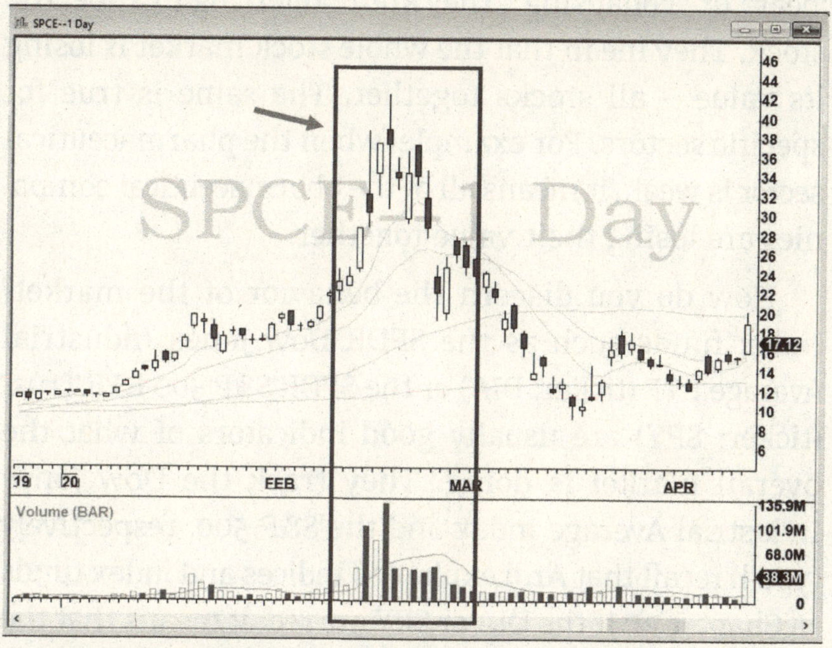

Figure 5.4: Daily chart of Virgin Galactic Holdings Inc. (ticker: SPCE) for the winter of 2020. I have placed a box around a group of days that SPCE had a high relative volume. Those days were suitable for day trading SPCE. You will see that those were the same days that the price of the stock gapped up or down.

The most important characteristic of high relative volume stocks is that these stocks trade independent of what their sector and the overall market are doing. When the market is weak, it means that the majority of stocks are selling off. When the market is strong, the prices of the majority of stocks will be going higher. It does not matter if it is Apple Inc. (ticker: AAPL), Facebook, Inc. (ticker: FB), Amazon.com Inc. (ticker: AMZN), or Exxon Mobil Corporation (ticker: XOM). Similarly, when you hear someone say the market is "bear" or "collapsing", they aren't referring to a specific stock. They mean that the whole stock market is losing its value - all stocks together. The same is true for specific sectors. For example, when the pharmaceutical sector is weak, it means all of the pharmaceutical companies are losing their value together.

How do you discern the behavior of the market? Index funds such as the SPDR Dow Jones Industrial Average ETF (ticker: DIA) or the SPDR S&P 500 ETF Trust (ticker: SPY) are usually good indicators of what the overall market is doing. They track the Dow Jones Industrial Average index and the S&P 500, respectively (you'll recall that Ardi explained indices and index funds in Chapter 2). If the DIA or SPY are red, it means that the overall market is weak. If the DIA or SPY are strong, then the overall market will be going higher.

Every day, only a handful of stocks are being traded independently of their sector and the overall market, and those are the only stocks that day traders should be trading. I sometimes call these stocks "*Alpha*", because in the animal kingdom, alpha is the predator at the top of a food chain upon which no other creatures prey. In day trading, alpha stocks are the ones that are independent of both the overall market and their sector. The market and high frequency trading cannot control them. We call these Stocks in Play.

A little earlier in this part of Chapter 5 I mentioned that a Stock in Play is often a stock with fresh news. Important news or events for companies can have significant impacts on their value in the market and therefore act as fundamental catalysts for their price action.

Here are some examples of the fundamental catalysts for stocks that make them suitable for day trading:

- Earnings reports
- Earnings warnings or pre-announcements
- Earnings surprises
- FDA approvals or disapprovals
- Mergers/acquisitions
- Alliances, partnerships or major product releases
- Major contract wins/losses
- Restructurings, layoffs or management changes
- Stock splits, buybacks or debt offerings

In the morning, day traders check the news on all stocks up or down more than 2% pre-market (before 9:30 a.m. ET) and create a shortlist. For finding those Stocks in Play which gapped up or down more than 2%, day traders use "scanners". Many scanners are free (*finviz.com* is a popular choice), but some advanced ones charge a fee to use. At Bear Bull Traders, we use Trade Ideas software for scanning stocks (*trade-ideas.com*) and publish our daily Stocks in Play to our Bear Bull Traders YouTube channel each trading day between 8:30 and 9 a.m. ET.

An example of a Trade Ideas scanner is shown in Figure 5.5 below. The screenshot of the scanner shows those stocks gapping up or down in price by more than 2% on April 16, 2020 at 9 a.m. I then selected some of those stocks for day trading based on their price range, volatility, volume and chart patterns, as well as my own past experience with them. As you can see, scanners are powerful tools. Out of over 7,000 companies traded daily in the U.S. stock market, I have now reduced my options to only a handful of them!

Gappers Watch List (Pre-Market Movers): 9:00:00 - 9:04:59 4/16/2020

Symbol	Price ($)	Vol Today	Chg Close	Chg Close	Flt (Shr)	Avg True	Shrt Flt (%)	Sector
THMO	7.30	879,119	2.71	59.0	4.48M	0.65	6.56	Manufacturing
RCUS	24.25	143,585	8.67	55.6	36.3M	1.51		Manufacturing
BBBY	5.17	1.02M	0.73	16.4	127M	0.69	85.82	Retail Trade
INO	7.65	650,877	0.51	7.1	90.3M	0.83	14.49	Manufacturing
TSM	52.07	273,012	2.41	4.9	5.17B	1.87		Manufacturing
CODX	9.89	471,856	0.39	4.1	15.8M	1.07	17.29	Manufacturing
ROKU	116.79	242,937	3.79	3.4	81.5M	7.09		Information
AMD	56.19	959,027	1.20	2.2	1.07B	2.88	5.70	Manufacturing
M	5.85	180,090	0.12	2.1	308M	0.77	32.25	Retail Trade
JD	45.53	129,736	0.93	2.1	1.22B	2.06		Retail Trade
SPCE	20.38	346,944	0.40	2.0	65.2M	2.05	27.06	Other Services (except Public Administration)
TWTR	26.90	375,617	-0.61	-2.2	751M	1.65		Professional, Scientific, and Technical Services
MS	37.42	299,300	-0.98	-2.6	1.60B	2.53	4.14	Finance and Insurance
BP	22.25	522,331	-0.59	-2.6	3.59B	1.58		Mining, Quarrying, and Oil and Gas Extraction
SBSW	7.20	130,276	-0.20	-2.7	575M	0.68		Mining, Quarrying, and Oil and Gas Extraction
TLRY	6.60	175,931	-0.19	-2.8	79.8M	1.45	71.25	Manufacturing
PFGC	23.32	521,883	-0.68	-2.8	103M	2.78	2.78	Retail Trade
UAL	30.90	502,356	-0.96	-3.0	247M	4.17	10.58	Transportation and Warehousing
SQ	59.20	299,879	-2.18	-3.6	331M	5.09	8.92	Information
HTZ	5.55	370,034	-0.25	-4.3	84.1M	0.83	31.05	Real Estate and Rental and Leasing
PSTI	9.30	310,623	-0.54	-5.5	14.5M	1.27	1.28	Manufacturing
RAD	12.86	815,258	-1.62	-11.2	53.4M	1.42	24.83	Retail Trade
CALA	6.74	172,240	-1.11	-14.1	34.1M	0.74	5.07	Manufacturing

Figure 5.5: Screenshot of the Bear Bull Traders/Trade Ideas scanner on April 16, 2020 at 9 a.m. showing several stocks that had gapped up or down in price by more than 2%.

In this next part of Chapter 5, I outline two specific day trading strategies: the ABCD Pattern and Opening

Range Breakouts (ORBs). They are easy to locate on your charts as well as to plan and execute a trade with. In addition, and very importantly, they also offer a high probability of success.

DAY TRADING STRATEGIES

In this section, I introduce two of the most common and well-known day trading strategies based on technical indicators and technical analysis and chart patterns. You will recall that I earlier explained *discretionary* and *mechanical* trading systems. The strategies in this section are directed heavily toward discretionary systems. I believe that many requirements of a successful trade, such as price action and recognizing chart patterns, can't be easily programmed into a computer. As I previously mentioned, I feel more in control when I myself evaluate each trade instead of relying on a computer to execute transactions.

As a day trader, you shouldn't care about companies and their earnings. Day traders are not concerned about what companies do or what they make. Your attention should only be on price action, technical indicators and chart patterns. I know more stock symbols than the names of actual companies. I don't mingle fundamental analysis with technical analysis while making a trade; I focus exclusively on the technical indicators. I don't care about the fundamental aspects of companies because I'm not a long-term investor – I'm a day trader. We trade very quickly – guerrilla trading! – at times we will trade in periods as short as a few seconds.

Every trader needs their own strategy and edge. You need to find your spot in the market where you feel comfortable. I focus on these two strategies in this chapter because they work for me. In theory, they are simple, but they are difficult to master and require plenty of practice. These trading strategies give signals relatively infrequently and allow you to enter the markets during the quiet times, just as the professionals do.

Another point to remember is that in the market right now, over 60% of the volume is algorithmic high frequency trading. That means you are trading against computers. If you've ever played chess against a computer, you know that you're eventually going to lose. You might get lucky once or twice, but play often enough and you are guaranteed to be the loser. The same rule applies to algorithmic trading. You're trading stocks against computer systems. On the one hand, that represents a problem. It means that the majority of changes in stocks that you are seeing are simply the result of computers moving shares around. On the other hand, it also means that there's a small handful of stocks each day that are going to be trading on such heavy retail volume (as opposed to institutional algorithmic trading) that you will overpower the algorithmic trading and you and I, the retail traders, will control that stock.

Each day, you need to focus on trading those particular stocks. These are what I earlier called the Stocks in Play, stocks that are typically gapping up or down by more than 2%. You must look for the stocks that have significant retail traders' interest and significant retail volume. These will be the stocks you will trade, and together, we the people, the retail traders, will overpower the computers, just like in a storyline for the next *Terminator* sequel.

I personally use the candlestick charts explained by Ardi in Chapter 4. Each candlestick represents a period. You can choose any intraday (same day) time frame, depending on your personality and trading style: hourly charts, 5-minute charts, or even 1-minute charts.

And please, remember, my philosophy of trading is that you must master only a few solid setups to be consistently profitable. In fact, having a simple trading method will work to reduce confusion and stress and allow you to concentrate more on the psychological aspect of trading. That is what separates the winners from the losers.

1-Minute ORBs

A very well-known day trading strategy is the so-called Opening Range Breakout (ORB). Right at the market Open (9:30 a.m. New York time), Stocks in Play usually experience violent price action that arises from heavy buy and sell orders that come into the market. This heavy trading in the opening seconds is the result of the profit or loss taking of the overnight position holders as well as new investors and traders. If a stock has gapped up, some overnight traders start selling their position for a profit. At the same time, some new investors might jump in to buy the stock before the price goes higher. If a stock gaps down, on the other hand, some investors might panic and dump their shares right at the Open before it drops any lower. On the other side, some institutions might think this drop could be a good buying opportunity and they will start buying large positions at a discounted price. Therefore, there is a complicated mass psychology unfolding at the Open for the Stocks in Play. Wise traders sit on their hands for at least a few moments and watch for the opening ranges to develop and allow the other traders to fight against each other until one side wins.

Typically, you should give the opening range at least 1 minute. This is called the 1-minute ORB. Some traders will wait even longer, such as for 5 minutes, 10 minutes, 30 minutes or even one hour, to identify the balance of power between buyers and sellers. They then develop a trading plan in the direction of that breakout. The longer the time frame, the less volatility you can expect. As with most setups, an ORB Strategy tends to work best with medium to large cap stocks, which do not show wild price swings intraday (the same day). I do not recommend trading this strategy with low float stocks that have gapped up or down. (Ardi discussed the terms "market cap" and "float" in Chapter 3 if you want to review their meanings again.)

For the 1-minute ORB, I wait for the 1-minute candlestick to close (which represents the end of the first minute of the battle between buyers and sellers). As soon as that candlestick closes at 9:31 a.m. ET, I (and all of the other traders around the world watching that particular stock) will decide whether or not to enter into a trade based on the breakout direction of that candlestick.

To gain a better understanding of this strategy, Figure 5.6(A) below shows a 1-minute ORB trade on Tesla Inc. (ticker: TSLA) that I took on January 3, 2020. As you can see, the stock closed as a hammer Doji within the first minute of trading (Dojis were explained by Ardi in Chapter 4). A hammer Doji in nature is a bullish sign. I then took the trade to the long side at $88/share and sold all the way up to $90!

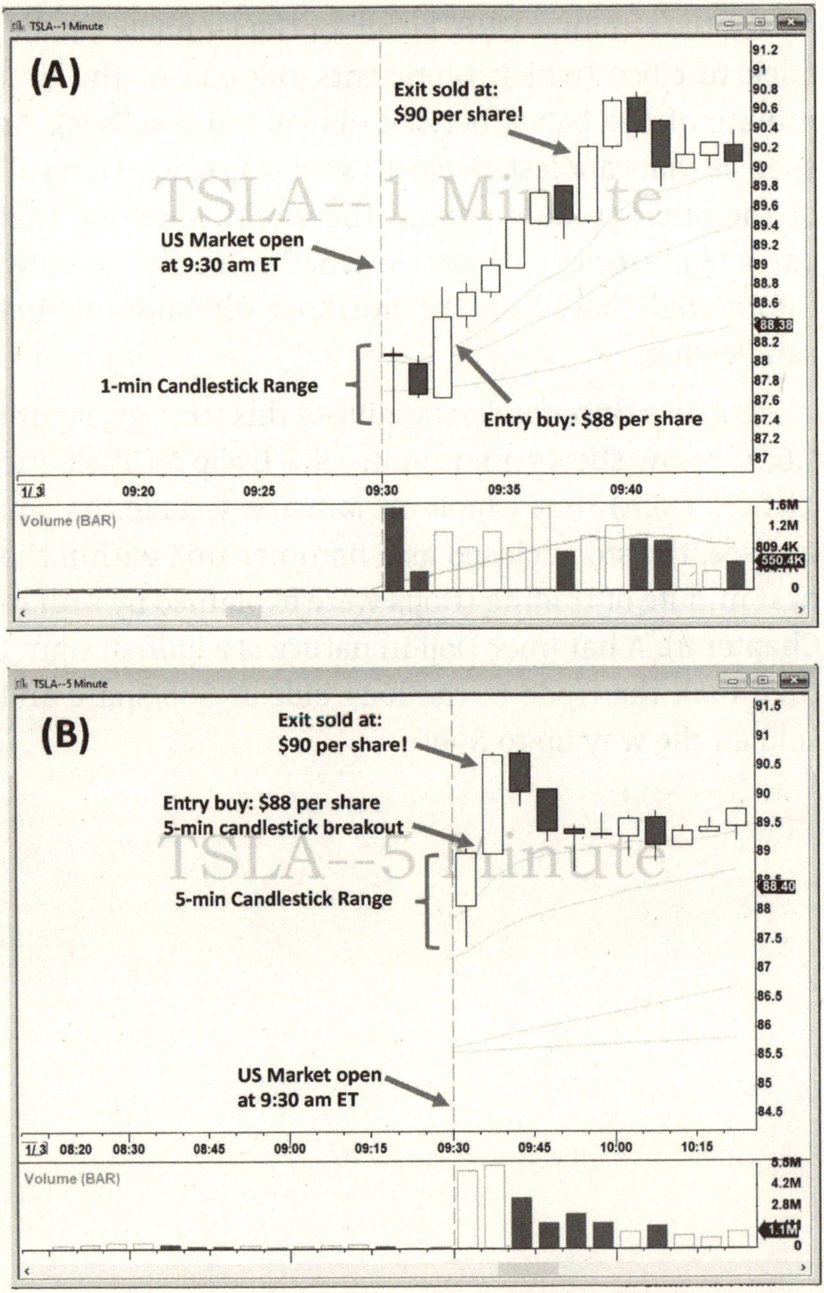

Figure 5.6: Examples of (A) 1-minute ORB and (B) 5-minute ORB on Tesla Inc. (ticker: TSLA) on January 3, 2020.

My strategy was for a 1-minute ORB, but the same process will also work well for other time frames such as a 5-minute ORB (as shown in the above Figure 5.6(B) for TSLA) or even higher time frames such as a 15-minute or a 30-minute ORB. If you look at this 5-minute chart for TSLA, this could also be a 5-minute opening range break up. Trading in the first 5 minutes after the market opens is usually very volatile and tricky. Therefore, new traders should definitely wait until the first 5 minutes of trading have ended and they have a better sense of the direction of the price action.

Another 1-minute ORB trade, but on the short side, is a trade I took on Aimmune Therapeutics Inc. (ticker: AIMT). You will see in Figure 5.7 below that AIMT opened weak and sold off between 9:30 and 9:31 a.m. As soon as it showed some weakness, I took the trade to the short side at $24.25/share and covered toward $23.25 with 1,000 shares short for a decent profit. Do you remember how short selling works from what Ardi wrote in Chapter 3? I borrowed 1,000 shares of AIMT from my broker, sold them at $24.25 per share, and when the price dropped, I purchased those shares back (what we call covered in day trading) at a lower price of $23.25. I then returned those shares back to my broker, but I kept the profit difference. With 1,000 shares, I made a $1,000 profit!

Remember, these patterns are easy to recognize and see in the past, after the fact, but they're not so simple in the heat of the moment. The perfect execution of trades requires considerable practice, the right tools and platform, and of course a good level of mental preparation and psychological resilience. Do not let these charts fool you. Day trading is a fast-paced, high-performing field, and you need to always be ready to deal with the unexpected.

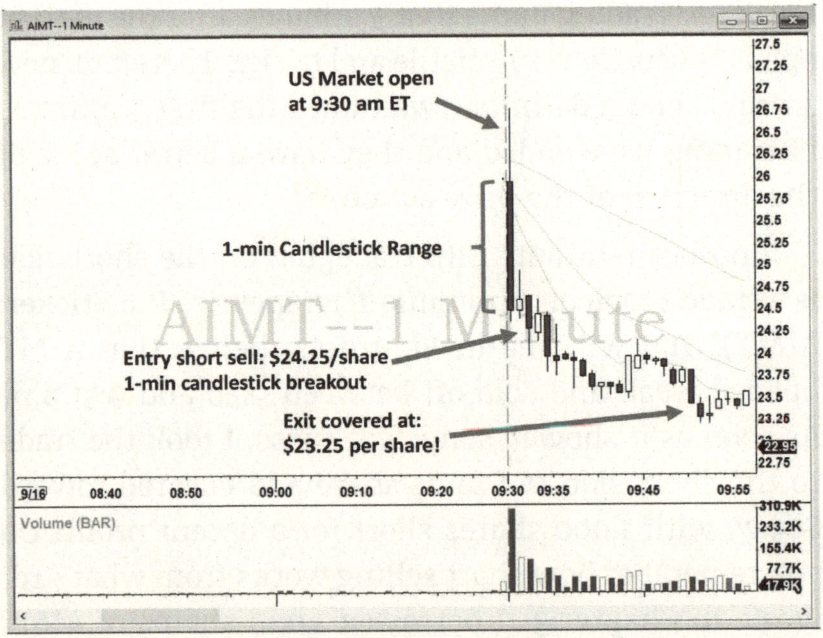

Figure 5.7: Example of 1-minute ORB (on the short side) on Aimmune Therapeutics Inc. (ticker: AIMT).

Another nice example of a 1-minute ORB is seen in Figure 5.8 below, a trade I took on December 11, 2019 on American Eagle Outfitters Inc. (ticker: AEO). The stock opened strong for 1 minute and, as soon as the breakout happened on the first candlestick, I went long at $13.90/share and sold toward $14.30, although the stock did move much higher to nearer $14.50. With my position of 2,000 shares, my profit was $800 in only a matter of minutes. That is the power of day trading. This example (and other examples in this book) may seem easy, but recognizing these patterns and executing them in the fast-paced environment of trading is definitely not easy. Trading looks deceptively easy when you are looking at the chart after the fact, but it is not, for it requires a certain level of dedication and experience similar to other high-performing fields such as professional athletics.

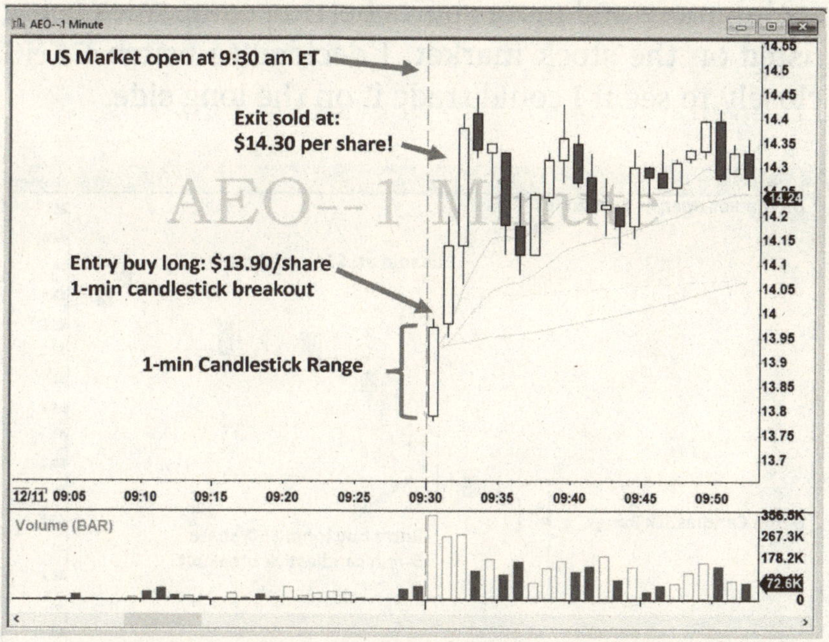

Figure 5.8: Example of a 1-minute ORB on American Eagle Outfitters Inc. (ticker: AEO) on December 11, 2019.

5-Minute ORBs

A slower-paced ORB Strategy that some day traders use is the 5-minute ORB. This is one of the easiest and more common strategies that many of our traders at both Peak Capital Trading and Bear Bull Traders use. Let's take a look at Figure 5.9 below, the September 17, 2020 5-minute chart for the American fantasy sports contest and sports betting operator, DraftKings Inc. (ticker: DKNG). DKNG was on the Bear Bull Traders Gappers watchlist that day. Thanks to stock market personality David Portnoy of Barstool Sports, we are seeing more and more sports betting companies being listed on the stock market. I decided to watch DKNG closely to see if I could trade it on the long side.

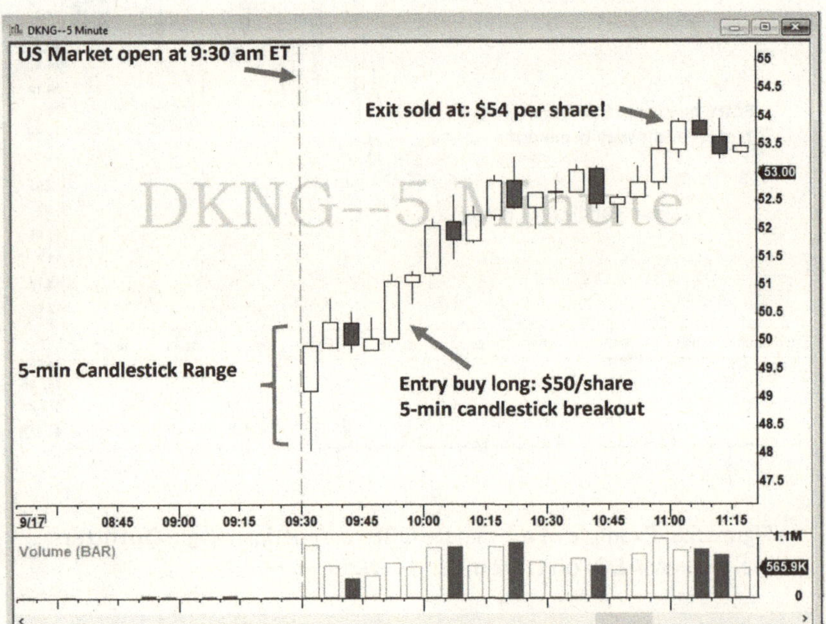

Figure 5.9: Example of a 5-minute ORB on DraftKings Inc. (ticker: DKNG).

As you can see in Figure 5.9 above, the stock opened at $49/share and sold off to below $48 within the first five minutes. It then bounced back and the first 5-minute candlestick closed at around $50. I ended up waiting some 15 to 20 minutes for the battle of buyers and sellers to settle down. At around 9:50 a.m., as soon as I saw that the price had broken the 5-minute opening range, I went long at about $50 and sold my position toward $54.

Another example of a 5-minute ORB is Micron Technology, Inc. (ticker: MU) on December 19, 2019. The stock hit my scanner and I had it on my watchlist at the Open.

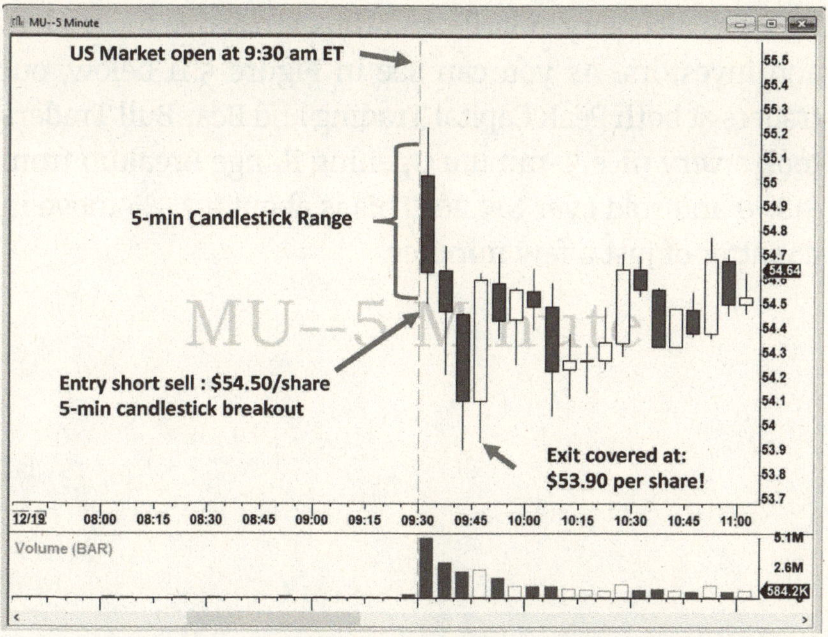

Figure 5.10: Example of a 5-minute ORB on Micron Technology, Inc. (ticker: MU) on December 19, 2019.

As you can see in Figure 5.10 above, when the market opened at 9:30 a.m., the price of the stock was represented by a big red (filled) candle which very quickly sold off. The first 5-minute candle was also red and that was a sign that sellers were in control of the price. I went short at the breakout for the 5-minute candlestick at $54.50/share, and covered at $53.90 with 1,000 shares, for a profit of approximately $600 for a few minutes of work.

A more recent example of a 5-minute ORB is on a chart for China's electric car manufacturer, NIO Inc., known as the Chinese Tesla. In the summer of 2020, there was a mania regarding electric car makers, and similar to Tesla, NIO was also very volatile and thus attractive for traders and investors. As you can see in Figure 5.11 below, our traders at both Peak Capital Trading and Bear Bull Traders took a very nice 5-minute Opening Range Breakup from $18.70 and sold over $19.20. This is about a 2.5% move in a matter of just a few minutes.

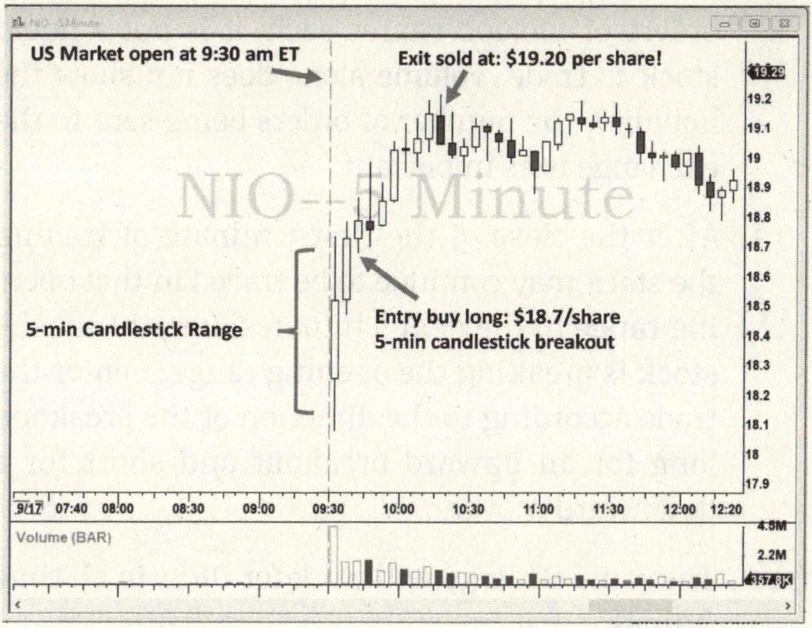

Figure 5.11: Example of a 5-minute ORB on NIO Inc. (ticker: NIO) on September 17, 2020.

To summarize the ORB Strategy:

1. After I build my watchlist in the morning, I closely monitor the shortlisted stocks when the market first opens.
2. I identify their opening range and their price action. How many shares are being traded? Is the stock jumping up and down or does it have a directional upward or downward movement? Is it high volume with large orders only, or are there many orders going through? I prefer stocks that have high volume, but also with numerous different orders being traded. If the stock has traded 1 million shares, but those shares were only ten

orders of 100,000 shares each, it is not a liquid stock to trade. Volume alone does not show the liquidity; the number of orders being sent to the exchange is as important.

3. After the close of the first 1 minute of trading, the stock may continue to be traded in that opening range in the next 5 minutes. But, if I see the stock is breaking the opening range, I enter the trade according to the direction of the breakout: long for an upward breakout and short for a downward move.

4. The same strategy will work for ORBs in all time frames.

5. It is often better to wait until 5 minutes of trading has elapsed. The 1-minute ORB is a volatile strategy and inexperienced traders need to be very careful trading it.

ABCD Patterns

The ABCD Pattern is one of the most basic and easiest patterns to trade, and it is an excellent choice for beginner and intermediate traders. Although it is simple and has been known for a long time, it still works effectively because so many traders are still trading it. You should do whatever all of the other traders are doing because a trend is your friend. In fact, a trend may very well be your only friend in the market.

Let's take a look at this pattern in Figure 5.12 below:

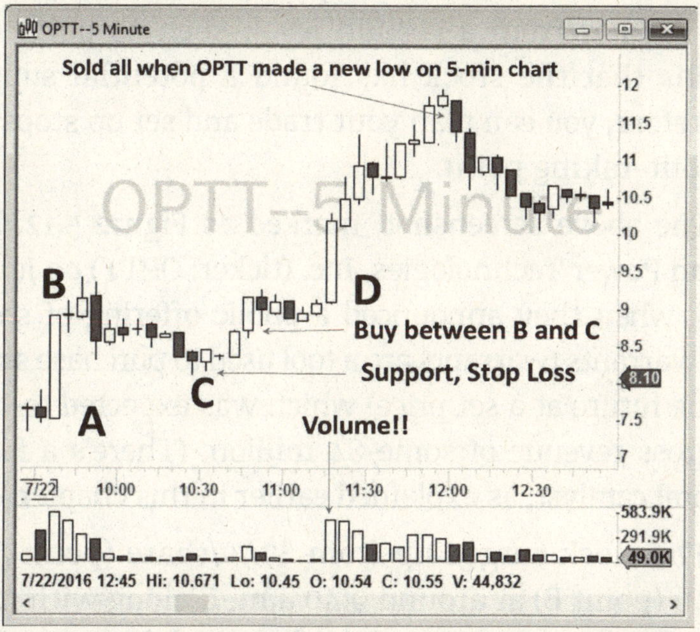

Figure 5.12: Example of an ABCD Pattern on Ocean Power Technologies, Inc. (ticker: OPTT).

ABCD Patterns start with a strong upward move. Buyers are aggressively buying a stock from point A and making constantly new highs of the day (point B). You want to enter the trade, but you should not chase the trade, because at point B it is very extended and already at a high price. In addition, you cannot say where your stop loss should be. You must never enter a trade without knowing where your stop is.

At point B, traders who bought the stock earlier start slowly selling it for profit and the price comes down. You should still not enter the trade because you do not know where the bottom of this pull back will be. However, if you see that the price does not come down any further from a certain level, such as point C, it means that the stock has found a potential support. Therefore, you can plan your trade and set up stops and a profit-taking point.

The above screenshot, marked as Figure 5.12, is of Ocean Power Technologies, Inc. (ticker: OPTT) on July 22, 2016, when they announced a public offering of shares and warrants (warrants are a tool used to purchase shares in the future at a set price) which was expected to bring in gross revenue of some $4 million. (There's a fundamental catalyst, as explained earlier in this chapter!)

The stock surged up from $7.70/share (point A) to $9.40 (point B) at around 9:40 a.m. I, along with many other traders who missed the first push higher, waited for point B and then a confirmation that the stock wasn't going to go lower than a certain price (point C). When I saw that point C was holding as a support and that buyers would not let the stock price go any lower than $8.10 (point C), I bought 1,000 shares of OPTT near point C, with my stop being a break below point C. I knew that when the price went higher, closer to point B, buyers would jump on massively. As I mentioned, the ABCD Pattern is a very classic strategy and many retail traders (people like you, the traders who trade from their home office and do not work for companies) look for it. Close to point D, the volume suddenly spiked, which meant that many more traders were jumping into the trade.

My profit target was when the stock made a new low on a 5-minute chart, which was a sign of weakness. As you can see in Figure 5.12 above, OPTT had a nice run up to around $12/share and showed weakness by making a new low on a 5-minute chart at around $11.60. That is when I sold all of my position.

Figure 5.13 below is another example, this time for SkyPeople Fruit Juice (ticker: SPU) on August 29, 2016. There are actually two ABCD Patterns in this example. I marked the second one as *abcd pattern*. Usually, as the trading day progresses, volumes become lower and therefore the second pattern is smaller in size. Please note that you will always have high volumes at points B and D (and in this instance also at points b and d). As an aside, less than two months after the date of this chart, the Nasdaq announced it was planning to delist SPU for failing to file various required reports.

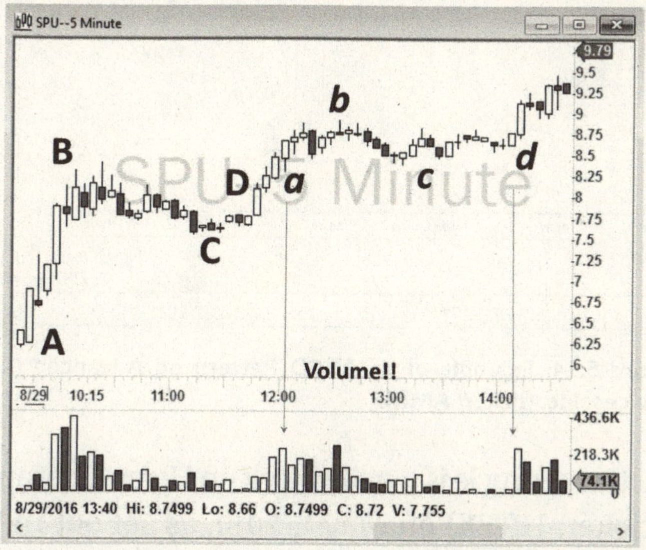

Figure 5.13: Example of an ABCD Pattern and an abcd pattern on SkyPeople Fruit Juice (ticker: SPU).

The next example, as shown in Figure 5.14 below, is for Advanced Micro Devices, Inc. (ticker: AMD) on May 28, 2019. Within about 30 minutes following the Open, AMD moved from $27/share to $28.44! For the first 20 minutes, from 9:30 to 9:50 a.m., I waited and watched the price action in order to identify points A, B, C and D. As the price started to move up again toward the then high of the day, I went long at $27.80 since a good entry could be identified from my 1-minute chart. The stop loss was a break below $27.75 (point C) and I profited toward the daily level of $28.44.

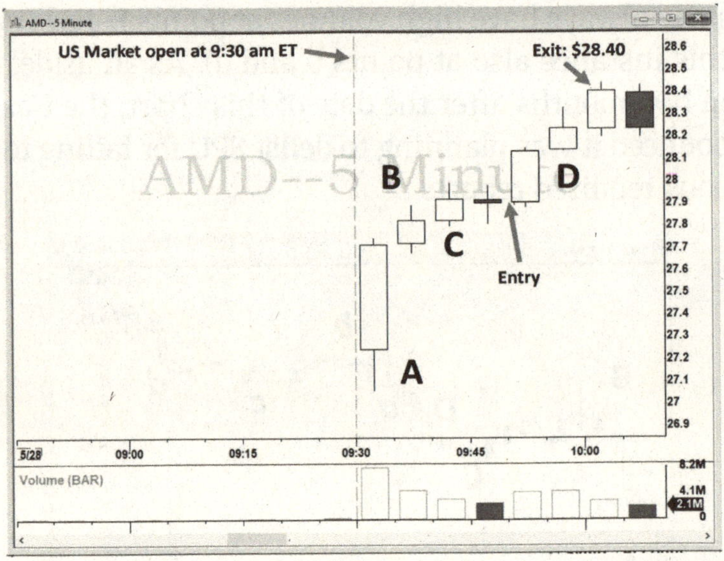

Figure 5.14: Example of an ABCD Pattern on Advanced Micro Devices, Inc. (ticker: AMD).

Another example is a trade I took on Heron Therapeutics Inc. (ticker: HRTX) on May 1, 2019, as set out in Figure 5.15 below. At 9:35 a.m., I went long at $17.44/share and sold for a decent profit at around $19. As you can see, on the 5-minute chart the candlesticks appear like a 5-minute ORB, and on the 1-minute chart they present as an ABCD Pattern. There is no issue with one trade fitting into two strategies at the same time. This actually can be a good sign, meaning you have a better confirmation. Remember, no matter what you call these strategies, the idea behind them is the same. Your job as a trader is to analyze the power between buyers and sellers and bet on the winning group. If the winners are going to be buyers, you go long; if the winners are going to be sellers, you go short. You may come across different names for what in essence is the same basic strategy: momentum, Bull Flag, Bear Flag, etc. In the end, they are all the manifestation of reading the battle between buyers and sellers.

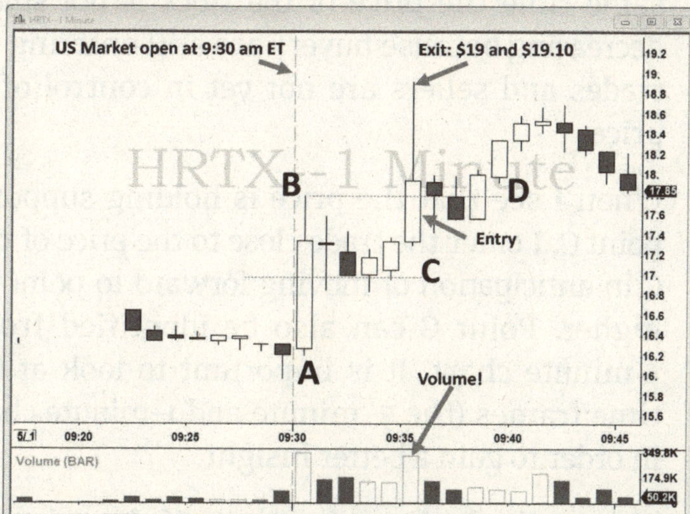

Figure 5.15: Example of a trade on Heron Therapeutics Inc. (ticker: HRTX).

To summarize my trading strategy for the ABCD Pattern:

1. When I find a Stock in Play, either from my Gappers watchlist or from one of my scanners, or when I'm advised by someone in our chatroom that a stock is surging up from point A and reaching a significant new high for the day (point B), I wait to see if the price makes a support higher than point A. I call this point C. I do not jump into the trade right away.

2. I watch the stock during its consolidation period. I choose my share size and stop loss and profit target exit strategy. A consolidation period occurs when traders who bought stocks at a lower price are selling and taking their profits while at the same time the price of the stock is not sharply decreasing because buyers are still entering into trades and sellers are not yet in control of the price.

3. When I see that the price is holding support at point C, I enter the trade close to the price of point C in anticipation of moving forward to point D or higher. Point C can also be identified from a 1-minute chart. It is important to look at both time frames (the 5-minute and 1-minute charts) in order to gain a better insight.

4. My stop is the loss of point C. If the price goes lower than point C, I sell and accept the loss. Therefore, it is important to buy the stock close to point C to minimize the loss. Some traders

wait and buy only at point D to ensure that the ABCD Pattern is really working. In my opinion, that approach basically reduces your reward while at the same time increasing your risk.

5. If the price moves higher, I sell half of my position at point D, and bring my stop higher to my entry point (break-even).
6. I sell the remaining position as soon as my target hits or I sense that the price is losing steam or that sellers are acquiring control of the price action. When the price makes a new low on my 5-minute chart, it is a good indicator that buyers are almost exhausted.

More Day Trading Strategies

The ABCD Pattern and Opening Range Breakouts are of course not the only day trading strategies. There are many other trading strategies that day traders use, some include more complex mathematical indicators, and some are purely based on candlesticks and chart patterns. A great day trader is a well-diversified expert who can understand various strategies; however, you do not need to be an expert in all of them. Being conversant in one or two good strategies is usually enough to be a consistent trader. In this book, Ardi and I can only scratch the surface of trading. Therefore, please, do not start day trading and risking your hard-earned money once you have finished reading this book. If day trading is of interest to you, I highly recommend doing a thorough search online in order to learn about other available resources. Two books that can give you a better understanding are *How to Day Trade for a Living* and *Advanced Techniques in Day Trading*, both written by me, and both available in various formats from Amazon. Of course, this unsolicited advertisement is only a suggestion for you, and there are many other very worthwhile free and paid resources you can find out about on the net.

CHAPTER 6

THE PATH TO BEING A SUCCESSFUL DAY TRADER

By Andrew Aziz

Every single day, countless individuals are launching their career in day trading. They join chatrooms, participate in various classes, and start trading in real accounts or simulators. They enter day trading with all kinds of different expectations. Let's deal with one that I encounter often. People will say to me something along the lines of:

"I'll become a full-time trader, and I can make a living out of that. I'll have financial freedom and become independent and be able to quit my job."

Unfortunately, that is not likely to happen very early in their trading career. Of course, it's possible for anyone after three months of training and study to become a full-time trader. That's the easy part. But if you want to actually make a living out of trading, preferably while lounging in a beach house on the Caribbean and sipping tall, cool drinks, that outcome is highly unlikely.

Trading is a career and a business. And in no career and in no business can you become profitable in just three months. Look at doctors, attorneys and engineers. They go to school for years and take examinations and serve internships and practice, and practice some more, before they can truly call themselves professionals. They are all long and challenging processes that take considerably more than three months.

Basically, what you will learn in those first three months are the answers to two vital questions:

1. Is day trading for you?
2. And if yes, how do I plan out my trading business?

The first and most fundamental question is: "*Is this for you or is it not?*" And if it is for you, you need to learn how to go about planning for it and you must understand that your trading business will grow slowly. You cannot rush it.

Many often ask if there is a guarantee that they will become a profitable trader? The answer is no, there is no guarantee for success. This is also true in all other careers and businesses. I personally know many doctors and engineers who are in financial trouble, carrying literally huge student loans and personal debts. An education or training program is an investment that you make, and maybe it works, and maybe it doesn't. If it doesn't, it's not the end of the world for you. You will survive and go on with your life. And if it works, well, that's good for you. Knowing how to manage expectations is extremely important, especially for beginner traders.

Some people tell me they need to get into trading with real money as quickly as possible, saying, "I don't have time to practice in a simulator. I really need the income. I quit my job, I don't have any savings, and I can't wait."

This is a common discussion I have almost every day with a new trader. They want to get into live trading as quickly as possible. In the summer of 2017, one trader emailed me and explained he had experienced some heavy losses and was wanting my advice. His sister had given him my first book as an early birthday gift. I did not know him before, and I had no idea what he was doing, but I urgently asked him to stop trading with real money and switch to a simulator so we could get to work on figuring out his problems. He emailed me back:

> *"I have never used a simulator. I can't afford to earn fake money for 3 months. I am on a mission to rebuild my battered portfolio."*

He later got into even deeper trouble with his account. Trading in a simulator and taking the time to gain a proper education is vital. I often receive negative feedback about why I place so much emphasis on these two points. Some traders think I want to push them toward buying my software, but in all honesty, I don't own any software. My desire is to try to save traders from themselves.

Trading in a simulator is a must. You should go live and begin trading with real money only after earning consistent profits when trading in a simulator for several months. The bottom line is that there is still no guarantee, even if you are consistent in the simulator, that you will make money when you use your real account. But, if you are not consistent in the simulator, failure is guaranteed when you begin trading with a real account, and especially given all of the psychological factors that will come into play.

Another problem for beginners is that many of them think that trading is easy, often because they have been misled by online marketing. If you search the Internet, you will find plenty of advertising for different training programs featuring people who say, "*Oh, it's easy,*" and constantly use catchy buzzwords and phrases like "financial freedom" and "becoming independent". The truth is that trading is not easy, and you have to be really skeptical about anyone who says otherwise.

NEXT STEPS FOR BEGINNER DAY TRADERS

I appreciate you taking the time to read thus far in this book, and I thank Ardi for asking me to write these two chapters for his book. I hope you've found lots of valuable information and ideas to help you move forward in your day trading career.

An important takeaway from my chapters in this book is to know whether or not day trading is for you. Day trading requires a certain mindset, as well as a discipline and a set of skills that not everyone possesses.

Interestingly, most of the traders I know are also poker players. They enjoy speculation and the stimulation that comes from it. Although poker is a type of gambling, in my opinion, day trading is definitely not. Day trading is the serious business of selling and buying stocks, at times in a matter of seconds. You should be able to make decisions quickly, with no emotion or hesitation. Doing otherwise results in losing real money.

A goal for these two chapters is to introduce you into the world of day trading, but you still have a long way to go to become a trader. Can you be a mechanic by just reading a book or two? Can you perform surgery after reading a book or taking First Aid 101? No. These chapters develop a basic foundation that you can build upon. If day trading is your passion and you feel you would like to pursue it, I encourage you to read more books and find online or in-person courses on day trading.

Another key message I desire you to take away from these chapters is that under no circumstances should you think day trading is easy and a fast way to get rich.

In my books on day trading, I emphasize how difficult a day trading career is and the potential risks involved in trading. Some readers, such as D. Carroll, did not like this approach, as set out in Figure 6.1 below:

"Book was very negative, depressing. Stopped reading it because of the constant reminder of failure."

★☆☆☆☆ **Negative outlook**

By D. Carroll on June 4, 2017

Format: Paperback | **Verified Purchase**

Book was very negative, depressing. Stopped reading it because of the constant reminder of failure.

5 people found this helpful

Helpful | ▸ 1 comment | Report abuse

Figure 6.1: What one reader did not like about my first book.

Five people found that comment helpful!

THE SEVEN ESSENTIALS FOR DAY TRADING

In order to become a consistently profitable trader, I believe that you need to follow these seven "essentials" before entering into the world of trading with your real money. Some should be focused on before and after each and every single trade you make:

1. Education and simulated trading
2. Preparation
3. Determination and hard work
4. Patience
5. Discipline
6. Mentorship and a community of traders
7. Reflection and review

Education and Simulated Trading

As I just mentioned, I encourage you to read more books and find online or in-person courses on day trading. You should never start your day trading career with real money. Sign up with one of the brokers that provides you with simulated accounts with real market data. Some brokers give you access to delayed market data, but don't use those. You need to make decisions in real time. Most of the simulated data software is a paid service, so you need to save some money for that expense. Many trading rooms and trading educators offer simulator accounts. The good news is that the cost of trading simulators has gone down significantly in recent years and now we also have many web-based or even mobile app simulators for trading. DAS Trader offers the best simulated accounts for a reasonable price. Check out their website (*dastrader.com*) or contact *support@dastrader.com* for more information. This completes my unpaid advertisement for them!

Trading education costs might be annoying at the beginning and seem unbearable, but they really are not that onerous when you consider trading as a new business or career. If you use a simulator for six months, and trade only with simulated money, it will cost you somewhere around $1,000. This is the cost of a proper education. If you are seriously considering day trading as a career, it's a small expenditure compared to the cost of an education for a new profession. For example, imagine that you want to go to school to get an MBA – it will easily cost you over $50,000. Likewise, many other diploma or postgraduate programs cost significantly more than the education required for day trading.

Once you have a simulated account, you will need to develop your strategy. Try the two strategies that I have discussed in this book. There are a lot of other strategies out there which you could also try. Ensure that you master one or two of them that fit with your personality, available time, and trading platform. There is no best strategy among them, just like there is no best automobile in the market. There might, however, be a best car for you. You need to only master a few of them to always be profitable in the market. Keep your strategy simple. When you have a solid strategy that you've mastered, make sure there is no emotion attached to it. Keep practicing it, and then start practicing a second strategy, and learn to incrementally add size in those strategies.

Practice with the amounts of money that you will be trading in real life. It is easy to buy a position worth $100,000 in a simulated account and watch it lose half of its value in a matter of seconds. But could you tolerate this loss in a real account? No. You will probably become an emotional trader and make a decision quickly, usually resulting in a major loss. Always trade in the simulator with the size and position that you will be using in the real account. Otherwise, there is no point in trading in a simulated account. Move to a real account only after at least three months of training with a simulated account and then, start small, with real money. Trade small while you're learning or when you are feeling stressed.

New traders often try to skip steps in the process, lose their money, and then give up their day trading career forever and tell themselves that it is impossible to make money by day trading. Remember, baby steps. Success in day trading is one foot forward and then the next. Master one step, and then and only then move on to the next.

Most traders struggle when they first begin, and many do not have sufficient time when the markets are open to practice in real time. Those who can give trading more time when they start have a better chance to succeed. How long does it take to be a consistently profitable trader? I don't think anyone can become a consistently profitable trader in less than six or seven months. After three months of paper trading, you need at least another three months of trading in small share size to master your emotions and practice self-discipline while trading with your real money. After six months, you may become a seasoned trader. Eight months is probably better than six months, and twelve months is better than both. Are you patient enough for this learning curve? Do you really want this career? Then you should be patient enough. Do you have this much time to learn the day trading profession?

It always amuses me when I see books or online courses and websites that offer trading education that will make a person money starting on day one! I wonder who would believe such advertisements.

You must define a sensible process-oriented goal for yourself, such as: I want to learn how to day trade. I do not want to make a living out of it for now. Do not set an absolute income for yourself in day trading, not at least for the first two years. This is very important. Many traders think of inspiring goals such as making a million dollars or being able to trade for a living from a chalet in the Swiss Alps. These goals may be motivating, and they definitely have their place, but they distract you from focusing on what you need to do today and tomorrow to become better. What you as a new trader can control is the process of trading: how to make and execute sound trading decisions. Many think a profitable day is a good trading day. They're wrong. A good trading day is a day when you are disciplined and you trade sound strategies. Your daily goal should be to trade well, not to make money. The normal uncertainty of the market will result in some days or weeks being in the red.

Often new traders email and ask me how they can become full-time traders while they are working at a different job from 9 a.m. to 5 p.m. New York time. I really don't have any answer for that. They probably cannot become a full-time trader if they cannot trade in a simulator in real time between 9:30 and 11:30 a.m. New York time. You do not need to have the whole day available for trading, but you at least need the first two hours that the market is open. If you insist, I would say the first one hour that the market is open (9:30 to 10:30 a.m. New York time) is the absolute minimum time you should be available for trading and practice, in addition to any time you need for preparation before the market opens at 9:30 a.m. New York time. Sometimes I am done with trading and hit my daily goal in the first fifteen minutes, but sometimes I need to watch the market longer to find trading opportunities. Do you have this flexibility in your work-life schedule?

Trading is a full contact sport. You are competing with the brightest minds on the planet. Traders all over the world, either in their home offices or in the proprietary Wall Street firms, are sitting in front of the most sophisticated tools imaginable, ready to take your money. Anything less than your full effort and attention is disrespectful and will very likely result in your trading account suffering a heavy and tragic loss.

You need to take trading seriously. Day trading is not a casual activity. For those who think it's cool to know a few things about the markets before jumping in, but nothing more, it always ends in regret. For those who cannot devote the necessary time, there are other kinds of trading that are not quite as demanding as day trading, such as the currency market, and that might be a better fit for people whose schedules cannot accommodate the intense commitment that day trading requires. So, in a nutshell, do it right or just don't bother doing it. If you can't do day trading, that's okay. You don't have to do it, and you can always look for another challenge that complements your budget and/or schedule. I feel obligated though to warn every reader of this book that it is very easy to lose your life savings when day trading. As I wrote at the beginning of this paragraph, you need to take trading seriously.

A very excited Trader Dwight emailed me to share his trading endeavor. He is passionate about trading and he is working hard to save more capital for it, but his schedule does not allow him to properly focus on day trading. Let's read this excerpt from his email together, as it's both educational as well as entertaining:

"Hello Andrew,

"I purchased your audible Version 4 from amazon and started to listen to it as I do my morning deliveries. First day of listening I was hungry to learn more. So I stop all trading in my account......I continued to listen.

"I work for a plumbing supply in N.Y.C. and start my day roughly around 7 a.m. I was active with real $$$ on Scottrade [a now former stock brokerage firm] since March 2017 and have been doing due diligence at night and trading during the day and was fortunate to be one of the lucky ones to make some gains. (Roughly from 2k to 5k). Now this is all happening as I drive the streets of New York delivering supplies. Sometimes stuck in traffic I can make a trade, and if I need to I pull over to watch Level 2 [the real-time Nasdaq TotalView Level 2 data feed] and make a trade or two. I have been doing straight kamikaze instead of Guerrilla warfare. Lol.

"I started to lose these gains and felt I had no control and realized I was lucky. This is where I am at now in writing to you......Today as I finished listening to the book (which I will listen to again in front of my desktop to follow all your charts and examples I missed while I was driving and listening to the audible), I started to map out and set goals for the next 12

to 18 months. I keep saying to myself, "how will I be able to learn on a simulator live time when I am driving during these hours?" I have evenings to educate myself which I will continue to do, but how will I be able to manage this hump? ...

"Thanks for taking the time to read this. Enjoy your weekend."

His story is an excellent example of why you should not even try day trading if you cannot dedicate sufficient time and energy to it. You don't open a restaurant only because you may have some time during the week to run it. No, you need to be able to run it perfectly or else you are destined to fail. I was unemployed when I started day trading. Then I had to find a job to pay the bills because I was losing my savings on day trading. I am lucky that I live in Vancouver, Canada (in the Pacific Time Zone), which is 3 hours behind the New York Time Zone, because I could trade and practice between 6:30 and 8:30 a.m. (in my time zone) and then be at work for 9 a.m. If you don't have this luxury, maybe swing trading is better for you. But making a living out of swing trading is more difficult. The best swing traders can expect an annual return of 20% on their account size. Day traders, on the other hand, look to profit between 0.5% and 1% of their account size daily. The currency market (Forex) is open 24 hours/5 days per week, and perhaps you could consider trading currencies and commodities if you do not have sufficient free time to practice day trading or swing trading.

You must always be continuing your education and reflecting upon your trading strategy. Never stop learning about the stock market. The market is a dynamic environment and it's constantly changing. Day trading is different than it was ten years ago, and it will be different in another ten years. So keep reading and discussing your progress and performance with your mentors and other traders. Always think ahead and maintain a progressive and winning attitude.

Learn as much as you can, but keep a degree of healthy skepticism about everything, including this book. Ask questions, and do not accept experts at their word. Consistently profitable traders constantly evaluate their trading system. They make adjustments every month, every day, and even in the midst of the trading day. Every day is new. It is about developing trading skills, discipline, and controlling emotions, and then making adjustments continually.

Traders who are consistently profitable have studied the fundamentals of trading and have learned how to make well-thought-out and intelligent trades. Their focus is on the rationale for their actions rather than on making money. Amateurs, on the other hand, are focused on making money every single day. That kind of thinking can be their worst enemy. I am not consciously trying to make money as a trader. My focus is on "doing the right thing". I am looking for excellent risk/reward opportunities, and then I trade them. Being good at trading is the result of mastering the skills of trading and recognizing the fundamentals of a good trade.

Money is just the by-product of executing fundamentally solid trades. Your goal is to develop trading skills. You must focus on getting better every single day, one trade after another. Push your comfort zone to find greater success.

Preparation

John Wooden (or as some call him, the Wizard of Westwood), the famous American basketball player and coach, often quoted Benjamin Franklin:

> *"By failing to prepare, you are preparing to fail."*

Indeed. New traders will often think that trading strategies can be reduced to a few rules that they must follow in order to be profitable: always do this or always do that. Wrong. Trading isn't about "always" at all; it is about each single trade, and each situation. Every trade is a new puzzle that you must solve. There is no universal answer to all of the puzzles in the market. Therefore, you need to make a plan for each trade and each day. After a few months of simulated trading you will learn how to quickly develop and review the trading plans in your mind for each trading situation. That is one of the most important outcomes of trading in a simulator. That is why at least three months of live simulated trading is essential as you begin your day trading career. (Ardi provides some thoughts in Chapter 8 on what should be included in a trading plan.)

Education and practice give you a perspective on what matters most in trading: how you trade, how you can control your emotions, and how you can grow and develop your skills. Once you have a perspective on what matters, you can proceed to identify the specific processes on which to focus. The key to success is knowing your exact processes. Often you will learn them the hard way - by losing money.

Determination and Hard Work

Hard work in day trading is different from what you might originally assume. A trader should not work 100 hours a week like investment bankers or corporate attorneys or other highly paid professionals do because, for us day traders, there are no end-of-the-year bonuses. More than anything else, as Ardi wrote earlier in this book, day trading is perhaps most similar to being a professional athlete because it is judged by one's daily performance. Having said that, day traders should work hard, consistently and productively, each and every day. Watching your trading screens intently and gathering important market information is how we define hard work in day trading.

It is essential to develop the routine of showing up every day to trade, whether it is in your real account or in a simulator. Searching for support and resistance levels each day, including before the market opens, will benefit your trading in the long run. Turning off the PC early after a few bad trades is a strategy that should be reserved for the rare occasions when it is absolutely essential to give your brain a break. Usually, spending time in a simulator after some losses will clear your mind sufficiently.

Novice traders using a simulator should keep on trading and practicing until the markets close at 4 p.m. ET. After all, trading in the simulator is not nearly as stressful as real trading with real money. Using a simulator with no commissions being paid to brokers and no profit (or loss) is still no excuse for overtrading. (Overtrading can mean trading 20, 30, 40, or even 60 times a day. You'll be commissioning your broker to do each and every one of those trades, so you are going to lose both money and commissions. Many brokers charge fees for each trade, so for 40 trades, for example, you may end up paying hundreds of dollars to your broker. That is a lot. If you overtrade, your broker will become richer, and you will become, well, broker!) At all times the focus must be on sound strategies with excellent risk/reward opportunities.

I am often asked, "*In your first months of trading, did you ever feel like you couldn't do it?*" The answer is "*Yes, and often!*" I still, at least once a month, get really frustrated after a few bad losses and consider quitting day trading. Frequently in my trading career I have wanted to quit, and at times I have actually believed the myth that day trading is impossible. But I did not quit. I really wanted to be a successful trader and to have the lifestyle and the freedom that come with it. I paid the price for my mistakes, focused on my education, and eventually survived the very difficult learning curve of trading.

Patience

Becoming a consistently profitable day trader requires hard work, extensive preparation, and considerable patience. Successful trades usually look easy after they're done, but actually finding them is far from easy and requires more patience and hard work than you might imagine if you have not day traded before. (Don't forget how I defined hard work for a day trader just a few paragraphs ago: watching your trading screens intently and gathering important market information.)

You need to watch, watch some more, and then keep watching. If a stock you're watching isn't offering excellent opportunities, it's time to move on. Check out other stocks on your watchlist, and then monitor them closely. Consistently profitable traders often spend their trading days searching and watching for excellent opportunities.

Successful traders are patient and resist the temptation to be involved in every move. Traders need to wait for opportunities to arise where they feel comfortable and confident.

Discipline

Success in trading comes with skill development and self-discipline. Trading principles are easy, and day trading strategies are very simple. I have a Ph.D. in chemical engineering and I have worked as a research scientist at a world-class facility. I have published numerous scholarly publications in high impact and respected scientific journals on my nanotechnology and complicated molecular level research. Believe me, I had to study and understand extremely more difficult concepts, so I can assure you that day trading, in theory at least, is easy.

What makes day trading, or any type of trading for that matter, difficult is the discipline and self-control that you need. You have no chance to make money as a trader without discipline, no matter your style, the time you commit to trading, the country you live in, or the market you are trading in.

New traders who fail to make money in the markets will sometimes try to improve themselves by learning more about how the markets work, studying new strategies, adopting additional technical indicators, following new traders, and/or joining other chatrooms. What they don't realize is that the main cause of their failure is often not their lack of technical knowledge but their lack of self-discipline, their impulsive decisions, and their sloppy money management.

Professional institutional traders often perform significantly better than private retail traders (individual traders like you, trading from your home office). Most private traders are university-educated, literate people. They are often business owners or professionals. In contrast, typical institutional traders are loud 20-something-year-old cowboys who used to play rugby in college and haven't read a book in years. Why do these "youngsters" outperform private traders year after year? It's not because they are younger or sharper or faster.

And it's not because of their training or platforms, because most retail traders have almost the same gear as they do. The answer is the strictly enforced discipline of trading firms.

Some successful institutional traders go out on their own after asking themselves, "*Why am I sharing my profits with the firm when I know how to trade and could be keeping all of the profits for myself?*" Most of them end up losing money as private traders. Even though they work with the same software and platforms, trade the same systems, and stay in touch with their contacts, they still fail. After a few months, most of them are back at a recruiting office, looking for a trading job. Why could those traders make money for their firms, but not for themselves?

The answer is self-discipline.

When institutional traders quit their firm, they leave behind their manager and all of the strictly enforced risk control rules. A trader who violates risk limits is fired immediately. Traders who leave institutions may know how to trade, but their discipline is often external, not internal. They quickly lose money without their managers because they have developed no self-discipline.

We private retail traders can break any rule and change our plan in the middle of a trade. We can average down to a losing position, we can constantly break the rules, and no one will notice. Managers in trading firms though are quick to get rid of impulsive people who break any trading rule for a second time. This creates a serious discipline for institutional traders. Strict external discipline saves institutional traders from heavy losses and deadly sins (such as the averaging down of a losing position), which quite often will destroy many private accounts. (If you are not familiar with the term "averaging down", Ardi includes an explanation of it in Chapter 8.)

Discipline means you execute your trading plan and honor your stop loss (your stop loss is the maximum loss you allow yourself on a particular trade based on your risk tolerance), without altering either in the middle of a trade. Discipline is executing your detailed trading plan every single time.

Do not be stubborn about your decision if you are wrong. The market does not reward stubbornness. The market is not interested in how you wish stocks would trade. Traders must adapt to the market and do what the market demands. And that is the way day trading works and that is how it will always work.

Trading teaches you a great deal about yourself, about your mental weaknesses and about your strengths. This alone ensures that trading is a valuable life experience.

I have found that trading, sticking to my trading plan and the discipline inherent in my trading methodology have had a snowball effect of positive habits in my life in general, and these habits have contributed to even more trading success. For example, I start my trading process by following the same routine when I get up each morning. I always go for a morning run before the trading session starts. As I mentioned before, I live in Vancouver, Canada, and the market opens at 6:30 a.m. my time. I wake up at 4:30 a.m. every morning. I go for a 45- to 60-minute run (usually between 7 and 10 kilometers (some 4 to 6 miles)). I come home, take a shower, and at 6 a.m. start developing my trading plan.

I have found that when my body has not been active prior to trading, I will make poor decisions. There are scientific studies showing that aerobic exercise has a positive effect on the decision-making process. People who regularly participate in an aerobic exercise (such as running for at least thirty minutes) have higher scores on neuropsychological functioning and performance tests that measure such cognitive functions as attentional control, inhibitory control, cognitive flexibility, working memory updating and capacity, and information processing speed. You can easily read about these topics on the Internet. Very often, our moods are influenced by our physical state, even by factors as delicate as what and how much we eat. Keep a record of your daily trading results as a function of your physical condition and you will see these relationships for yourself. Begin preventive maintenance by keeping body, and thus mind, in their peak operating condition. I stopped drinking coffee and alcohol, and I have stopped eating animal-based food, and my performance levels have increased significantly. Not eating meat and fish (any living beings that are marked with blood), and not using alcohol, coffee and tobacco lifts you above the curse and accelerates you forward in every facet of life. Likewise, in trading, your focus should be about being better than your current state, in all aspects of your life.

In 2014, I was visiting New York City and decided to go for a walk along Wall Street during lunchtime on a working day and perhaps take a selfie with Charging Bull, the famous 3.5-ton bronze sculpture of a bull located near Wall Street that symbolizes New York's financial industry. I assumed that most of the people walking around in that area on a weekday must either be traders or working in the financial sector. I knew there was a good chance that the person sitting next to me in a restaurant was taking home a bonus of $2 million at the end of the year. I tried to observe people's attitudes, how they walked, how they dressed and how they treated themselves. I rarely saw anyone who was not well-dressed, without confidence and without being in excellent physical shape. I wondered to myself, are these people well-dressed, confident, in great physical shape and disciplined because they are rich and successful <u>or</u> did they become rich and successful because they were disciplined, confident and ambitious? This is possibly a "chicken and egg" problem with no real answer, but I personally believe it is the latter. Based on what I saw, successful traders have often succeeded in almost everything they have done. They are ambitious and they expect a lot from themselves and they expect it at an early age. They expect to be the best. Success has been their history, so why should trading be any different?

Research has shown that winners think, feel, and act differently than losers. If you want to know if you have the self-discipline of a winner, try right now, starting today, to stop a habit that has challenged you in the past. If you have always wanted to be in better physical shape, try adding exercises such as running into your routine, and also take control of your salt and sugar intake. If you drink too much alcohol or coffee, try to see if for one month you can stay away from them. These are excellent tests to see if you are emotionally and intellectually strong enough or not to discipline yourself in the face of a losing trade. I am not saying that if you drink coffee or alcohol, or that if you are not a regular runner, you cannot become a successful trader, but if you make a try at these types of improvements and fail, then you should know that exercising self-control in trading will not be any easier to accomplish. Change is hard, but if you wish to be a successful trader, you need to work on changing and developing your personality at every level.

Mentorship and a Community of Traders

Dr. Brett Steenbarger, the author of outstanding books such as *The Psychology of Trading* and *The Daily Trading Coach*, once wrote:

> *"There is no question in my mind that, if I were to start trading full-time, knowing what I know now, I would either join a proprietary trading firm or would form my own "virtual trading group" by connecting online (and in real time) with a handful of like-minded traders."*

You need to be part of a mastermind group that will add value to your trading career. To whom can you turn to ask trading questions? I encourage you to join a community of traders. Trading alone is very difficult and can be emotionally overwhelming. It is very helpful to join a community of traders so that you can ask them questions, talk to them, learn new methods and strategies, get some hints and alerts about the stock market, and make your own contributions. You will also notice that senior traders often lose money. It can be comforting to see that losing money is not limited to you, and that everyone, including experienced traders, has to take a loss. It's all part of the process.

There are many chatrooms that you can join on the Internet. Some of them are free, but most of them charge a membership fee. You may also want to find a trading mentor. A good mentor can positively impact your trading career in so many different ways. Today, because of algorithmic programs and market volatility, it's much harder for new traders to survive the learning curve. A good mentor can make a huge difference. A mentor demonstrates the professionalism required to be successful. A mentor can lead you to discover the talent inside of you. Sometimes you just need to be told that you can do it. In online trading communities, experienced traders mentor new traders at times for a fee, but often for free. I personally mentor a few traders at a time, and of course, I myself did and still have a trading mentor. It is important to note though that mentorship does not work unless you are receptive, listen, and then put in the work necessary to adapt successfully. You should find a mentor whose trading style fits with your personality.

It is extremely important to remember, however, that after joining a trading community, you should not follow the pack. You need to be an independent thinker. Don't blindly follow the crowd but do partake of the benefits inherent in being part of a trading community that fits with your personality. People often change when they join crowds and become more unquestioning and impulsive. Stressed traders nervously search for a leader whose trades they can mirror. They react impulsively with the crowd instead of using their own common sense and reason. Chatroom members may catch a few trends together, but they will also get killed together when trends reverse. Never forget that successful traders are independent thinkers. Simply use your judgment to decide when to trade and when to not.

Reflection and Review

By now, you may correctly think that trading psychology and self-discipline, a series of proven trading strategies, and excellent money and risk management are the essential elements of success in trading. But there is another element that ties all of your trading fundamentals together: record-keeping.

Keeping records of your trades will make you a better trader as it will enable you to learn from your past successes and failures. In fact, the most important and the most effective way to continuously improve as a trader is to keep a diary of your trades. There are many consistently profitable traders around the world, trading different markets with different methods, but they all have one thing in common: they keep excellent records of their trades. It is a very tedious and boring task; but it is also a very necessary task. Journal your trades daily. Make sure to include the following points in your trading journal:

1. Your physical well-being (lack of sleep, too much coffee, too much food the night before, etc.).
2. The time of the day you made the trade.
3. The strategy you were anticipating to use.
4. How you found the opportunity (from a scanner, a chatroom, etc.).
5. Quality of your entry (risk/reward).
6. Sizing/management of your trade (scaling in and out as planned).
7. Execution of exits (following profit targets or stop losses).

I personally take a screenshot from my screen (with a free app called *Lightshot*) and journal my trades in my blog with that software. Please visit our community's website for ideas from some experienced traders on how they journal their trades. Many of them have shared their Excel spreadsheet or other tools they are using in our publicly available forum. You do not have to follow any of our styles, but you should find what works best for you because, in order to be successful, you must journal your trades daily.

There are also several online tools you can use for journaling your trades such as *Chartlog.com*. The founders of Chartlog are experienced traders and know the importance of proper journaling.

New traders often ask me how to improve after a series of losses and a period of struggling. I recommend to them that they review their journal and look more specifically at what precisely they are doing poorly at in their trading. I am doing poorly doesn't mean anything. You cannot improve if you don't have a proper record of your daily trades.

- Is it your stock selection?
- Is it your entry points?
- Is it your discipline or psychology?
- Is it your platform or clearing firm (broker)?
- What about other traders, is it a bad month for everyone or just for you?

One time a trader complained about her order execution speed. I remotely connected to her PC (using TeamViewer, a remote control/remote access software) and evaluated the CPU performance. I had to remove many unnecessary programs and apps from her PC, run a malware scanner and remove a variety of intrusive software, computer viruses, spyware, adware, scareware, and other malicious programs. I freed up a lot of the PC's memory and CPU capacity and her trading execution speed increased significantly. Your PC, just like your body and mind, needs to be kept clean, lean and fast, all of which have a direct effect on your trading platform and eventually your trading results.

My friend, Mike Bellafiore, co-founder of SMB Capital (a proprietary trading firm in New York City), writes in his book, *One Good Trade*, that the professional traders at his firm video record all of their trades during the day. In their afternoon session, they sit around their conference room tables, enjoy a lunch catered by the firm, review their trades and groupthink about better ways to take your money.

I personally live video record all of my trades during the morning session (as I rarely make any trades Mid-day or at the Close). I believe traders, like athletes, should watch their trading videos. The best athletes and teams watch films of themselves to see what they're doing right and wrong, and how best to improve. I will review my tapes during Mid-day and make sure to note important observations on my entry, exit, price action, Level 2 signals (the real-time Nasdaq TotalView Level 2 data feed) and so on. I try to learn as much as possible from my trades. Sometimes I look for new algorithmic programs that I must be aware of. I search for areas where I could have added more size. This is one of my trading weaknesses. I also do a poor job of holding for a longer time the stocks that are going in my favor (basically, I exit from a trade too soon and thus don't profit as much as

I could have). I therefore consider trades that I could have held longer. I make sure to find spots where I was too aggressive. I look for times where I took a trade even though it did not offer a good risk/reward opportunity. I review my position sizing and why and where I added more. That is how to day trade for a living. There is no other way to get better. There are no excuses in trading.

Watching trading videos also shows me how easy trading is when there are no emotions attached to a trade. When I review my work, I am not invested in a trade in real time with real money. Trading live, the market seems fast and unpredictable. When you watch back your trading video, you see that the market is actually very slow. There are times when I see the pattern in a stock by watching my video and recognize how I traded the stock backward, and that is embarrassing for someone of my experience.

I later review my videos over the weekend to create educational series to use in teaching day trading. Over the weekend, after I celebrate the winning week on Friday night with my friends and family, I lock myself into my home office and cut tape after tape to develop and update my training programs.

Watching your videos is an exercise that can benefit all traders no matter their experience. New traders need to watch the markets trade. Watching your videos increases your trading experience and confidence and significantly shortens your learning curve. But I agree with what you may be thinking, it takes time and it is indeed boring.

FINAL WORDS

You need to practice. You need experience deciphering market patterns. Every day is a new game and a new puzzle to solve. Showing up every day is important. Many people believe that trading can be reduced to a few rules that they can follow every morning. Always do this or always do that. In reality, trading isn't about "always" at all; it is about each situation and each trade. You must learn how to think in day trading, and that is no easy task.

You must start recognizing patterns and developing trading strategies. And these strategies must be practiced in real time and under stress. Trading in a simulator can help and is absolutely necessary, but there is no substitute for trading with your real hard-earned cash where your results actually matter.

When you begin as a trader, you most likely will be horrible. As I mentioned not too many pages ago, many times at the beginning of my career I came to the conclusion that day trading was not for me. Even now that I am an experienced and profitable trader, there is at least one day almost every month where I wonder if I can trade in the markets any longer. Of course, this feeling of disappointment goes away faster these days, usually after the next good trade. But for you, because you have not seen success yet, surviving the learning curve is very difficult. I know that. However, this does not mean you should lose a lot of money when you trade live at the beginning. Trading in a simulator will help to prepare you for real trading with real money.

If you are signing up for a training course or mentorship program, you should very carefully read about their plan. A good training program will encourage you to trade only the easiest setups when you start and will walk you through the trading process slowly and methodically. But most importantly, it must teach you how to think as a trader, rather than merely give you some rules and alerts. There are major differences between a trading community, an educational course and an alert service.

New traders often expect to make money immediately, and when they don't, they let this affect their work. When they do not see the results that they expected, they start to focus on the wrong things. Some increase their share size, hoping that this will help them make more money. Many will not prepare as thoroughly as they should because they become discouraged. They ask themselves, "*What's the point of preparing hard if I can't make money?*" They start to take chances that a successful and experienced trader would never take. They become gamblers. This leads to even more significant losses and only adds to their problems.

While there is no one right way to make money by trading, there is only one right way to begin your trading career. When you first begin, you must focus on the process of trading, not on how to make money for a living. You must allow at least eight to twelve months before you will become consistently profitable. If you are unwilling or unable to do this, then you should find another career. Some are not able to either financially or psychologically commit this much time to this pursuit. If this is the case, then again, you should find another profession.

Again, I cannot emphasize enough to you how unimportant the results are from your first six months of trading. They do not matter. During these first months, you are building the foundation for a lifetime career. Do you think in year ten that your results in your first six months will be significant?

Becoming a consistently profitable trader could turn out to be the hardest thing you will ever do. The intensive training process that you must follow takes eight to twelve months and requires much hard work. It will enable you to find out how good you can be, but to do that you need to genuinely believe that you will become great.

All of us have mental weaknesses that we must conquer. If we stubbornly insist on trying to prove to the market that we are right, we will pay a high price. Some traders cannot accept a loss and exit stocks that trade against them. Some exit from a trade too soon and take small profits, instead of sticking to their well-thought-out trading plan which would result in larger profits. Some are afraid to make a decision to enter a trade, even with an excellent risk/reward ratio that they recognize. The only way to get better is to work on your weaknesses.

There is no shame in failing as a trader. The real shame is in not pursuing your dreams. If you are passionate about trading, or anything else, and never try it, then you will live your life wondering what might have been. Life is too short not to embrace new challenges. To take on any challenge in life and fail is very honorable. If you have the courage to take a chance and day trade, that decision will serve you well later in life. The next career change or challenge you accept might be the one that works out for you, and what you learn about yourself in the process can be invaluable.

If you're ever interested in connecting with me, check out my website at *BearBullTraders.com* or send me an email at *andrew@BearBullTraders.com*. Teaching people and helping them to start a new career fulfills something inside of me that motivates me every day, so I truly would be happy to have a chat with you.

CHAPTER 7

SWING TRADING IN THE STOCK MARKET

As introduced in Chapter 2, swing trading is the "*art and science*" of profiting from the short-term price movement of stocks (generally periods of a few days to a few weeks — one or two months, max). It is a trading technique used by everyone from retail traders (people who work from their home offices and not for companies) all the way up to hedge fund managers and institutional traders.

Unlike day traders, swing traders generally analyze their trades overnight and do not require expensive charting tools or platforms. Many swing traders can use free charting software found on the Internet (such as tradingview.com or stockcharts.com). Even mobile apps are now becoming more sophisticated and have added the technical indicators that most swing traders require. This is one of the additional benefits of being a swing trader.

Stock Selection

While the vast majority of day traders only look at chart patterns (what is called technical analysis), some swing traders also look at the fundamentals of a company (and not just its price charts). Investors, on the other hand, rely mostly on fundamental analysis and they conduct technical analysis and review chart patterns only when deciding on the timing and entering of their positions, not for the initial decision on whether or not to invest in a company. For example, when Warren Buffett or Ray Dalio, the "biggest" investors and hedge fund managers in the world, decide whether or not to invest in a company like Apple Inc. (ticker: AAPL), they do not look at Apple's candlestick charts. They analyze the fundamentals of the company, its sales, growth, potential, etc. and then decide whether or not to invest. However, they will look at the company's charts in order to find a proper time to buy. Technical analysis helps them to time when it is best to enter into a particular investment, but technical analysis does not impact their overall decision on whether or not to invest in that company. Although I discussed the differences between technical and fundamental analyses in detail in Chapter 4, I believe a brief refresher at this point in the book is in order for those readers who are new to trading and investing.

Technical analysis includes studying price action charts, understanding what the current value of a stock is on the market in comparison to previous time periods, and identifying specific patterns in charts which you can then use to accurately predict the stock's future price movement. Fundamental analysis is principally concerned with the product or service a company sells, its earnings, its valuation, corporate events (such as takeovers and acquisitions), and anything and everything that is contained in its financial statements. If you wish, please don't hesitate to refer back to Figure 4.1 in Chapter 4, which summarizes in visual form some of the key elements of fundamental and technical analyses.

While very short-term traders (day traders) focus exclusively on technical analysis, and long-term investors focus primarily on fundamental analysis but also use technical analysis to assist them in entering into an investment, swing traders fall somewhere in the middle, albeit with an emphasis on technical analysis. Although both fundamental and technical analyses can play a role in how a swing trader selects stocks to trade as well as how they enter and exit their trades, the majority of swing traders lean toward either solely or primarily using technical analysis. Technical analysis is particularly important for swing traders with a very short time horizon for entering and exiting their trades (such as a couple of days). The shorter your time horizon, the more prominently technical analysis should figure in your trading plan (I provide some thoughts in Chapter 8 on what should be included in a trading plan).

I encourage new swing traders to learn both technical and fundamental analyses, but I've found in my experience that newcomers are typically attracted to focusing mainly on technical analysis because:

1. Technical analysis doesn't require nearly as much work as fundamental analysis does.

A fundamental analyst has considerably more variables to deal with and considerably more calculations to compute. To properly analyze a company, a fundamental analyst must understand many, many aspects of the business including, but certainly not limited to, the dynamics of the firm's industry, its competitors, its cost structure, its management team, and its financial statements.

2. Trading decisions based on fundamental analysis take more time to play out than those based on technical analysis. A company may be deeply undervalued relative to the market and its industry, but being undervalued doesn't necessarily mean shares will rise tomorrow or the day after. Some companies' shares stay undervalued for weeks, months, or even years. That's why long-term investors rely so heavily on fundamental analysis — they can afford to be patient.

As mentioned earlier, each day, Andrew and other day traders look for the handful of stocks that are in play for that day. They look in part for stocks that have gapped up or down in price by at least 2% and have high relative volume. That's what day traders do. In this section, I will discuss how to find Stocks in Play for swing trading.

Stock selection in swing trading is very different from how it is done in day trading. Swing traders use two approaches: (A) top down and (B) bottom up.

A top-down swing trader finds potential stocks for trading by beginning at a macro level and drilling down to firstly an industry and then secondly to a particular company's stock. A bottom-up trader finds potential stocks by beginning at the bottom (that is, with individual companies) and then narrowing down their own selection based on the overall direction of the market and other macro-level fundamentals.

For example, as you know, during the COVID-19 pandemic, the airline industry was severely affected and the stock price of many airline companies sold off heavily. Imagine for a moment that you want to select a stock because of this event. You firstly search to find out what are the largest public companies in this industry. We'll pretend you initially settle on United Airlines Holdings Inc. (ticker: UAL), Delta Air Lines, Inc. (ticker: DAL), American Airlines Group Inc. (ticker: AAL), and a couple of others. You review each company and then select one of them which you believe has the best trading opportunity and is the most undervalued. This is a top-down approach. You decide to trade based on the overall market conditions, you then select an industry group (airlines), and you then choose a specific stock to trade (for example, American Airlines) based on your criteria.

Another approach is that you hear in the news that Tesla Inc. (ticker: TSLA) is releasing a new and affordable car. You expect this news will affect the price of their stock. You go and have a look at the TSLA daily chart, evaluate the market conditions and see if it is a good time to trade TSLA or not. This is a bottom-up approach. Both top-down and bottom-up approaches also work for investors and hence I will briefly review this topic again in Chapter 9.

For either of these approaches to work, you firstly need to define your trading strategy, and then, based on your trading strategy, you select the stock you wish to trade. There are of course many different swing trading strategies, and all of them are correct if, but only if, you execute them properly. As explained in the day trading chapters, there is no one correct way to trade, there are many different ways and all of them can lead to success. Every swing trader might also have a different approach to the criteria they use for finding stocks. You need to learn that part for yourself. In the next section, I will discuss how to find stocks based on particular trading strategies. Overall though, I have three rules of thumb for narrowing down stocks which might be in play.

I recommend utilizing these criteria:

» Stock price ≥ $5

» Average daily volume ≥ 100,000 shares

» Market capitalization ≥ $250 million (as I explained in Chapter 3, a company's market cap is calculated by multiplying the number of shares outstanding in the company with the price of its shares)

I do not recommend trading stocks priced at less than $5/share because, when you do so, you are entering into the world of speculative and gambling-prone penny stocks. Even if a stock is priced at less than $5, but is above $1, I still call them penny stocks, as they are for the most part issued by manipulated and/or bogus companies. Confirming an average daily volume equal to or greater than 100,000 shares is to ensure you have sufficient daily volume so that your orders can enter and exit the market. Andrew once met a trader who had invested his family's savings for their children's education ($50,000) into a penny stock and then, because of insufficient daily trading volume, was unable to sell and come out. Verifying a market capitalization of at least $250 million is to also assist you in avoiding putting your money into these bogus scam penny stock companies. If you want to see what is behind the scenes of these penny stocks, I encourage you to watch the 2018 documentary, *The China Hustle*, by director (and Academy Award nominee) Jed Rothstein.

SWING STRATEGIES

Chart Patterns

One of the key strategies in swing trading is to identify chart patterns and to then trade accordingly. In the next few sections, I discuss some of the most popular patterns in swing trading and share real-life examples of trades that I have made.

Head and Shoulders Trades

The Head and Shoulders Pattern is one of the more reliable forms of technical analysis and is widely used by swing traders. I provided some commentary regarding this bearish pattern in Chapter 4, however, in this chapter I want to showcase additional examples in order to further reinforce the concept. Figure 7.1 below is the daily chart of Apple Inc. (ticker: AAPL) in autumn 2018. Buyers were able to rally up the price to $232/share. Sellers brought the price back down to form the pattern of a head on this daily chart, but buyers were not able to bring the price back up to the same $232/share level and instead could only reach the earlier price level (which at that time had formed the pattern of a left shoulder). This price action thus formed the pattern of a head and two shoulders, indicating a lack of conviction amongst buyers.

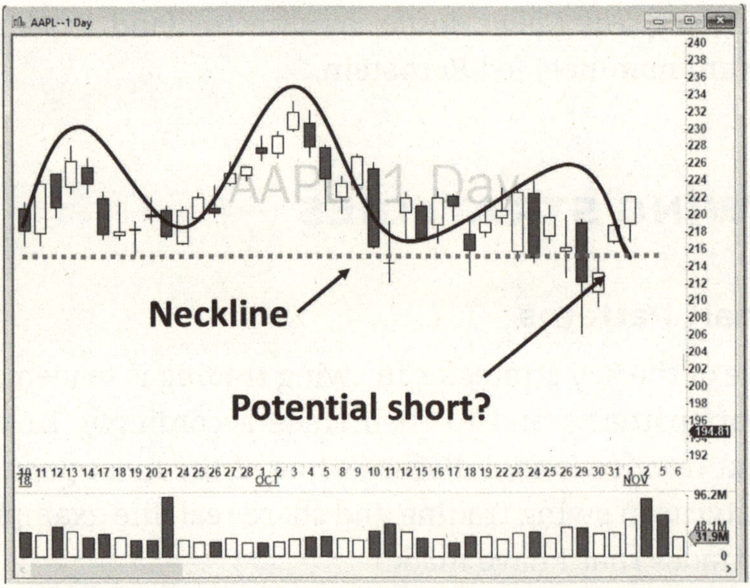

Figure 7.1: Example of the share price of Apple Inc. (ticker: AAPL) forming a perfect Head and Shoulders Pattern on a daily chart in the autumn of 2018. Buyers were not able to push the price back up to the level of the head, and thus the pattern of a right shoulder was formed.

Identifying the pattern, I knew that the stock would sell off with a minimum drop of $17/share. You'll recall that the price drop can be calculated by taking the difference in price between where the image of the right shoulder's neckline placed on the chart ($215) and where the top of the image of the head reached on the chart ($232). As predicted, the price of Apple's shares did go down, even further actually than $17, to levels of around $180, as shown in Figure 7.2 below.

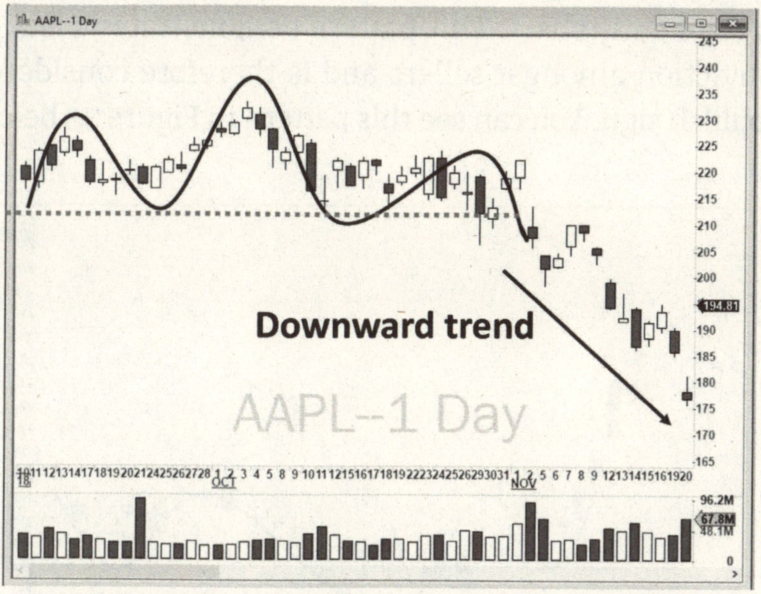

Figure 7.2: Continuing the example of the Head and Shoulders Pattern set out in Figure 7.1, the price of shares of Apple Inc. (ticker: AAPL) dropped after buyers were not able to return the price to the $232/share level. One would expect the price of the stock to fall the difference between where the image of the right shoulder's neckline placed on the chart ($215) and where the top of the image of the head reached on the chart ($232). Accordingly, $232-$215=$17. The price of the stock in fact fell to the $180 level.

The Head and Shoulders Pattern also works in the reverse situation. Let's take Home Depot Inc. (ticker: HD) again as an example, this time from late 2019 and early 2020. Sellers were able to push the price down to the $212/share level. Buyers pushed the price back to the $222 level (the price level which had initially formed the pattern of a reversed left shoulder on HD's daily chart). Sellers tried pushing the price down again but could not reach the previous level and buyers brought the price back up, forming a Reverse Head and Shoulders Pattern on HD's daily chart. This pattern demonstrates a lack of conviction amongst sellers and is therefore considered a bullish sign. You can see this pattern in Figure 7.3 below.

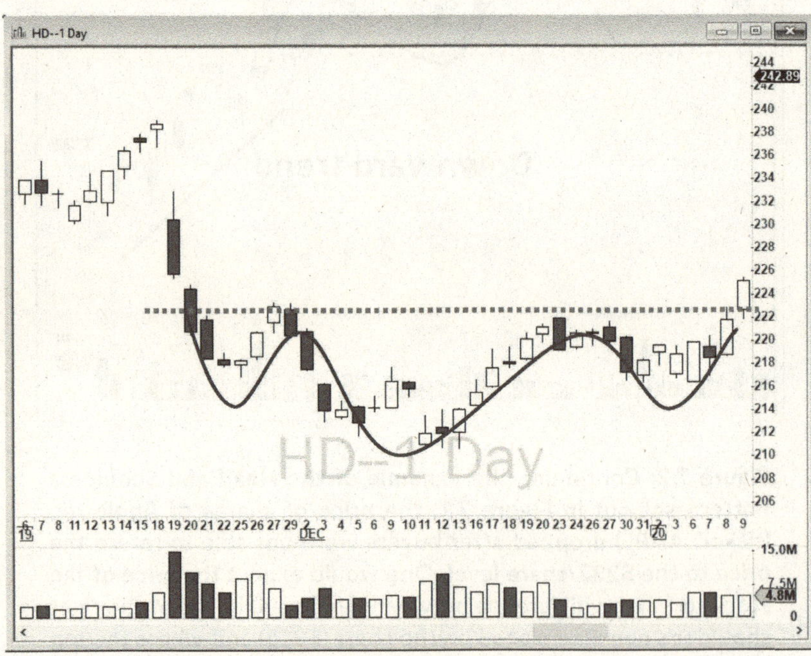

Figure 7.3: Example of the share price of Home Depot Inc. (ticker: HD) forming a Reverse Head and Shoulders Pattern on its daily chart in late 2019 and very early 2020.

As set forth in Figure 7.4 below, buyers took control and were able to push the price up to the $232/share level. The difference between where the image of the right shoulder's neckline placed on the daily chart and where the top of the image of the head placed on the chart is around $10 ($222–$212). Thus, one could safely predict that the share price would increase by a minimum of $10 to $232.

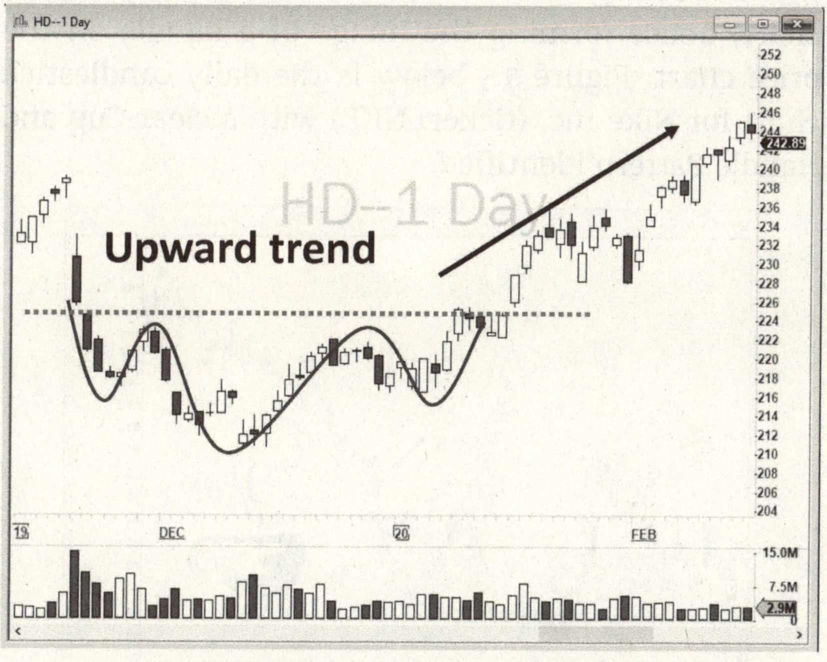

Figure 7.4: Continuing the example of the Reverse Head and Shoulders Pattern set out in Figure 7.3, the price of shares of Home Depot Inc. (ticker: HD) increased after sellers were not able to push the price down to the previous $212/share level. Buyers then took control and pushed the price higher.

Cup and Handle Trades

As I referenced in Chapter 4, Cup and Handle is a bullish pattern. The pattern is formed on a price chart when sellers initially take the price of the stock down, and then buyers recover the price, therefore creating the pattern of a cup on the price chart. Sellers will later take control of the price again and push the price down, but they will not be able to take the price back down to where the image of the bottom of the cup placed on the chart, hence forming the image of a handle on the price chart. Figure 7.5 below is the daily candlestick chart for Nike Inc. (ticker: NKE) with a clear Cup and Handle Pattern identified.

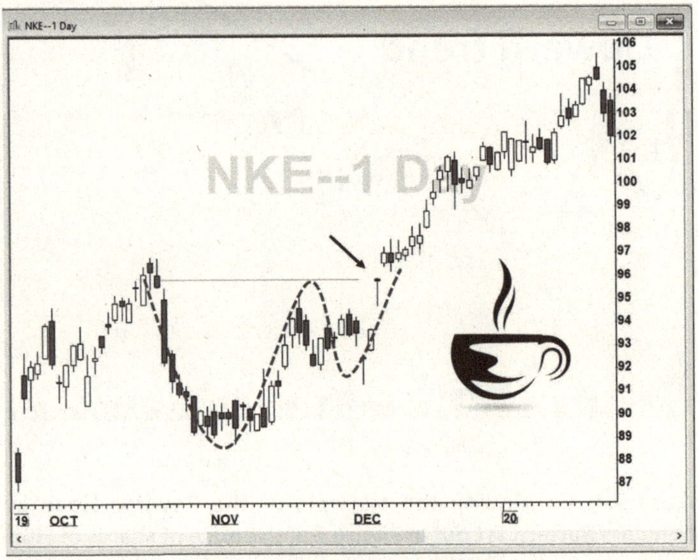

Figure 7.5: Example of a Cup and Handle Pattern (followed by an uptrend) formed on the price chart of Nike Inc. (ticker: NKE) in late 2019.

Figure 7.5 above is from late 2019 and early 2020. Sellers were able to bring the price of Nike's shares down to $89, and then buyers were able to recover the price of the stock, forming the cup pattern shown in the chart. Later, sellers tried to bring the price back down to the $89 level, but they were not able to do so, showing a lack of conviction amongst sellers. Buyers were therefore able to again take control and push the price up in the weeks that followed.

Figure 7.6 below demonstrates a Reverse Cup and Handle Pattern on the early 2020 price chart of the tech giant, Facebook, Inc. (ticker: FB). In this instance, buyers were not able to take control of the price action, and that led to the stock selling off.

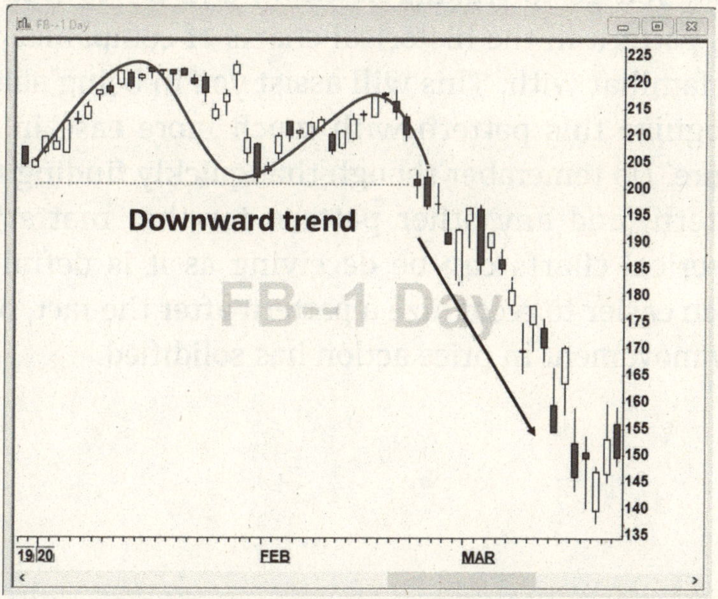

Figure 7.6: Example of a Reverse Cup and Handle Pattern on the price chart of Facebook, Inc. (ticker: FB). Sellers took control after buyers were not able to return the price of the stock to the level where the image of the bottom of a cup was formed on the price chart. This resulted in the formation of an image of a reversed handle on the price chart. This Reverse Cup and Handle Pattern indicated a breaking of the upward trend in the price of Facebook's stock.

Buyers in this example were able to push the price up to $220/share. Afterward, the price was brought down to around $200, forming the image of a reversed cup on the price chart. Later, buyers tried without success to push the price back up to the initial $220 level. This lack of confidence and conviction amongst buyers showed that sellers were in control of the price action and that led to the stock selling off.

In my opinion, Cup and Handle Patterns are one of the cleanest chart patterns in technical price chart analysis. I recommend that before you move on in this book, you go to tradingview.com and try to identify this pattern in the historical charts of companies you are familiar with. This will assist you in being able to recognize this pattern with much more ease in the future. Do remember though that quickly finding this pattern (and any other pattern for that matter) in historical charts can be deceiving as it is definitely much easier to recognize a pattern after the fact, once any movement in price action has solidified.

Darvas Box

Figure 7.7: Nicolas Darvas standing outside the New York Stock Exchange in 1959, after he made his first million dollars using his strategy.

One of the other well-known and reliable strategies used in the swing trading community is known as the Darvas Box. It is reliable in part because it made Nicolas Darvas a millionaire in less than two years! Before discussing the details of the strategy, it is worth mentioning the story of the man behind it, pictured in Figure 7.7 above. Darvas was not a financial guru or a fund manager. He was the exact opposite of who you would imagine a financier to be. Darvas was a professional ballroom dancer who was fascinated by the market and spent most of his free time studying it. He turned $25,000 of his savings into an astonishing $2.25 million in just 18 months. Let his story (which is easily available online in much more detail) be an inspiring tale for any reader who is starting their own journey in trading or investing.

Figure 7.8 above are pictures of the front and back cover of Darvas' 1960 book, *How I Made $2,000,000 in the Stock Market*. As of the time of writing, both updated and reprinted editions are available on Amazon.

As for Darvas' strategy, he believed certain securities tend to trade between two levels before rallying up. Darvas therefore looked for stocks that were trading clearly between two support and resistance levels. The support level marks the price where buyers bought the stock, leading to an increase in its price. The resistance level on the other hand is the price where sellers stepped in and sold their shares, causing the stock price to fall. After identifying stocks that were trading between their support and resistance levels, Darvas would wait patiently for the stock to break above the resistance level. Knowing that action is usually followed by heavy volume, he would then go long on the stock, with his stop loss at the support level.

The Darvas Box works in reverse too. If a security breaks below the support level and starts selling off, Darvas would go short, with his stop loss being at the resistance level.

Let's look at how the Darvas Box presents itself on price charts. Figure 7.9 below is the daily chart of Walmart Inc. (ticker: WMT). In September and October of 2018, Walmart was trading between $93.91 and $96.72/share. There were clear support and resistance levels which were allowing Walmart to trade within that range. As soon as Walmart broke the resistance level at $96.72, this signaled to the market that buyers were now in control and that led into new volume and the value of the stock going up.

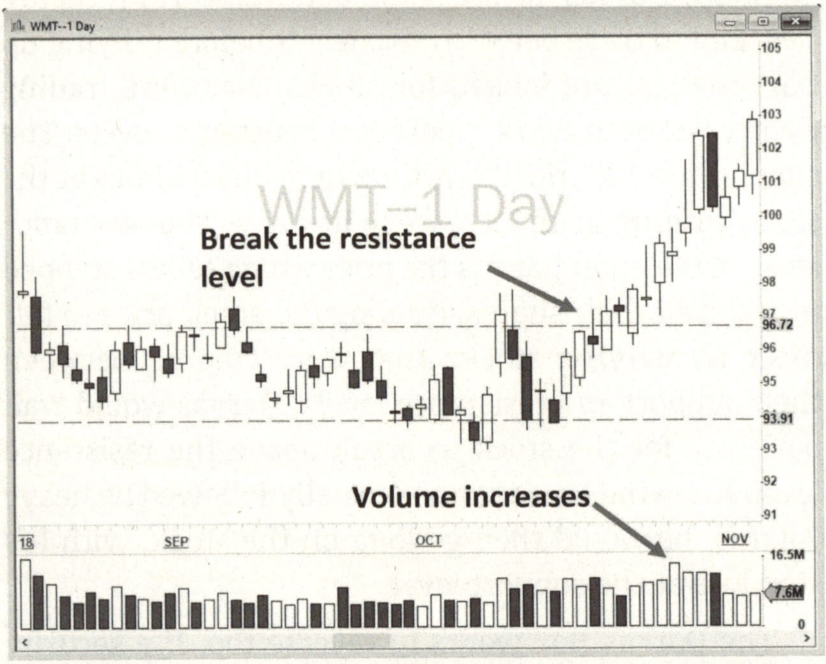

Figure 7.9: The daily chart of Walmart Inc. (ticker: WMT), showing Walmart trading between support and resistance levels in September and October 2018. As soon as the stock broke above the resistance level of $96.72/share, the volume of shares being traded increased and the stock was pushed into an uptrend.

Figure 7.10 below is a good example from the first part of 2020. Coca-Cola Consolidated Inc. (ticker: COKE) had been trading between (approximately) the $257 and $295/share levels for several months with steady volume. Due to a catalyst (in this case, poor earnings results), the stock broke the support level at $257, and that was followed by a significantly higher trading volume. This led into the stock selling off.

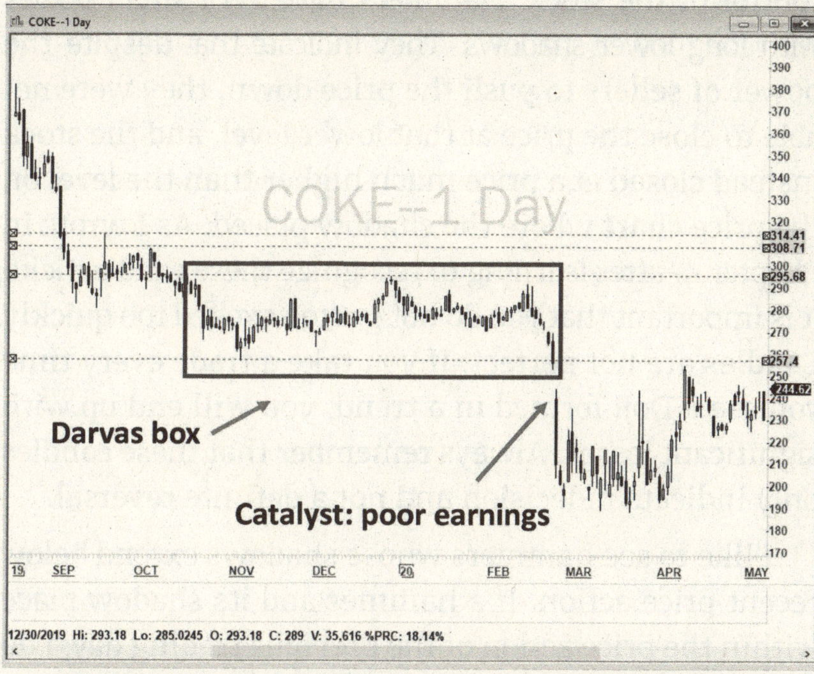

Figure 7.10: The price chart of Coca-Cola Consolidated Inc. (ticker: COKE) for the last months of 2019 and the first months of 2020. This is an excellent example of a Darvas Box. The stock had been trading between clear support and resistance levels for almost 5 months. As soon as the price of shares broke the support level, trading volume increased and pushed the price of the stock into a downward trend.

Hammer Doji Reversal

This strategy works well in identifying a potential change in a trend and that can then signal that a profitable swing trade awaits. The hammer Doji (do review Chapter 4 if you do not recall my earlier commentary on Dojis) is a bullish indicator which often presents at the end of a downtrend. It signals to the market that sellers are exhausted and that buyers may be able to take control of the stock. Hammers have very small bodies with long lower shadows. They indicate that despite the power of sellers to push the price down, they were not able to close the price at that lower level, and the stock instead closed at a price much higher than the level on the price chart where the shadow placed. As I wrote in Chapter 4, after learning to recognize these candlesticks, it is important that you do not get too excited too quickly. Candles are not perfect. If you take a trade every time you see a Doji formed in a trend, you will end up with significant losses. Always remember that these candles only indicate indecision and not a definite reversal.

I like to see hammers whose shadows extend below recent price action. If a hammer and its shadow place within the price action of the previous trading day, I do not consider it to be a reliable indicator.

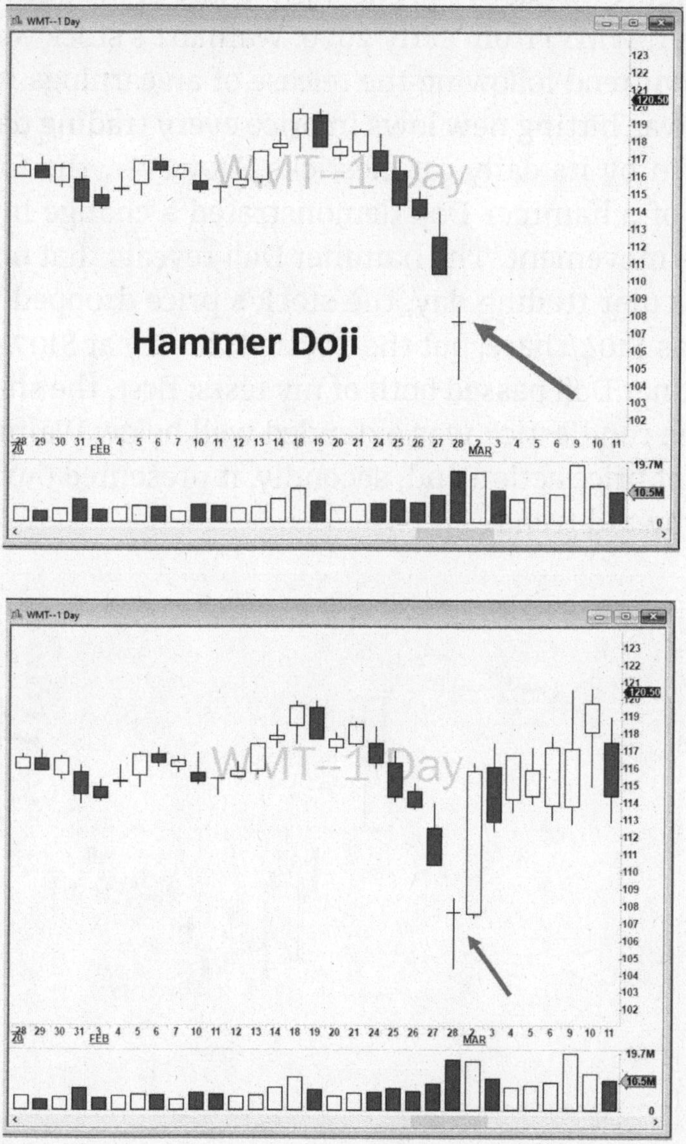

Figure 7.11: The price chart of Walmart Inc. (ticker: WMT). The formation of a hammer Doji (as I've marked) demonstrated a lack of conviction amongst sellers. This signaled that buyers might very likely take control and push the price of the stock back up, and that is indeed what happened.

Figure 7.11 above is the daily chart of Walmart Inc. (ticker: WMT) from early 2020. Walmart's stock was on a downtrend following the release of an earnings report and was hitting new lows in price every trading day, as shown by its daily candlesticks. However, the formation of a hammer Doji demonstrated a change in that price movement. The hammer Doji reveals that on one particular trading day, the stock's price dropped to as low as \$104/share, but then closed the day at \$107. This hammer Doji passed both of my tests: first, the shadow of the candlestick was extended well below Walmart's recent price action and, secondly, it presented during a downward trend.

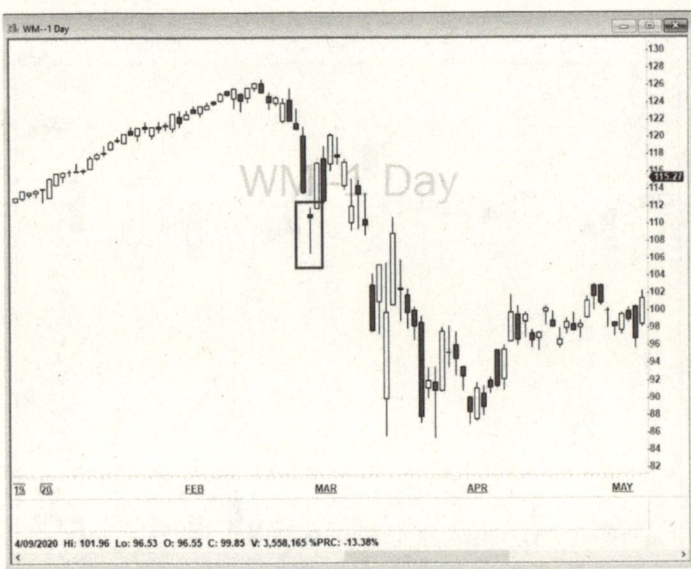

Figure 7.12: The price chart of Waste Management, Inc. (ticker: WM). The formation of a hammer Doji (as I've marked) demonstrated that sellers were exhausted. This signaled to buyers that the downtrend in the price of the stock may be coming to an end. Buyers then in fact did take control and pushed the price of the stock back up.

Another example is found in Figure 7.12 above, the price chart of Waste Management, Inc. (ticker: WM). Waste Management's stock began to fall in price in the days following the release of its Q4 (fourth quarter) earnings on February 13, 2020. The price action on February 28, 2020 resulted in the formation of a hammer Doji that again passed both of my conditions in order to be identified as a Hammer Doji Reversal: the price of the stock was in a downward trend and the shadow of the candlestick was lower than the candlesticks formed as a result of recent price action. This showed that sellers were exhausted and could not push the price of the stock any lower. The resulting hammer Doji confirmed that although the stock went down as low as $106/share, buyers were able to push the price back up and the stock closed at $111. Buyers then took control and over the next few trading days pushed the price back up to $120.

Lastly, Figure 7.13 below is another example, this time from The Kroger Company (ticker: KR) in the first months of 2020. You will see that the price of its stock is on a downtrend. On February 28, 2020, however, the price of the stock formed a hammer Doji which passed both of my criteria to be categorized as a Hammer Doji Reversal: it was in a downward trend and the shadow of the Doji was lower than the candlesticks formed by recent price action. As one might expect, the price of the stock bounced and began to then move up, which of course resulted in a great potential for trading.

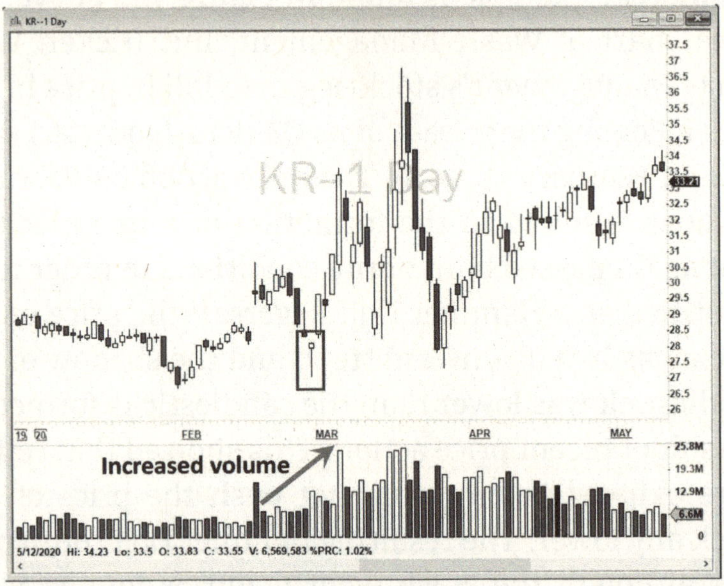

Figure 7.13: The price chart of The Kroger Company (ticker: KR), with the hammer Doji marked that was formed on February 28, 2020. This hammer Doji demonstrated exhaustion amongst sellers. The next trading day (March 2, 2020), the price of the stock bounced back and began its upward move.

While chart patterns such as Head and Shoulders, Cup and Handle and Hammer Doji Reversal seem intuitive and easy to recognize, it is important not to get too excited because there are definitely cases where these patterns fail. Just like any other strategy, it is important to have clear risk management rules before entering into any trade based on these indicators. In the next chapter, I will provide details on how to both journal your trades and set clear risk and reward ratios, to make sure you are not blowing up your account if any of these patterns fail. Proper risk management will dictate your longevity in the stock market.

Hot Sector Mania

Another strategy for successful swing trading is called hot sector mania. Hot sector mania refers to the situation where many individuals (traders, investors and the general public) rush to buy a specific stock, or rush to buy in a specific sector, all without any rationale other than a "massive" fear of missing out on something perceived to be great.

I am sure many readers remember the "tulip mania" of Bitcoin at the end of 2017, when Bitcoin was being traded at up to around $20,000 per Bitcoin. Tulip mania refers to a period in the 17th century, during the Dutch Golden Age, when the Netherlands was the world's leading economic and financial power. At that time, the prices of some fashionable tulip bulbs reached extraordinarily high levels and then in February 1637 dramatically collapsed, essentially becoming the first recorded speculative bubble, which is when the prices of assets or commodities deviate considerably from their real intrinsic values. Tulip mania, similar to the cryptomania craze of 2017, was more a socio-economic phenomenon than a major economic issue or crisis, as tulip bulbs were not a significant part of the Dutch economy, just as cryptocurrency is not (yet at least!) a significant part of our global economy.

Similarly, in 2017, ordinary people, uneducated investors, and people with limited financial literacy were rushing to buy cryptocurrencies. The market was unbelievable. The blockchain stocks were the hot new thing. The value of companies which simply mentioned the word *"blockchain"* in a press release would skyrocket.

For example, a company called "Long Island Iced Tea Corp." (ticker: LTEA) changed their name to "Long Blockchain Corp." (ticker: LBCC) and decided to shift their focus from beverages to blockchain technology. The stock ran nearly 500% in a single day, as you can see in Figure 7.14 below. The company's shares moved from below $2 to $9.47 with heavy trading volume. On April 10, 2018, the Nasdaq announced the delisting of LBCC, but it is still available in the over-the-counter (OTC) markets (which are briefly described in Chapter 2). As of June 11, 2020, LBCC was being traded at $0.10 per share. The company has abandoned its plans to purchase Bitcoin mining equipment.

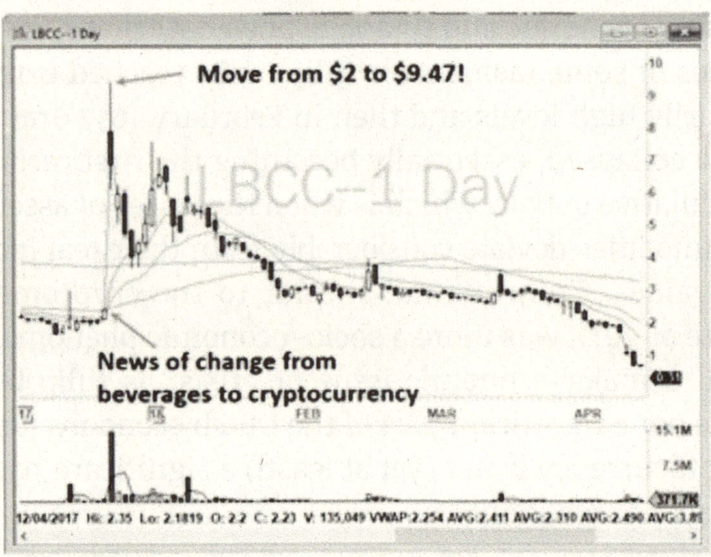

Figure 7.14: The daily chart of Long Blockchain Corp. (ticker: LBCC), formerly known as Long Island Iced Tea Corp. (ticker: LTEA). In December 2017, the corporation rebranded as part of a corporate shift toward "exploration of and investment in opportunities that leverage the benefits of blockchain technology" and reported that they were exploring blockchain-related acquisitions.

A more recent mania involved the famous electric car company, Tesla Inc. (ticker: TSLA). Very suddenly, TSLA became a new hot stock and everyone wanted to jump on the bandwagon and benefit from the move. Figure 7.15 below shows how the price of TSLA stock changed between the spring of 2019 and the spring of 2020.

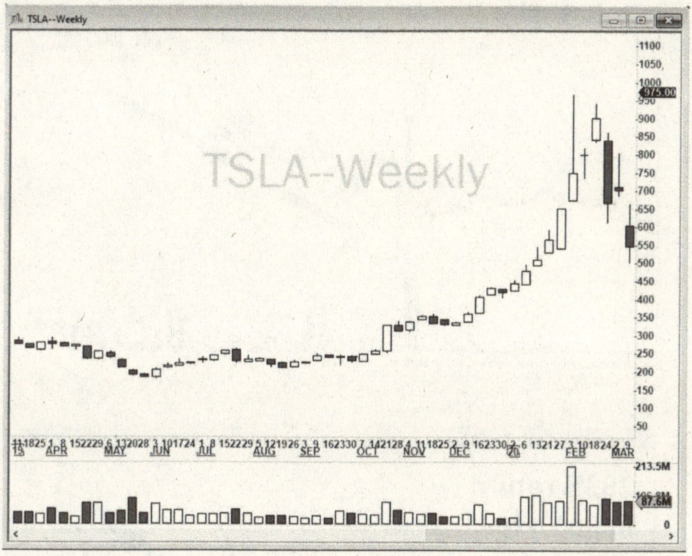

Figure 7.15: The weekly chart for Tesla Inc. (ticker: TSLA) demonstrates a perfect example of a hot sector mania.

Another very recent mania involved companies developing potential COVID-19 vaccines and manufacturing personal protective equipment. As the coronavirus pandemic spread throughout the world, these types of companies and sectors became "hot". An example of this is shown in Figure 7.16 below. You can see the significant changes in the price of shares in the daily charts of Moderna, Inc. (ticker: MRNA), a Cambridge, Massachusetts-based biotechnology company that is focused on drug discovery and drug development, and Novavax, Inc. (ticker: NVAX), a clinical-stage vaccine company.

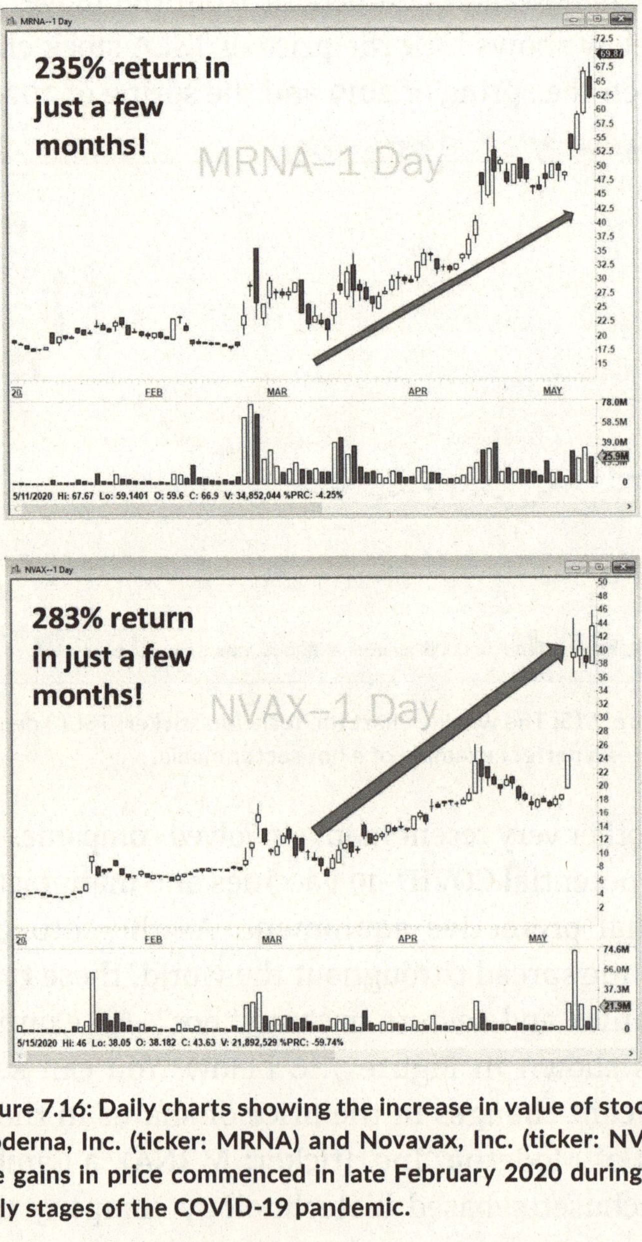

Figure 7.16: Daily charts showing the increase in value of stock of Moderna, Inc. (ticker: MRNA) and Novavax, Inc. (ticker: NVAX). The gains in price commenced in late February 2020 during the early stages of the COVID-19 pandemic.

Another example of a hot sector mania involved the stock of companies focused on the medicinal and recreational use of marijuana. "Pot mania" was very real for a season! Figure 7.17 below is the daily chart of Tilray, Inc. (ticker: TLRY) from the summer and early autumn of 2018. It was not only TLRY, but many other stocks in the marijuana market, which made crazy moves. You will see in Figure 7.17 below that TLRY reached around $300/share one day in September 2018. It's important to remember thought that a specific hot sector mania doesn't last forever. As of June 11, 2020, TLRY was trading at $8.37/share.

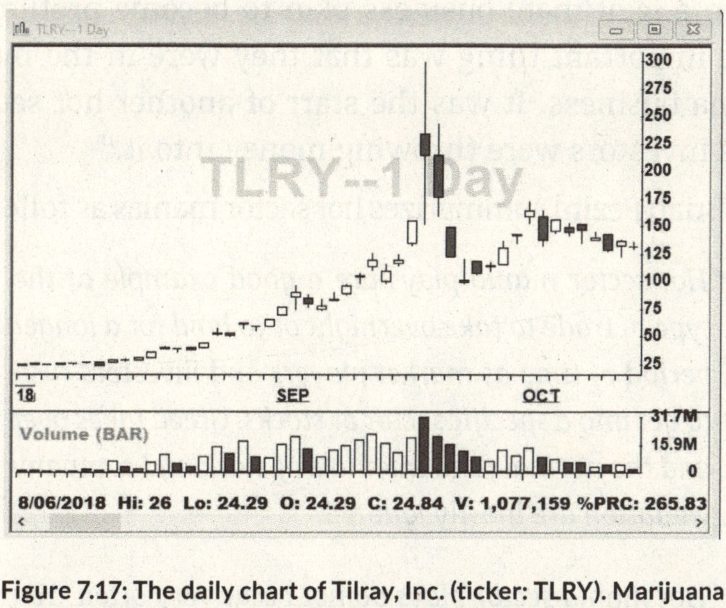

Figure 7.17: The daily chart of Tilray, Inc. (ticker: TLRY). Marijuana stocks were once upon a time a hot sector mania. As of June 11, 2020 though, TLRY was trading at $8.37/share.

Often, so-called ordinary people want to get in on the action when these types of manias hit the news.

And then, the fear of missing out on something "big" impacts the drastic moves in price even more. Andrew's friend, Brian Pezim, in his book, *How to Swing Trade*, referenced the following regarding "pot mania":

"Marijuana stocks started sprouting up like tulips in spring, particularly in Canada because of the more favorable legal environment and the support of the Canadian federal government, in comparison to the US. Old publicly traded mining companies that were dormant got renamed, becoming marijuana companies, and the money started to flow. Like most mania investing, nobody cared that the management had no experience or knowledge or even a legitimate business plan to become profitable. The important thing was that they were in the marijuana business. It was the start of another hot sector and investors were throwing money into it."

Brian Pezim summarizes hot sector manias as follows:

> *"Hot sector mania plays are a good example of the type of trade to take overnight or to hold for a longer period of time as market players and investors rush to get into a specific sector or stocks. Greed takes over and the normal fundamentals of stock and company valuation are mostly ignored.*
>
> *"Hot mania sector plays do not occur very often. You might have to wait 6 months to a year or more for one to occur. Patience and diligence is the key to making money using the hot sector mania strategy. Monitoring news feeds, chat rooms, social media sites, scanning*

the market with tools and using any connections you might have in the brokerage or venture capital industry are all ways to keep up to date on where the hot money is flowing."

Moving Average Crossovers

Another strategy that is useful when trading a trending stock is the Moving Average Crossover. When a stock is in a very bullish uptrend, you can buy and sell off at the crossover of 9 and 20 moving averages (most trading platforms come with these indicators already programmed and their "lines" will automatically appear on your charts). For example, Figure 7.18 below is the daily chart for the SPDR S&P 500 ETF Trust (ticker: SPY) for part of 2018. You can see the 2 faint lines that present from left to right on this chart. Those are the 9 and 20 moving average indicators. You will also see they cross each other at 2 points, which I have marked on the chart. That is where you could have successfully bought long (in July 2018) and then sold (in October 2018). As you may know, 2018 was a bull market and most stocks were trending higher. The Moving Average Crossover is one of the best strategies in a trending market.

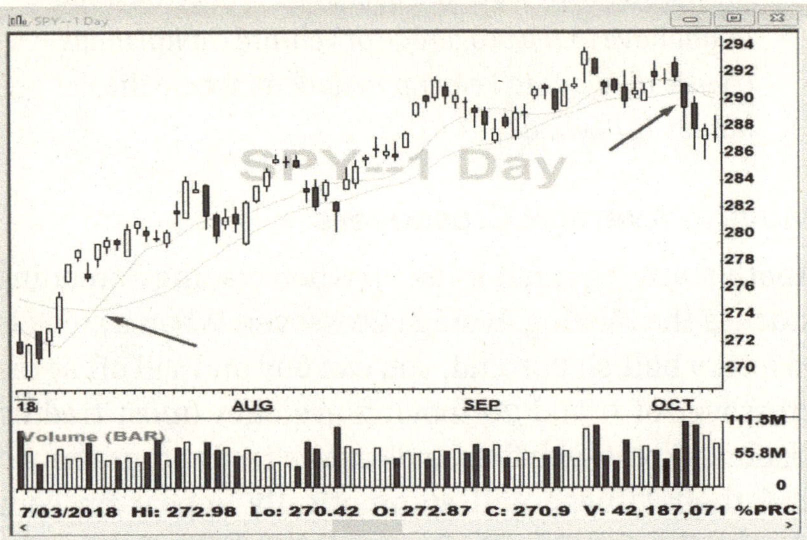

Figure 7.18: An example of a Moving Average Crossover Strategy marked out on the daily chart of SPDR S&P 500 ETF Trust (ticker: SPY). The first time the 9 and 20 moving average indicators crossed each other marked the place to enter your trade (in July 2018). When the 9 and 20 moving averages crossed again, it was a signal to sell and take your profit (in October 2018).

Figure 7.19 below shows the stock price of Apple Inc. (ticker: AAPL) in early 2020, during the bear market and recession brought on by the COVID-19 pandemic. As you can see, I marked on the chart where you could go short and then where you would cover this swing trade position.

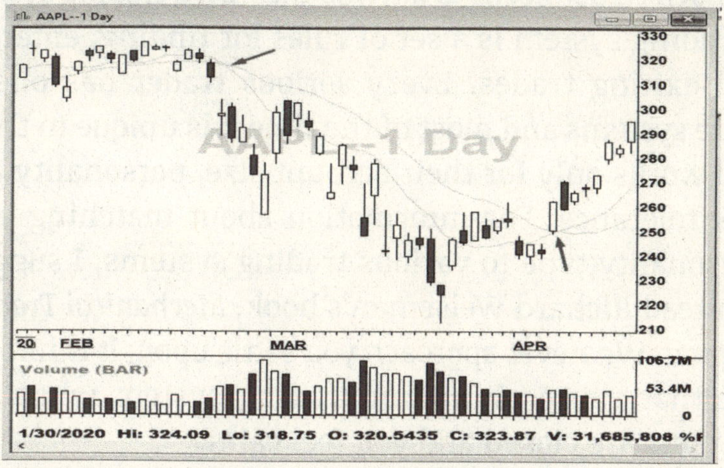

Figure 7.19: An example of a Moving Average Crossover Strategy on Apple Inc. (ticker: AAPL). You could go short and enter the trade when the 9 and 20 moving averages cross each other on your chart (which I have marked in February 2020) and you would cover your position and take your profit when the 9 and 20 moving averages cross each other again on your chart (which I have marked in April 2020).

Other Swing Trading Indicators / Importance of a Trading System

Another well-known technical indicator is the MACD (short for moving average convergence divergence). The MACD was developed in the late 1970s by Gerald Appel, a professional money manager and investment advisor. I highly recommend his 2005 book, *Technical Analysis: Power Tools for Active Investors*, should you be wanting to learn more about technical indicators such as the MACD. Two other well-known indicators are the Impulse System and the Channel Trading Systems, both introduced by Dr. Alexander Elder, author of the book, *Trading for a Living*.

Each trader needs to develop their own trading system. A trading system is a set of rules for finding, entering, and exiting trades. Every serious trader has one or more systems and most of the time it is unique to them, and works only for their account size, personality and risk tolerance. For information about matching your personality type to various trading systems, I suggest you read Richard Weissman's book, *Mechanical Trading Systems*. Whatever approach you settle upon, it is important that you design your trading system when the markets are closed and you feel calm.

A proper trading system includes the following:

» What is my entry? (Under what conditions do I enter a trade?)

» What is my exit? What is my stop loss? What is my profit target?

» What are my scanners set to search for? (How do I find the best stocks to swing trade?)

» What is my confidence level in this trade?

In the next chapter I go into more detail on what it takes to be successful in swing trading and what are some of the key mistakes novice traders make while trading. Before moving to the next chapter, however, I encourage you to go online and search for swing trading strategies. Millions of strategies will come up and soon you will realize that it is not so much about the strategy, but more about the trading system you implement for yourself. Not every strategy will work every time. If you could make a trade and profit every time you saw a Cup and Handle Pattern or a Head and Shoulders Pattern, everyone, and I mean everyone, would be a "market millionaire". Strategies fail, but what will prevail is the system you can develop for yourself. That is why Andrew and I in this book have both hammered down the importance of journaling your trades and developing a trading system.

At Peak Capital Trading, we have multiple mentors, several risk analysts, and an in-house psychologist, who all are committed to helping our traders develop their own proprietary system.

CHAPTER 8

THE PATH TO BEING A SUCCESSFUL SWING TRADER

"People who think they know all the answers, probably don't even know the question."

—Sir John Templeton,
Founder of the Templeton Growth Fund

MANAGE EXPECTATIONS

Managing key expectations when you are swing trading is one of the most important things you must do. As referenced previously, a professional swing trader can reasonably expect to make an average of 20 percent per year on their trades. In order to generate these types of returns however, you need to maintain a minimum balance in your account, and traders will have different minimum balance requirements depending on their goals and profit targets.

DON'T START WITH TOO LITTLE CAPITAL

So, how much capital do you need to get started in swing trading? I've tried to provide in this section some guidelines to help you generate reasonable returns but, of course, the following are just my recommendations. They are not hard-and-fast rules.

- **Trading for retirement:** If you are swing trading your retirement account, you are not depending on the trades to provide you with your current income. You can therefore begin with an account in the range of $10,000 to $20,000, and that will allow you to hold around 10 positions at any given time.
- **Trading for a living:** If swing trading is your full-time job, then you need to start with a reasonably sized nest egg. A professional swing trader can expect to make a return of 20 percent per year. If your living expenses total $5,000 per month, your account must hold at least $300,000. (Achieving 20 percent on $300,000 equals $60,000 per year, or $5,000 per month.) I must caution though, this calculation is based on ideal conditions. What if you only average 15% in your first year? That equals $3,750 per month. 10% equals $2,500 per month. The larger your account is, the more of a cushion you have. You could use margin to increase your returns, but you must be very

careful when using margin. As I explained in Chapter 3, while using a margin account can amplify your returns, a margin account can also easily (and dramatically) increase your losses.

» **Trading for fun:** By now you should know that Andrew and I do not recommend trading for fun. Trading is a serious business and we both have watched too many amateur traders lose their savings because they did not treat it as such. If you have a few thousand dollars saved up, and you do not plan to diligently prepare before making your first trade, I suggest you instead either save your money for that proverbial rainy day, make a donation to a cause or two you feel passionate about, or treat yourself and your loved ones to something special.

All things considered, I find it difficult to believe that you can swing trade well on less than $10,000. The costs of commissions, taxes, slippage, and other factors work against you so much that you can't generate reasonable returns.

CREATE A TRADING PLAN

A cliché that I hear over and over again is, "*Plan your trade, then trade your plan.*" I hate to regurgitate that here, but I can't phrase it any better. Your trading plan is your road map. It answers the following questions:

- » What are you trading?
- » How did you identify this particular stock for a trade? What chart pattern did you recognize? Did you use a top-down approach? Did you use a bottom-up approach?
- » What technical analysis have you done? What fundamental analysis have you done?
- » What is your time horizon for this specific trade?
- » How will you trade? Will you go long? Will you go short? What strategy will you use?
- » How much capital will you allocate to your position?
- » What are your entry signals?
- » When will you exit the position for a profit?
- » When will you exit the position and take a loss?

Trading plans must be carefully thought through and then written down. You should keep a paper copy of your trading plan right at your trading station or a digital version should be easily accessible on your device. You must create a trading plan before you enter each and every trade. Not after the fact! After you enter a trade is the correct time to journal about the trade but it is not the right time to be identifying what you hope to achieve from the trade. Friends will get into a trade and then ask me for advice on what to do with their position. My response is always the same, "Where is your trading plan?"

DON'T LET EMOTION CONTROL YOUR TRADING

Your emotions are your worst enemy when trading. Traders who lose billions of dollars at major hedge funds often start out losing a small amount and then try to break-even or prove themselves right. I have seen this happen far too often in my line of work. Their ultimate failing lies not in their analysis, nor in their market knowledge, but in their inability to control their emotions. As the famous economist, John Maynard Keynes, said in the 1930s, "*Markets can stay irrational longer than you can stay solvent.*" Far too many funds have been wiped out due to one wrong bet.

The markets aren't personal. When you lose money, it's not because you made money last time. Your losses and profits are a function of your trading ability and the markets in which you trade. The true, professional trader is a master of their emotions. Profits don't lead to extreme joy, and losses don't lead to extreme sadness. If you sat across the table from a professional trader, you wouldn't be able to tell whether they were up

$50,000 or down $100,000. Professional traders are calm and don't let their emotions take over their cognitive functions.

Another factor in controlling your emotions is keeping tabs on your trades. Don't brag to others about your profits. Don't tell others about any trades you're in at the moment. Do so and you become married to your positions. If you tell your best friends that you hold shares of Tesla Inc. (ticker: TSLA) and you believe the share price is going to skyrocket, you'll be less likely to exit if the trade turns against you. You may say to yourself, "*Oh no! Everyone knows I hold Tesla. I can't bail now. I've got to hold to prove I was right.*"

Controlling your emotions isn't something that just happens one day and you never have to worry about it again. Rather, it's an ongoing battle. The two strongest emotions you are going to face are greed and fear. When markets are roaring in one direction and you are riding that wave, you'll want to hold positions longer than you need to as you amass more profits. And when markets roar in the opposite direction and your profits evaporate, you'll want to take more risks to make up for those losses.

Somehow you have to learn to keep your emotions in check and to make trades based on your well-thought-out trading plan. That is why it is so important to practice trading in real time in a simulator before risking your own money in actual trades.

DIVERSIFY

As a swing trader, you must hold a diversified portfolio of positions (basically, the swing trades you have "in process" at any given time). You should aim to have **ten** different positions, and they should be in different sectors. If you can, you should also incorporate a variety of asset classes into your swing trading. For example, include exchange-traded funds that track international markets, or commodities such as gold.

Each swing trade you are in the midst of represents a different way to diversify your portfolio. Holding more than one position reduces *idiosyncratic risk* (a fancy way of saying the risk you face in focusing your trading on one company or sector or asset class). Similarly, having both long and short positions reduces your market direction risk. And diversification allows your portfolio to withstand market volatility — the gains from a few positions can offset the losses from others.

Should you be interested in jumping ahead and reading more about this topic, I have included further commentary on diversification in Chapter 10.

TRADE MANAGEMENT

I am a strong believer that each trader has to develop their own technique and plan in order to become successful. I have taught you many different strategies and theories professional traders use to make money.

It is obvious that not all would work equally for everyone. As an example, my most profitable trades have come from the Head and Shoulders Strategy. You on the other hand might find that Doji Reversals or Engulfing Patterns are a more reliable strategy. Regardless of the strategy you choose, what can set you apart as a consistently profitable trader is how you manage your trades. Below I discuss two common methods I use to manage my open positions:

Use a Stop Loss Order

You may think that stop loss orders are nothing more than training wheels. "*I'm an adult. I don't need these pesky stop loss orders. I can exit when I see weakness.*" Unfortunately, that kind of thinking may get you killed (financially speaking, of course). Financial markets aren't playgrounds or appropriate places to find out who you really are. Stop loss orders are necessary for several reasons — even if you watch the market 24 hours a day, 7 days a week:

» **They help you deal with fast-moving markets.** If you swing trade ten different positions, it's quite possible that many of them may start acting up on the same day. And they can move fast and furious if negative news is in the air. Because of the speed at which markets move, you need a stop loss to save you if you are unable to act. In 2020, for example, we saw one of the fastest ever bear markets unfold over a time frame of just 2 weeks. Yes, you read that correctly, the market dropped by more than

20% in just 9 trading days, wiping out trillions of dollars in value. Imagine if you were trading the SPDR S&P 500 ETF Trust (ticker: SPY) on the long side without a stop loss!

» **They limit your downside.** Without a stop loss order, your downside may be all your capital (or worse, if you're shorting, as explained in Chapter 3). Stop loss orders serve to protect you, because they place some upper limit on the losses you may suffer. Nevertheless, a security could gap through your stop loss order, but your loss would be realized then regardless of whether a stop loss order existed.

» **They help take your emotions out of the game.** When you place a mental stop loss, you may start to arbitrarily move your imaginary stop loss as the markets move against you. With a stop loss order, when you are long a stock and its price starts to fall, you cannot talk yourself out of exiting this losing position.

» **They give you time to take your eye off the ball.** If you travel or are unable to watch the markets on a day when you are sick, stop loss orders ensure that your portfolio value is preserved. If you didn't have stop loss orders, you should fear being away from your device and thus out of touch with the markets. One or two lousy positions can quickly change a top-performing account into a poor performer.

Set a Profit Target or Technical Exit

I will again stress the importance of risk management. The reason is simple: You can't last long without it. But when it comes to profits, you must set your profit target or technical exit. Your profit target is often based on a previous support or resistance level. Some swing traders set predefined profit targets of selling 50 percent of a position after it achieves a 5 percent gain from entry and selling the other 50 percent after it reaches a 10 percent gain. When trading based on a pattern like Head and Shoulders, your profit target may be determined by the projection price implied in the chart pattern. My preference in taking profits is to rely on a signal from a technical indicator rather than a preexisting support or resistance level. Some securities trend longer and farther than anticipated, and they can be very profitable. Hence, I prefer to exit after a security breaks below an indicator, such as a moving average, or on a sell signal from a trending indicator.

KEEP A TRADING JOURNAL

Most of the successful traders I have met during my career have several things in common. One of those commonalities is that they keep a journal of all of their trades. And this process is not limited to traders only. For any system to function properly, there has to be a feedback loop where an individual can learn from their mistakes and build upon their strengths. For example, successful companies hold regularly scheduled reviews with their employees. Writing a trading journal is exactly like an employee review at work. Your manager will tell you what you have been doing well, and on what you can improve. Writing a journal does the same thing for traders. It is a great moment of self-reflection that if done properly can lead to improvement in performance. You can identify your reasoning for each trade you entered. Why did you get into this trade? What was the technical signal for your early exit? Etc. Etc. In general terms, you can identify your mistakes. You can group your winning trades and losing trades together in order to find similarities and to identify patterns. If you are struggling with how best to journal your trades, I encourage you to review that section of Chapter 6 again. Andrew includes some very useful commentary on journaling in that chapter.

Andrew and I both understand that journal keeping can be cumbersome and tough in the beginning, but there is considerable research to indicate that writing a journal correlates with better performance. Although many believe the study does not exist, some motivational speakers share of a study from Yale University which showed that only 3% of their 1953 graduating class wrote down career goals. Twenty years later, those 3% who wrote their goals on paper were worth more than the rest of the class combined. By no means will writing a trading journal be the only factor that will turn you into a successful trader, but it does lay the necessary foundation.

The trouble is, more often than not, traders who do not journal find themselves continually making the same errors, and that leads them to step out of the game prematurely. We all know that the definition of insanity is doing the same thing over and over again while expecting different results. If you are not journaling your trades, you are bound to repeat, and repeat, and repeat yet again, the same mistakes.

As I wrote earlier, one of my professors was a major advocate of KISS (Keep it Simple, Stupid). I've learned that the key to consistency is keeping it simple. That principle works for many aspects of life, including journal keeping. If you desire to consistently maintain a journal, try to keep it as simple as possible. Over the years, I have developed a "three what" strategy in which I use my journal to answer three simple questions:

» **What** triggered the trade? What were the technical indicators behind entering the trade?

» **What** was my position? How many shares did I trade? Long or short? Margin or cash? Etc.

» **What** was the result? (The simplest way to answer this question is to include a screenshot of my chart, with my entry and exit marked, along with some brief comments about what triggered the exit and what was the rate of return.)

Below I have shared two examples of trades I took and the journal entries I subsequently made based on them. First, as Figure 8.1, is a profitable trade I took on the software company, Oracle Corporation (ticker: ORCL).

I entered the trade on June 19, 2019 after Oracle's share price gapped up due to a positive earnings report. You will see that I recorded what indicator triggered the trade, what my position was, and what the results were based on that. This process helps me to keep track of what strategies are working best for me.

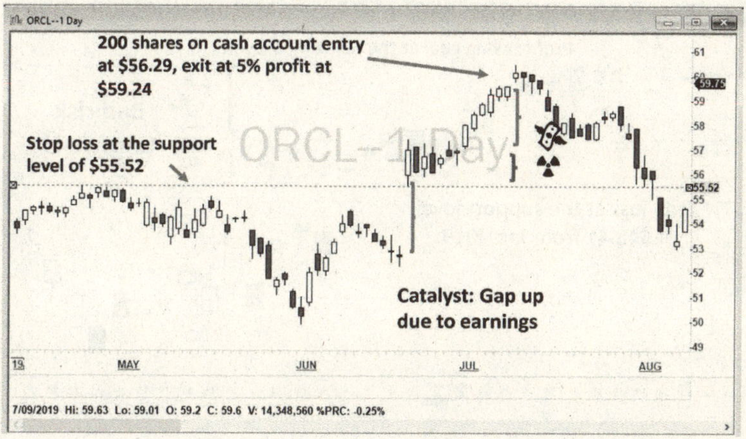

Figure 8.1: An example from my trading journal. I include simple commentary on what led me to enter this trade of shares in Oracle Corporation (ticker: ORCL) as well as the end result of the trade, all in order to help me fine-tune my strategies.

It is also very important to journal all of your unprofitable trades. There are far more learning opportunities when a trade goes against you than when it works out to your favor. Below, as Figure 8.2, is an example of one of my losing trades. The price of stock of the Canadian financial institution, Toronto-Dominion Bank (ticker: TD), was on a downward trend, but on February 27, 2020, I identified a hammer Doji. The hammer Doji signaled that sellers might be exhausted and hence I went long in the hope of a reversal. The stock (of course!) continued to fall and I was stopped out of my trade with a loss. After journaling my trade, I realized that my error was entering this position too close to the earnings. The result of the earnings pushed the stock into a further downward spiral.

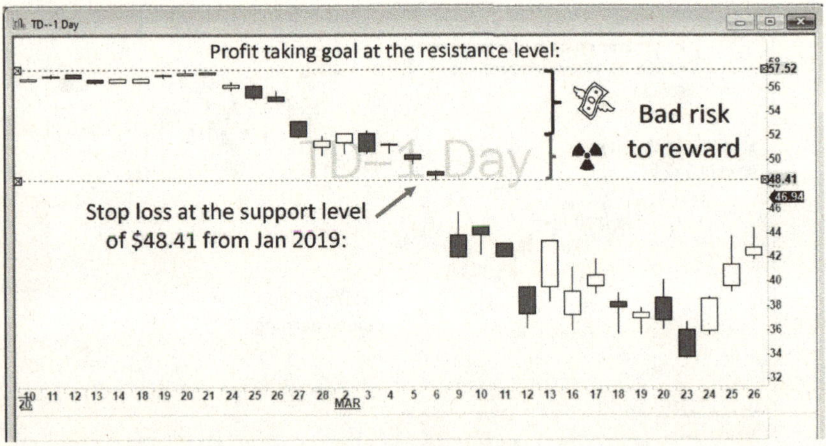

Figure 8.2: An example from my trading journal of an unprofitable trade in early 2020 on Toronto-Dominion Bank (ticker: TD). It is important to journal your losing trades as well as your winning trades.

GAMBLING ON EARNINGS DATES

The period right before earnings are released is usually the worst time to enter into a stock. Why? For one, you do not know which way the stock price is going to go after the earnings are announced. You might say in response, for example, that you are confident Apple Inc. (ticker: AAPL) will beat analysts' expectations for their earnings and the value of their stock should therefore go up. Let me tell you, it is not as easy as that. In some cases, a stock will beat the expectations in terms of both earnings per share and revenue, but their price will still fall. Perhaps, during an earnings call, management will unexpectedly mention in passing that they plan to increase capital expenditures and R&D. That type of announcement will usually take the price of stock into a downward trend because the stock market is a future-looking vehicle and much emphasis is placed on future earnings. When a company plans to increase capital expenditures and R&D, it signals to investors that next year's net income will be lower, and hence the price of the stock will generally fall. It's important to remember that the calculations involved in predicting what will happen to the price of a stock after an earnings report is far more complicated than merely beating or missing expectations.

Another reason not to trade before earnings calls is a phenomenon called "post earnings announcement drift" or PEAD. When a stock has a strong earnings report and gaps up, it will have a tendency to continue moving in the same direction for many days or even weeks. As a small investor, you can ride the wave, but if you were betting against the stock, you are in trouble.

AVOID OVERTRADING

Swing trading is principally defined by the short-term nature of the price swings it attempts to capture. Obviously, those price swings require more trading than a buy and hold investment strategy (see Chapter 2), but you should still trade as few times as possible in order to achieve your objective. Why? The more often you trade, the more work you need to do:

- » Trading entails costs, and costs hurt returns. Even with commission-free trading, you still might lose on exchange rates.
- » Overtrading also increases your administrative work. You need to journal your trades and review them on a weekly or monthly basis. Once you start overtrading, you will find yourself spending more and more time on your trading journals. As a result, in order to save time, you will skip journaling your trades which, as I set out not too many pages ago, will not be a wise decision.

Swing trading is supposed to fit in the happy medium between the day trader who trades minuscule price movements and the buy and hold investor who sits on their hands until they become numb. The more often you trade, the more likely you're simply trading *market noise* (moves driven by non-fundamental reasons). Buying and selling often or intraday (during the same day) makes your success as a swing trader that much more difficult — so get in before a major price move and get out after you capture it.

I can't give you a set number of trades to place per week or per month, but on average, your trade length should last several days to several weeks. If you're holding positions for shorter amounts of time, you need to examine that part of your trading system. Are losses that force liquidation causing you to trade this way? Or are you becoming impatient and trading in and out because you're looking for the elusive stock that will make a major move the day after you buy it?

AVOID PENNY STOCKS AND LOW FLOAT STOCKS

There is a saying on Wall Street that penny stocks are "fool's gold in the market". The reason for this is that inexperienced novice traders are often the ones who lose "big time" when trading these penny stocks. The stocks with low floats and low prices are easy targets for market manipulation. You'll recall from earlier in this book that I consider any stock priced under $5/share to be a penny stock. It is not that I am inherently against these stocks, but I know how easy it is for them to make large moves and wipe out your entire account within minutes. The additional risk factor associated with trading penny stocks is their liquidity. Believe it or not, many OTC (over-the-counter) stocks do not even trade on certain days. Trust me, you do not need to trade junk to become a successful trader. Penny stocks quite often represent companies that are financially distressed. You would recognize the names of many companies (Blockbuster LLC and E*TRADE Financial Corporation being two) which became penny stocks before they either went out of business or were acquired (very cheaply) by larger competitors. As a rule of thumb, avoid trading stocks where their float is less than 5% of their shares outstanding.

Too many people become greedy and try to trade these penny stocks. Andrew receives plenty of emails from traders who have ignored his advice (and the advice of many others) and lost thousands of dollars within a few minutes.

Andrew is famous for one particular quote: "low float stocks garbage". Some of the members of his trading community actually had a T-shirt made up for him as he had said this so many times. You can see this T-shirt in Figure 8.3 below.

Figure 8.3: Andrew and his famous "low float garbage stock" T-shirt. You are right, Andrew! Low floats are garbage!

STAY HUMBLE: AVOID BEING OVERCONFIDENT

If you string together several winning trades, you will no doubt start to build confidence in your strategy and skills as a swing trader. Good for you! But if your confidence turns into arrogance, you're going to cut corners and take greater risks. This is when traders usually stop writing in their journals and no longer use stop losses for their trades. Regardless of how good you think you are, plenty of other traders are out there who are better prepared and ready to take your lunch money. A humble trader isn't afraid to admit mistakes. An arrogant trader thinks the market's wrong and they are right. A humble trader looks at their education as a journey and not a destination. You need to understand that at no point does your education in trading stop, regardless of your account size or your trading resume. I look at every trading day as a learning opportunity where I can teach, improve and potentially make my clients and myself some money.

Some traders falsely believe that once you know the so-called tools of the trade, there's nothing more to figure out. They're wrong. The market is a living organism that keeps evolving.

Try setting a goal for yourself to read at least one trading-related book every quarter. I personally read one finance-related book every two months, and this is in addition to 5 years of university education and work experience. If you're constantly taking in new information, you're less prone to thinking that you're the be-all and end-all when it comes to trading, and you can avoid the fate of those "smart" traders who are brilliant on an IQ level but not in practice. So please, stay humble and continue to learn.

AVERAGING DOWN: NEVER ADD TO A LOSING POSITION

What is averaging down? Pretend for a moment that you, as a trader or investor, purchase some stock, and then watch the price of that stock move in a downward direction. "Rats," you think to yourself. Instead of humbly admitting defeat and getting out of the trade with hopefully not too large of a loss, you purchase more shares, at a now lower price, in the hope that the stock's price will eventually increase to a level where you can sell them all and recoup the money you've put into the trade. This is called "averaging down" because, as you buy more shares at a cheaper price, your average price paid per share decreases. There is a saying in the trading community that "only losers average down losers". This expression is true, trust me, because there is no guarantee that the share price will come back up. It may very likely keep going down and you will suffer a much more significant loss than if you had got out of the trade early on. You must pick a stop loss level when you enter a trade and then stick to it. To create that proper stop loss though really depends on your risk tolerance and how large your account is.

Let's explain this further with a practical example. If you buy $10,000 worth of Tiffany & Co. (ticker: TIF) stock for $100 per share (which results in you owning 100 shares), and its price immediately falls to $90, you're facing a $1,000 loss. Yikes! No trader wants that to happen. You might think to yourself, if I buy another 100 shares of TIF at the new price of $90, I will have averaged my purchase price to $95 per share, and it will be much easier to break-even.

Averaging down, or doubling down, does not work. If the price of the shares you bought march down in value even more, your losses will be compounded because you've now exposed yourself to double your initial investment. Never send good money after bad. If you have a loss on a trade, then your original trade idea was wrong. Adding more money to the trade doesn't make you right.

The only time doubling down might be acceptable is when you have done your fundamental analysis and you are looking at a longer term timeline. As an example, if you are holding shares in Apple Inc. (ticker: AAPL) as a result of your fundamental analysis, and you have a timeline of 5 to 10 years, it might be a good idea to add to your position when the stock is dropping in price in order to bring your average cost per share lower. In fact, retirement professionals often advocate this version of doubling down. Investors who have long-term time horizons do not concern themselves with short-term losses the way swing traders do.

"Scary" averaging down stories do not only include retail traders. They can involve hedge fund and institutional traders as well. Here's a good example. Brian Hunter was a superstar trader with an impressive track record at Amaranth Advisors, a massive hedge fund with over $9 billion in assets in 2006. This 32-year-old trader from Calgary, Alberta, Canada was up $2 billion from trading in natural gas earlier in 2006. That summer though, natural gas dropped to below $4 in a terrible, unusually steep down move. With a deep billion-dollar pocket, Brian Hunter ignored the market and repeatedly averaged down on a risky, volatile bullish position on natural gas. JPMorgan, his broker, kept calling for more collateral to support his enormous positions, and when the collateral didn't arrive, he was forced to liquidate his positions. Amaranth Advisors went from $10 billion in managed assets to $4.5 billion, accepting a $6.6 billion loss which led to the company being dissolved entirely. Regardless of your account size, averaging down on losers could bankrupt you, even if your account is worth $10 billion. Jim Cramer, former hedge fund manager and host of *Mad Money* on CNBC says, "Stocks are not like parents when you lose them at the mall, they do not always come back." Next time you are averaging down on a stock, I encourage you to remember this quote and reconsider your position.

As Andrew writes in his first day trading book, for the trader at home with many dollars less than billions, you cannot withstand such draw downs. Brian Hunter believed that the price had to go up and not down. He was wrong at that time. I don't know why, but traders such as Brian Hunter will at times stubbornly put being right about their decision over making money. These are the types of traders who conveniently forget that the market can remain irrational longer than they can survive in the game. You cannot let your pride get the best of you. If you've made a bad decision, take a loss and get out early. Predictions and speculations have their place, but the price action of the stock is the most important indicator for traders like us. If you believe in an irrefutable trading opinion and the price action does not confirm your bias, then simply do not make the trade. Predictions without validation from the price action are not advisable if you wish to enjoy a long trading career. Your job is not prediction and anticipation, but the *identification* of trends and then the taking of a successful ride on them.

HAVE FUN AND ENJOY YOUR NEW BUSINESS

I want to end this chapter on a very positive note. You must remember to have fun. Would you open a sushi restaurant if you hate fish? Well, why would you treat swing trading any differently? I know too many people who dislike their jobs, even those receiving large paychecks. My close friend is a lawyer at a major firm here in Canada and he never seems to be happy. I, on the other hand, am the happiest person I know. Honestly!

I love my job, even if it sometimes requires me to stay in the office for well beyond the standard 8 hours that many people work. I love looking at charts, building complex forecast models and reading income statements.

If you have to force yourself to research positions, then swing trading may not be for you. If logging on to your brokerage account is a painful exercise you prefer not to do because you feel ashamed, swing trading may not be for you. Even when your account is down, you have to be optimistic that profits will come soon. And that optimism is what helps make those profits a reality.

So, please, enjoy swing trading and all that it entails. Remember to have fun and to be patient.

CHAPTER 9

INVESTING IN THE STOCK MARKET

"The stock market is a giant distraction from the business of investing."

John Bogle, Founder, The Vanguard Group

I wanted to start this section of the book with a quote from one of my favorite people in the world of investing and trading, John Bogle. Bogle was the founder of The Vanguard Group, which now has over $6 trillion under asset management. They offer some of the best, low-cost ETFs (exchange-traded funds) in the market.

As Bogle put it, there is much noise and many distractions in the market that a true investor should ignore. Investing is very analytical. You look at a stock and its fundamentals, and then at the prospects of the industry the stock is part of, followed by a review of the overall economy (you'll recall that this is called the bottom-up approach). Share prices going up or down a few percentage points should not distract you from all of the research you have done which led you to determine that a particular stock is a good buy for the long haul.

In this chapter, I will teach you the necessary tools to identify solid investment opportunities and how not to be distracted by the noise in the market. I will review how to read income statements, balance sheets and cash flow statements, as well as what to look for in those documents, and I'll do that without getting "super" technical. I will also review some key ways to value stocks in addition to how to go about finding undervalued companies and good buys.

DEFINE YOURSELF AS AN INVESTOR

The first step in becoming a successful investor is to define your goals and your timeline. You have to be honest with yourself in regard to your investing time horizon and your risk tolerance. When I sit down with high-net-worth clients, we first break down their financial goals and timeline. Most of my clients want to earn a certain amount before their retirement, while some prioritize a steady cash flow from their investment. Some younger clients want more aggressive returns and are willing to take on more risk. Regardless of your goals, it is important to be realistic and know what is attainable, and how much risk you are able or willing to take on to achieve that.

"Expected market risk premium" is the amount of additional return an investor expects for taking on additional risks of being in the equity market. This is a very key concept in the world of finance. Let me explain this further by an example. As an investor, you have the option of simply buying U.S. Treasury bonds and receiving a secured return of less than 1.5% per year. These bonds are risk free with a low chance of default. However, as a more aggressive investor, you will expect a higher return for taking on the additional risk of being in the stock market. During good times, investors expect around 7%-10% return from their investment in the market. Nevertheless, in 2020, given that there are so many uncertainties related to COVID-19, the expected market return is far lower at 5%.

I discussed the above example to help you understand the realistic expectations when you are investing. If you produce returns of 6 to 8% annually in the market, you are beating many fund managers on Wall Street. In 2019, the average return among hedge funds on Wall Street was 6.96%, failing to beat the index. I myself am down 5% in my portfolio in the spring of 2020 (although many of my colleagues are down double digits). If you are looking for higher returns than an annual 5 to 10%, you might want to consider trading instead. Many successful day traders are able to add 1% to their portfolio daily. With that being said, higher returns usually mean higher risks as day trading can be more difficult and requires much more time and energy to master.

I would like you to take a few minutes, right now, to define yourself as an investor. What is your timeline? Your risk tolerance? What returns are you expecting? In the next chapters, I will teach you the necessary skills to pick the right stocks based on your timeline. I will also teach you about diversification and hedging so you can manage your risk. Throughout this book, I have tried not to give any investment advice but to simply provide you with the tools required to succeed in the market. I do, however, mention some of my favorite stocks and ETF investments which I have in my own portfolio along with why I selected them.

One of my favorite sayings about investing comes from Chamath Palihapitiya, founder of Social Capital, a venture capital firm in Silicon Valley. He states that your job as an investor is to be an "observer of the market" and to identify trends which will happen in the future. Let me explain this concept by sharing an example. A few years ago, I, alongside some colleagues, were reviewing growth stocks in the market. We all knew that e-commerce was growing at an unprecedented level and "direct to consumer" was the future of online commerce. Based on that "observation", we suggested Shopify Inc. (ticker: SHOP) to our manager for investment. Our suggestion was denied due to SHOP's lack of cash flow and profitability. Needless to say, as set out in Figure 9.1 below, a $56,000 investment in SHOP in 2016 would have been worth over a million dollars by 2020.

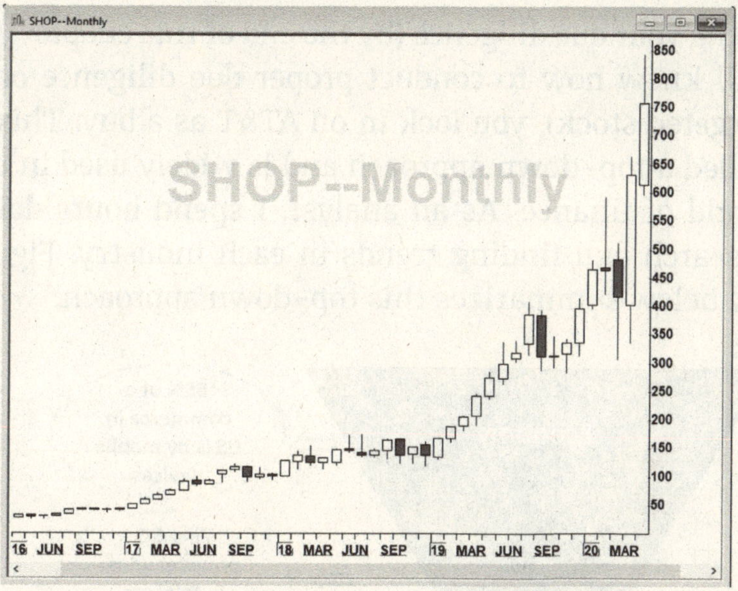

Figure 9.1: Performance of Shopify Inc. (ticker: SHOP) between June 2016 and May 2020. A $56,000 investment in 2016 would have been worth more than $1,000,000 in 2020.

On that note, there are two ways you can find worthwhile stocks for investing: by using either a top-down or bottom-up approach.

The top-down approach identifies promising candidates by starting with market analysis (looking at the stock and commodity markets). It then drills down into specific industries before finally examining individual stocks. Let's say you have an opinion on the Communication Services Sector. You believe that 5G is the future of communications and that whatever company has an edge in implementing it properly will grow tremendously over the next 5 years. You then conduct more research and realize that AT&T Inc. (ticker: T) is ahead of the competition in implementing 5G. After doing your due diligence (by the end of this chapter you will know how to conduct proper due diligence on a targeted stock), you lock in on AT&T as a buy. This is called a top-down approach and is widely used in the world of finance. As an analyst, I spend hours doing research and finding trends in each industry. Figure 9.2 below summarizes this top-down approach.

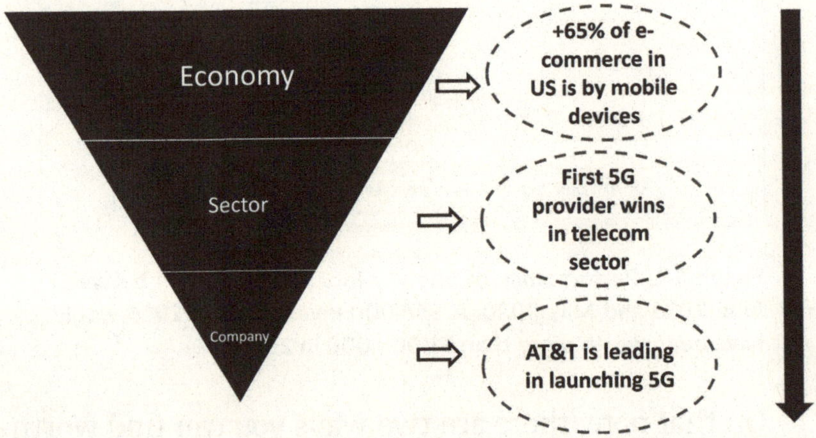

Figure 9.2: Example of a top-down approach in identifying a target company. You start with a review of the overall economy and then you work your way down.

This approach implicitly argues for greater weight on markets and industries over the merits of an individual company because these big-picture items are more important in determining a stock's return than company-level factors are. Again, let's go back to the Shopify Inc. (ticker: SHOP) example. At the time, my colleagues and I knew that e-commerce and entrepreneurship would rise in the U.S. and around the world, and we were willing to bet on companies which were going to empower entrepreneurs.

The bottom-up approach is the opposite. In this case, you start with a stock that you are bullish toward. After conducting your initial due diligence on the company, you then move on to the industry trends and examine macroeconomic factors in order to decide whether or not your stock is well positioned to prosper over the next few years. Let's break this down with an example. It's the summer of 2020. You are an Apple user and love the company. The bottom-up approach starts with you doing your due diligence on Apple Inc. (ticker: AAPL). After examining their income statement, balance sheet and cash flow statement (I will later teach you techniques on how to look at these intimidating documents and in no time at all be able to analyze a company's health), you realize that the company's fundamentals are solid. You then look at the industry and after hours of research, you realize the market is moving toward wearable technology. In addition, on a macro level, the economy is on pace to make at least somewhat of a recovery by 2021. The bottom-up approach is useful when you have selected a company and want to ensure the industry and economy support your decision. Figure 9.3 below summarizes this bottom-up approach.

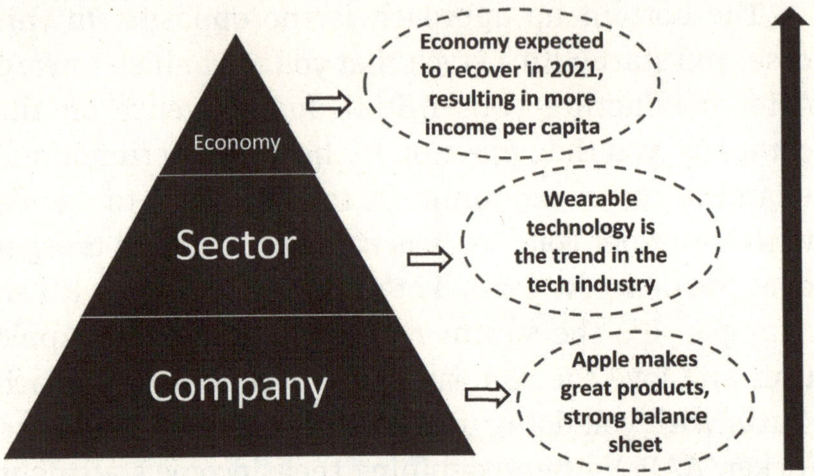

Figure 9.3: Example of a bottom-up approach in identifying stocks for investing. You start by reviewing a specific company that interests you and you then work your way up, validating your hypothesis.

Peter Lynch, the iconic mutual fund manager and author of *Beating the Street* (one of my favorite books), used to go to various stores and consumer outlets to observe what products were being offered for sale and how consumers were responding to certain brands. He desired to understand as much as possible about both business and consumer behavior. And he certainly did understand them. During his 13 years at Fidelity Investments, he had an annual average return of more than 29%!

The point is, as an investor, if you can observe where the market is going, and then make use of the tools and practices taught in the pages to come, you can make much more than whatever the expected market return is.

HOW TO START: FREE RESOURCES

There are many free resources available which can help you in your decision making. As a professional analyst, I have access to resources such as the Capital IQ platform and the Bloomberg Terminal, both of which provide the real-time financial data on companies that I need for my day-to-day research and analysis. Annual costs for the Bloomberg Terminal or the Capital IQ platform range from around $24,000 to $39,000 at the time of writing, and most retail investors of course cannot afford to pay that. This does not mean the game is completely rigged against the average Jane and Joe investor. There are many free resources available that can create the necessary edge a retail investor like you, working from your home office and not for a company, needs to be profitable. Below I have shared some of my favorite resources:

Yahoo Finance (*finance.yahoo.com*) is a great place to start your research for certain securities. It provides you with 3 important statements for each company: income statement, balance sheet and cash flow statement. Yahoo Finance displays income statements for the previous several years so that you can identify trends and make educated decisions about the future of a company. In addition, the website offers basic charting as well as the latest news and analysts' estimates. Figure 9.4 below is an example of an income statement from Yahoo Finance.

Apple Inc. (AAPL)
NasdaqGS - NasdaqGS Real Time Price. Currency in USD

☆ Add to watchlist

241.41 -3.52 (-1.44%) **241.25** -0.16 (-0.07%)

At close: 4:00PM EDT   After hours: 7:58PM EDT

Summary Chart Conversations Statistics Historical Data Profile **Financials** Analysis Options Holders Sustainab

Show: **Income Statement** Balance Sheet Cash Flow   **Annual** Quarterly Download Data

Income Statement All numbers in thousands

Breakdown	TTM	2019-09-30	2018-09-30	2017-09-30
Total Revenue	267,683,000	260,174,000	265,595,000	229,234,000
Cost of Revenue	166,105,000	161,782,000	163,756,000	141,048,000
Gross Profit	101,578,000	98,392,000	101,839,000	88,186,000
Operating Expenses				
Research Development	16,766,000	16,217,000	14,236,000	11,581,000
Selling General and Administrati...	18,659,000	18,245,000	16,705,000	15,261,000
Total Operating Expenses	35,425,000	34,462,000	30,941,000	26,842,000
Operating Income or Loss	66,153,000	63,930,000	70,898,000	61,344,000
Interest Expense	3,471,000	3,576,000	3,240,000	2,323,000
Total Other Income/Expenses Net	368,000	422,000	-441,000	-133,000
Income Before Tax	67,749,000	65,737,000	72,903,000	64,089,000
Income Tax Expense	10,222,000	10,481,000	13,372,000	15,738,000
Income from Continuing Operations	57,527,000	55,256,000	59,531,000	48,351,000
Net Income	57,527,000	55,256,000	59,531,000	48,351,000

Figure 9.4: Example of an income statement from Yahoo Finance for Apple Inc. (ticker: AAPL).

Reuters (*reuters.com/finance*) is another great source for the type of financial data you require in order to conduct a fundamental analysis of a company. Unlike Yahoo Finance, Reuters supplies its own data as opposed to simply aggregating existing data. One of the key features of Reuters is the "Stock Screener" section. This section allows you to search for specific stocks based on criteria such as growth, price-to-earnings ratio and sector. Later in this chapter, I will teach you strategies to select growth or value stocks (see Figure 2.3) based on these criteria and, hence, I know that the Reuters Stock Screener will be a useful tool in helping you to pick the right stock. Figure 9.5 below is a screenshot of the Reuters Stock Screener.

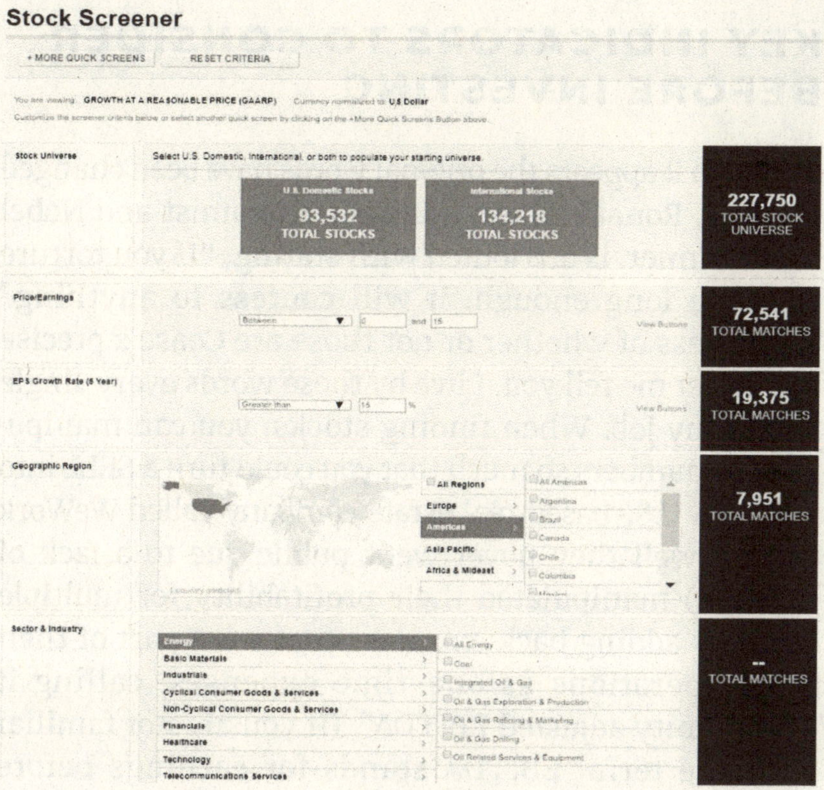

Figure 9.5: Screenshot of the Reuters Stock Screener. This is a very useful tool to identify worthwhile stocks in either the growth or value bucket.

There are many platforms that allow you to look at the bar and candlestick charts of different stocks. Some of the platforms I recommend using are BigCharts by MarketWatch (*bigcharts.marketwatch.com/*) and TradingView (*tradingview.com/chart/*). BigCharts allows you to see the latest news surrounding the stock. It also allows you to review analysts' estimates and ratings. *Briefing.com* is another great resource which provides live updates on analysts' estimates and offers the most recent earnings call transcripts of companies.

KEY INDICATORS TO CONSIDER BEFORE INVESTING

Although it appears the original words have been changed by time, Ronald Coase, a British economist and Nobel prize winner, is attributed with stating, "If you torture the data long enough, it will confess to anything." Regardless of whether or not those are Coase's precise words, let me tell you, I live by these words every single day at my job. When finding stocks, you can manipulate the numbers so much that you could turn a SELL into a BUY. A U.S.-based real estate company called WeWork (ticker: well they never went public due to a lack of demand) manipulated their profitability for multiple years by adding back expenses that were part of their daily operations as one-time expenses, calling it "community adjusted EBITDA". (If you are not familiar with the term, EBITDA stands for earnings before interest, taxes, depreciation and amortization.) They were torturing their numbers so they could confess "profitability". The same thing can happen while you are buying stocks. You could look at a company's income statement and ignore certain red flags in order to justify your buy.

Over the next few pages, I will show you some indicators to look for while selecting stocks. Looking at these indicators reduces the chance of you being fooled by certain numbers.

Dividend Yield

The dividend yield is the ratio of a company's annual dividend compared to its share price. The dividend yield is represented as a percentage and is calculated as follows:

$$\text{Dividend Yield} = \frac{\text{Annual dividend}}{\text{Stock price}} \times 100$$

This is an important concept to look at, especially during portfolio construction. In an optimal portfolio, you want to have some stocks that pay you every quarter in the form of a dividend. Figure 9.6 below includes information on the dividends paid by four well-known companies.

Company	Ticker	Annual Dividend	Price per share as of April 17th, 2020	Dividend Yield	Schedule
	AAPL	$3.08	$282.80	1.09%	Paid quarterly
Chevron	CVX	$5.16	$87.17	5.92%	Paid quarterly
	MCD	$5.00	$186.10	2.69%	Paid quarterly
The Walt Disney Company	DIS	$1.76	$106.63	1.65%	Paid semi-annual

Figure 9.6: Four of the 30 Dow Jones Industrial Average index companies along with their dividend yield.

Income Statement

Gross Margin and Net Margin

There are many things you can learn from reviewing a company's income statement. In my day job, I sometimes spend hours analyzing the income statement of a company. However, you yourself do not need to spend hours or go to business school to learn the skills necessary to effectively review and analyze a company. There are three items you can easily calculate which will tell you much about a company's health. The first key metric you learn from an income statement is the company's margins. In particular, there are two sets of margins which are important to review: gross margin (also called gross profit margin) and net margin (also called net profit margin or net profit ratio).

Gross margin is simply a company's gross profit (gross (total) revenue minus cost of goods sold (cost of revenue)) divided by its gross (total) revenue. Net margin is a company's net income divided by its gross (total) revenue. All of these figures can be found in a company's income statement. You want to calculate these important margins and compare them over a 5-year period to see if you can observe any trends. You ideally want each company in your portfolio to have either a consistent margin or an improving margin in comparison to their industry sector. As an example, the food industry has gross margins of 55% to 60%. Accordingly, you will want to be cautious if you are investing in a restaurant chain that has a lower margin.

$$\text{Gross Profit Margin} = \frac{\text{Revenue - Cost of Goods Sold}}{\text{Revenue}}$$

$$\text{Net Profit Ratio} = \frac{\text{Net Income}}{\text{Revenue}}$$

Income Statement All numbers in thousands

Breakdown	TTM	2019-09-30	2018-09-30	2017-09-30
Total Revenue	267,683,000	260,174,000	265,595,000	229,234,000
Cost of Revenue	166,105,000	161,782,000	163,756,000	141,048,000
Gross Profit	101,578,000	98,392,000	101,839,000	88,186,000
Operating Expenses				
Research Development	16,766,000	16,217,000	14,236,000	11,581,000
Selling General and Administrati...	18,659,000	18,245,000	16,705,000	15,261,000
Total Operating Expenses	35,425,000	34,462,000	30,941,000	26,842,000
Operating Income or Loss	66,153,000	63,930,000	70,898,000	61,344,000
Interest Expense	3,471,000	3,576,000	3,240,000	2,323,000
Total Other Income/Expenses Net	368,000	422,000	-441,000	-133,000
Income Before Tax	67,749,000	65,737,000	72,903,000	64,089,000
Income Tax Expense	10,222,000	10,481,000	13,372,000	15,738,000
Income from Continuing Operations	57,527,000	55,256,000	59,531,000	48,351,000
Net Income	57,527,000	55,256,000	59,531,000	48,351,000
Net Income available to common s...	57,527,000	55,256,000	59,531,000	48,351,000
Basic EPS	-	11.97	12.01	9.27
Diluted EPS	-	11.89	11.91	9.21
Basic Average Shares	-	4,617,834	4,955,377	5,217,242
Diluted Average Shares	-	4,648,913	5,000,109	5,251,692
EBITDA	-	81,860,000	87,046,000	76,569,000

Figure 9.7: Apple Inc. (ticker: AAPL) income statement. You can calculate a company's gross margin by simply dividing its gross profit by its gross (total) revenue. A company's net margin is calculated by dividing its net income by its gross (total) revenue.

Figure 9.7 above, from Yahoo Finance, is the income statement of Apple Inc. (ticker: AAPL). You can easily calculate Apple's gross margin by dividing its gross profit by its gross (total) revenue (October 2018 to September 2019: 37.8%, October 2017 to September

2018: 38.3%, October 2016 to September 2017: 38.5%). As you can see, Apple has been able to consistently maintain their top line margin (the "smart" way of saying gross margin) over these three fiscal years.

Similarly, you can look at Apple's net margins and see whether or not there is anything of concern. Apple's net profit margin for October 2018 to September 2019 was 21.2%. For October 2017 to September 2018, it was 22.4%. For October 2016 to September 2017, its net margin was 21.1%. Again, Apple has been able to consistently maintain its net margin. You would want to do this with all of the companies in your portfolio in order to see if any alarming trends are in the making.

Identifying Trends

You can also use a company's income statement to identify trends. Using the above Figure 9.7, you can for example compute year-over-year sales growth for Apple. You can see that from its 2016/2017 fiscal year to its 2017/2018 fiscal year, Apple's sales grew 15.86% (October 2017 to September 2018 sales (total revenue) - October 2016 to September 2017 sales (total revenue)) / October 2016 to September 2017 sales (total revenue). In its 2018/2019 fiscal year however, sales dropped by about 2%. This type of a trend analysis allows you to capture the health of a company and is an easy way to flag anything that might cause alarm. Figure 9.8 below is a trend analysis of the revenue/sales of Shopify Inc. (ticker: SHOP) vs. General Motors Company (ticker: GM).

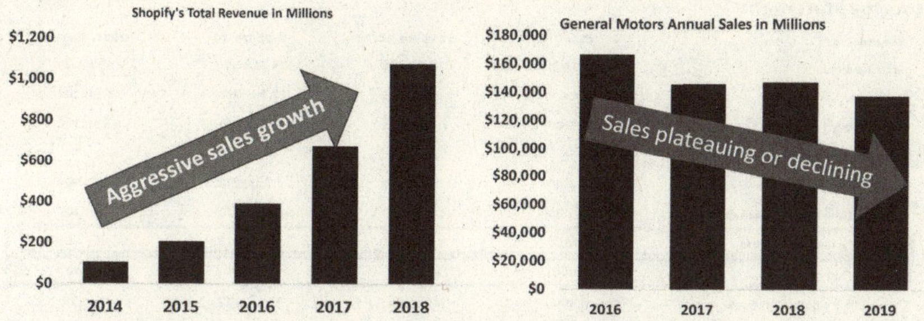

Figure 9.8: Shopify Inc. (ticker: SHOP) revenue vs. General Motors Company (ticker: GM) sales. With a simple trend analysis, you can see which company is growing and which has been stagnant. As a rule of thumb, avoid companies with declining sales.

Interest Coverage Ratio

Another figure that you should compute when reviewing an income statement is the company's interest coverage ratio. This will provide you with additional information about a company's health. It basically shows you as an investor if the company can pay the interest owing on its debt from the cash it earns from its operations (in finance, we call this EBIT, or earnings before interest and taxes, but you do not need to worry about understanding the technical term). Overall, you want to look for companies which have an interest coverage ratio of at least 2. You also want to compare the company's interest coverage ratio with the rest of their peers.

Interest Coverage Ratio = Operating Income or Loss / Interest Expense

Income Statement All numbers in thousands

Breakdown	**TTM**	**2019-09-30**	**2018-09-30**	**2017-09-30**
Total Revenue	26,973,000	26,508,600	24,719,500	22,386,800
Cost of Revenue	19,315,800	19,020,500	17,367,700	15,531,500
Gross Profit	7,657,200	7,488,100	7,351,800	6,855,300
Operating Expenses				
Selling General and Administrati...	1,810,300	1,824,100	1,759,000	1,393,300
Total Operating Expenses	3,580,400	3,572,400	3,545,300	2,958,500
Operating Income or Loss	4,076,800	3,915,700	3,806,500	3,896,800
Interest Expense	347,900	331,000	170,300	92,500
Total Other Income/Expenses Net	828,000	785,000	1,952,400	237,900
Income Before Tax	4,644,500	4,466,200	5,780,000	4,317,500
Income Tax Expense	925,000	871,600	1,262,000	1,432,600
Income from Continuing Operations	3,719,500	3,594,600	4,518,000	2,884,900
Net Income	3,724,300	3,599,200	4,518,300	2,884,700
Net Income available to common s...	3,724,300	3,599,200	4,518,300	2,884,700
Basic EPS	-	3.04	3.45	2.00
Diluted EPS	-	2.92	3.24	1.97
Basic Average Shares	-	1,184,600	1,309,100	1,431,600
Diluted Average Shares	-	1,233,200	1,394,600	1,461,500
EBITDA	-	6,246,500	7,256,200	5,477,100

Figure 9.9: Starbucks Corporation (ticker: SBUX) income statement. You simply divide a company's operating income or loss by its interest expense to calculate its interest coverage ratio. As you can see, Starbucks generates sufficient cash flow from its operations to easily pay the interest owing on its debt.

The above Figure 9.9 is the income statement of Starbucks Corporation (ticker: SBUX). Starbucks is one of the companies that I have in my long-term portfolio. It pays a dividend, its sales are growing in double digits and it sells an addictive drug! Those are some of my favorite criteria! You can see that Starbucks had an interest coverage ratio of 11.8 for the period of October 1, 2018 to September 30, 2019. This means that Starbucks can easily pay the interest owing on its debt 12 times over just from the cash it generates from its operations.

Balance Sheet

Similar to income statements, there are certain things you can easily find on the balance sheets of companies in order to identify good stock picks for your portfolio.

Cash Balance

You should first examine a company's cash balance. You want to make sure that the company you are selecting has sufficient cash on hand to be able to maneuver an economic downturn such as a recession or the COVID-19 pandemic. A rule of thumb is that a company's total cash should equal if not exceed its current liabilities. Please see Figure 9.10 below for an example of how to locate this on a balance sheet for Apple Inc. (ticker: AAPL). In the second column of numbers, you will see that Apple's total cash on hand at the end of its fiscal year in September 2019 was $66.3 billion. (Although not shown, this second column of numbers covers the period of October 2018 to September 2019. In addition, all numbers in this figure are in the thousands.)

Current Ratio

Another important figure to calculate from a company's balance sheet is its current ratio (its total current assets divided by its current liabilities). Please see Figure 9.10 below for an example of how to calculate this number on Apple's balance sheet. Using the second column of numbers in this figure, the current ratio for the fiscal year ending in September 2019 was 1.12. This ratio does differ industry by industry but a general rule is to look for a ratio of at least 1.5. Although there are some caveats, any company with a current ratio of less than 1.5 is considered to be financially distressed.

Current Ratio = Total Current Assets / Current Liabilities

Capital Structure

Another figure to take away from a company's balance sheet is the company's capital structure. This means how much of a company is in debt or leveraged versus how much is financed by equity. As an example, if you made a $200,000 down payment on a house you purchased for $400,000, and received a bank mortgage of $200,000 for the remainder, your capital structure is 50–50. You can easily compute a company's capital structure by dividing its long term debt by the total of its stockholders' (shareholders') equity and its long term debt. Any company that is more than 65% in debt is considered to be highly leveraged and is not a good candidate for investment. Using the second column of numbers in Figure 9.10 below, in the fiscal year ending September 30, 2019, Apple's capital structure was 46.7% debt, and thus 53.3% equity.

Capital Structure = Long Term Debt / (Stockholders' Equity + Long Term Debt)

˅ Cash				
Cash And Cash Equivalents	48,844,000	25,913,000	20,289,000	20,484,000
Other Short Term Investme...	51,713,000	40,388,000	53,892,000	46,671,000
Total Cash	100,557,000	66,301,000	74,181,000	67,155,000
Net Receivables	22,926,000	23,186,000	17,874,000	15,754,000
Inventory	4,106,000	3,956,000	4,855,000	2,132,000
Other Current Assets	12,352,000	12,087,000	13,936,000	8,283,000
Total Current Assets	162,819,000	131,339,000	128,645,000	106,869,000
› Non-current assets	175,697,000	234,386,000	246,674,000	214,817,000
Total Assets	338,516,000	365,725,000	375,319,000	321,686,000
˅ Liabilities and stockholders' eq...				
˅ Liabilities				
› Current Liabilities	105,718,000	116,866,000	100,814,000	79,006,000
˅ Non-current liabilities				
Long Term Debt	91,807,000	93,735,000	97,207,000	75,427,000
Deferred taxes liabilities	-	426,000	31,504,000	26,019,000
Deferred revenues	-	2,797,000	2,836,000	2,930,000
Other long-term liabilities	20,958,000	11,165,000	8,911,000	10,055,000
Total non-current liabilities	142,310,000	141,712,000	140,458,000	114,431,000
Total Liabilities	248,028,000	258,578,000	241,272,000	193,437,000
› Stockholders' Equity	90,488,000	107,147,000	134,047,000	128,249,000
Total liabilities and stockholde...	338,516,000	365,725,000	375,319,000	321,686,000

Figure 9.10: Apple Inc. (ticker: AAPL) balance sheet. You can use a company's balance sheet to locate its cash balance and calculate its current ratio and capital structure. All numbers are in the thousands.

Looking again at Figure 9.10 above, the balance sheet of Apple Inc. (ticker: AAPL), you will recall that the second column of numbers are for the period of October 1, 2018 to September 30, 2019. You can see that Apple's impressive cash balance (the total cash figure) on September 30, 2019 was $66.3 billion (all numbers in this figure are in the thousands). Their current ratio for the end of their fiscal year 2018/2019 was 1.12 and that is of course below the 1.5 threshold I previously referenced. You can however give Apple a pass because of their outstanding ability to turn inventory into cash and pay their suppliers. Lastly, their capital structure was 46.7% debt and 53.3% equity. Although the company was highly leveraged on September 30, 2019, its ability to generate cash flow makes it possible for it to pay down its debt.

Cash Flow Statement

A cash flow statement is one of a company's most important financial documents. It tells you both how the company is generating cash and what is it doing with the cash it generates. Analyzing a cash flow statement can be extremely difficult and is beyond the scope of this book, however, there are two key numbers I suggest you do look at when reviewing a company: cash flow from operations and share repurchase.

Cash Flow from Operations

The first number to look for is the trend of a company's cash flow generation from their operations. This demonstrates the company's ability to generate consistent cash flow. In Figure 9.11 below, a partial cash flow statement for Tesla Inc. (ticker: TSLA), I show where to look for the cash flow from operations. Tesla was one of the companies that many on Wall Street were betting on going into bankruptcy due to its inability to generate cash from its operations.

Cash Flow All numbers in thousands

Breakdown	TTM	2019-12-31	2018-12-31	2017-12-31	2016-12-31
˅ Cash flows from operating activ...					
Net Income	-862,000	-862,000	-976,091	-1,961,400	-674,914
Depreciation & amortization	2,154,000	2,154,000	1,901,050	1,636,003	947,099
Stock based compensation	898,000	898,000	749,024	466,760	334,225
Change in working capital	-349,000	-349,000	57,951	-496,603	-693,861
Accounts receivable	-367,000	-367,000	-496,732	-24,635	-216,565
Inventory	-429,000	-429,000	-1,023,264	-178,850	-2,465,703
Other working capital	968,000	968,000	-221,714	-4,142,008	-1,564,300
Other non-cash items	186,000	186,000	207,237	284,020	-9,216
Net cash provided by operatin...	2,405,000	2,405,000	2,097,802	-60,654	-123,829
˅ Cash flows from investing activi...					
Investments in property, plant a...	-1,437,000	-1,437,000	-2,319,516	-4,081,354	-1,440,471
Acquisitions, net	-45,000	-45,000	-17,912	-114,523	-
Purchases of investments	-	-	-	-	0
Sales/Maturities of investments	-	-	0	0	16,667

Figure 9.11: Tesla Inc. (ticker: TSLA) partial cash flow statement. Cash flow from operations is a good indicator to confirm whether a company is able to generate cash from its operations.

Share Repurchase

Secondly, a cash flow statement will tell you whether or not a company has been repurchasing its shares. As I mentioned in the second chapter, one of the key ways a company can generate value for its shareholders is through share buybacks.

Cash Flow All numbers in thousands

Breakdown	TTM	2019-12-31	2018-12-31	2017-12-31
› Cash flows from operating activ...	8,122,100	8,122,100	6,966,700	5,551,200
⌄ Cash flows from investing activi...				
Investments in property, plant a...	-2,393,700	-2,393,700	-2,741,700	-1,853,700
Acquisitions, net	-540,900	-540,900	-101,700	-77,000
Other investing activites	-628,500	-628,500	-302,900	-245,900
Net cash used for investing act...	-3,071,100	-3,071,100	-2,455,100	562,000
⌄ Cash flows from financing activ...				
Debt repayment	-2,061,900	-2,061,900	-1,759,600	-1,649,400
Common stock repurchased	-4,976,200	-4,976,200	-5,207,700	-4,685,700
Dividends Paid	-3,581,900	-3,581,900	-3,255,900	-3,089,200
Other financing activites	-23,500	-23,500	-20,000	-20,500
Net cash used privided by (use...	-4,994,800	-4,994,800	-5,949,600	-5,310,800

Figure 9.12: McDonald's Corporation (ticker: MCD) cash flow statement. You will see that McDonald's consistently buys back shares and pays dividends.

In the above Figure 9.12, the cash flow statement of McDonald's Corporation (ticker: MCD), you can see that McDonald's management pays a consistent dividend and does yearly share buybacks, which both lead into massive shareholder value creation! Needless to say, McDonald's is another one of my favorite stocks. Although I rarely eat there, *"i'm lovin' it"*.

Beta

There are multiple definitions for beta and many involve statistics and regression analysis, but a simple explanation of beta is that it is a way to gauge the riskiness of a stock in comparison to the overall market. If a stock is considered to be equally as risky as the overall market, the stock will have the beta of 1. As an example,

Amazon.com Inc. (ticker: AMZN) has a beta of 1 (at the time of writing), which means if the market as a whole goes down by 10%, Amazon's stock will likely go down by 10% as well. In comparison, Shopify Inc. (ticker: SHOP) has a beta of 1.40 (at the time of writing), which means that for every 1% movement in the market (up or down), Shopify's stock will likely move 1.4%. This is of course a simplified definition of beta as gaining a full understanding of the term would require a working knowledge of statistics. In general, growth stocks have a beta of 1.3 and above. You definitely do want to check a company's beta before investing in it.

Looking at beta is extremely important if you have a shorter term time horizon or if you are nearing retirement. Let me break this concept down with an example. WPX Energy Inc. (ticker: WPX) is a company in the Energy Sector with a beta of 2.9 (at the time of writing). During the 2020 market crash, the stock dropped dramatically in value (on February 18, 2020 it was at $11.71 and on March 18, 2020 it was at $2.11) and probably will not recover all that it lost for at least the next several years. This is important to understand. Imagine if you had 40% of your portfolio invested in this stock and you were retiring in the next 12 months! This would be a horrible and terrible event. It would seriously impact you and your loved ones. Sadly though, I see examples such as this almost every day. People need to be very, very careful in their stock selection. Figure 9.13 below is a graph comparing the value of WPX stock in comparison to the S&P 500 index.

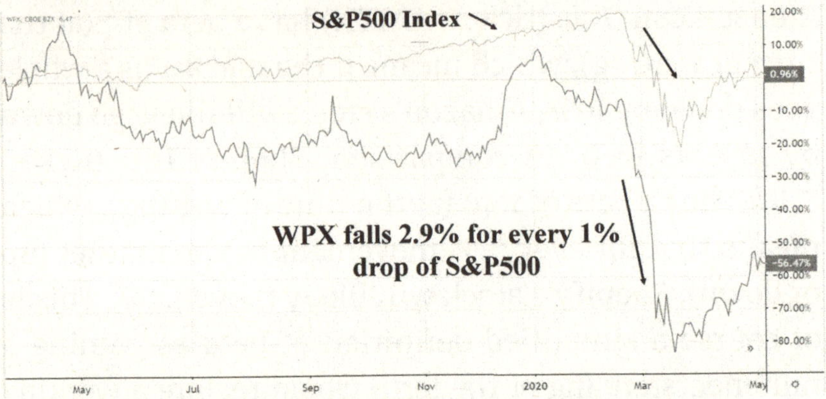

Figure 9.13: Value of WPX Energy Inc. (ticker: WPX) stock versus the S&P 500 index. WPX's larger beta is the result of it selling off much faster than the S&P 500 index.

52-Week High/Low

This indicator is quite self-explanatory. The 52-week high/low is the highest price and the lowest price of a stock in the past 52 weeks. Currently, as I am writing this book, almost 60% of S&P 500 stocks are near 52-week lows. As a rule of thumb, you want to be cautious of stocks that are trading near their 52-week high or low.

GROWTH STOCKS VS. VALUE STOCKS

By now you should well understand the differences between value and growth stocks, but you may still be wondering which one is best for investing in.

While I will share with you my opinion later in this chapter, the truth is that researchers have not been able to answer this question with certainty.

Research analyst John Dowdee published a report on Seeking Alpha (a great website, by the way, for investing ideas) where he broke stocks down into six categories that reflected both the risk and returns for growth and value stocks in the small, mid (referenced by others as "medium") and large cap sectors, respectively.

The study lasted for 13 years (from 2000 to 2013) and, on a risk adjusted basis, there was no clear answer as to which category provided the superior return.

Craig Israelsen published a different study in *Financial Planning* magazine in 2015 that showed the performance of growth and value stocks in small, mid and large cap sectors over a 25-year period from the beginning of 1990 to the end of 2014. Similar to previously conducted research, no definitive answer was found!

For an additional demonstration, Figure 9.14 below is a comparison of the performance of the iShares Russell 1000 Growth Index ETF (ticker: IWF) vs. the iShares Russell 1000 Value Index ETF (ticker: IWD) for the period of spring 2017 to spring 2020. You will see that the growth stocks being tracked by IWF have outperformed the value stocks being tracked by IWD.

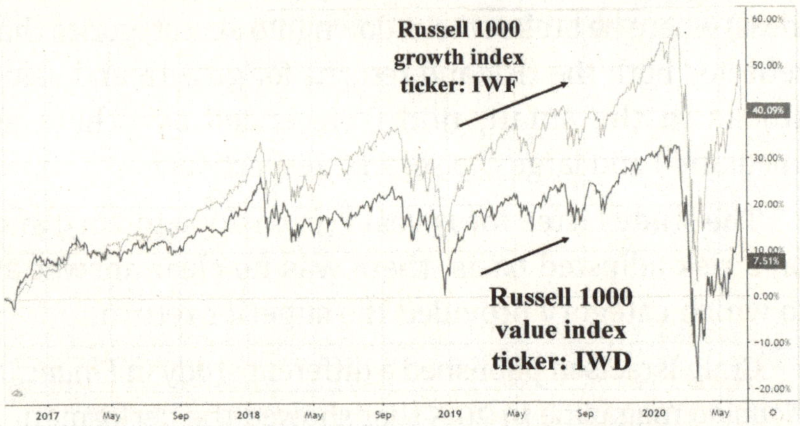

Figure 9.14: Performance of the iShares Russell 1000 Growth Index ETF (ticker: IWF) vs. the iShares Russell 1000 Value Index ETF (ticker: IWD) for the period of spring 2017 to spring 2020. The growth stocks being tracked by IWF have been able to outperform the value stocks being tracked by IWD.

While research might not be clear on providing certainty regarding which stocks provide a better return, it is important to have both types in your portfolio. I will teach you in what follows the important indicators used to identify quality stocks in each bucket. I will also share a personal anecdote on how I was able to make one of my client's money by finding him a few growth and value stocks in the Health Care Sector. Remember, it is far more important to pick the right stocks notwithstanding the bucket they fall into, rather than to blindly put your money exclusively in either the growth or value buckets.

Below, are the 5 key indicators that I look for in identifying **growth stocks**:

1. Last closing share price ≥ \$5: I consider stocks below \$5/share to be penny stocks.

2. Average daily volume (last 50 days) ≥ 100,000 shares: Unless you're trading \$5 million or more, an average daily volume of 100,000 shares with stocks priced \$5/share or greater should allow you to get in and out without too much trouble. (Average daily volume refers to the average number of shares traded each day in a particular stock.) I don't trade stocks with an average daily volume of less than 100,000 shares. You need sufficient liquidity to be able to get in and out of the stock without difficulty.

3. Earnings per share (EPS) growth (most recent quarter versus year-ago quarter) ≥ 25 percent.

4. Annualized five-year historical EPS growth rate ≥ 10 percent: William O'Neil, founder of *Investor's Business Daily*, recommends this number as well.

5. Price-to-earnings ratio (P/E ratio) must be > 20.

By using this simple 5-step guide, you can easily identify growth stocks worthy of inclusion in your portfolio. The Reuters Stock Screener is extremely handy in identifying stocks that can pass this test.

Below, are the 5 key indicators that I use to quickly identify **value stocks**:

1. Last closing share price ≥ \$5

2. Average daily volume (last 50 days) ≥ 100,000 shares

3. Price-to-sales ratio (P/S ratio) ≤ 1.25
4. Dividend yield > 1.5%
5. P/E ratio must be < 20

The first two fields restrict you to an investment universe that trades often and above $5 per share. The next ranking restricts you to so-called cheap stocks, as measured by their P/S ratio. This ratio is calculated by dividing a company's market capitalization by its total sales in a given year. Like the P/E ratio, the P/S ratio is also widely reported. (As I set out in Chapter 3, a company's market cap is calculated by multiplying the number of shares outstanding in the company with the price of its shares.)

Value stocks often pay dividends, so I like to see some dividend payout. But beware of companies that pay dividends of 10 percent or more. These companies are often distressed and are about to cut their dividend payments.

VALUATION OF STOCKS FOR INVESTING: INTRINSIC AND RELATIVE

If you have tuned into CNBC and listened for even just a few minutes during earnings season, you will have heard the terms "missing" or "beating" the analysts' expectations. Did you wonder: What do they mean by this? It's a fair question. As is: How do Wall Street analysts predict share prices and earnings? To be honest, it is quite complicated and, sometimes, they can be extremely wrong.

In early 2000, Pets.com (former ticker: IPET) was valued at about $300 million. Later that year, it was valued at zero, as the company went out of business. In the private equity world, WeWork was valued at $42 billion by late 2018 but, by the end of 2019, it was valued at (only) around $8 billion. In 1996, Apple Inc. (ticker: AAPL) was valued at less than $3 billion. Then the company brought back Steve Jobs, who introduced the iPod and the iPhone. The price of Apple's stock moved considerably higher and now its market cap is around one trillion dollars. Understanding how Wall Street deems some stocks buy worthy and some an immediate sell could help you with your own stock selection.

Overall, there are two primary methods that an analyst at Goldman Sachs or at any other major investment bank will use to value a stock. They will calculate its intrinsic value and its relative value. The intrinsic method uses a discounted cash flow model, while the relative method compares the value of the particular stock or asset against similar ones (also known as comparable or comp for short). I will not delve into extensive details on these two methods in this chapter, but I will provide you with enough knowledge in order to level the playing field so that you can value stocks and find the underpriced ones. After all, the objective of any investor is simple: buy low and sell high.

INTRINSIC VALUATION

Discounted cash flow models, or DCF, is the most common way analysts on Wall Street value stocks. In this method, analysts forecast a company's revenues and costs for the next 5 to 10 years in the future, and then discount the cash flow (think of it as the net income) with the appropriate discount rate to today's date. Now, there are many complexities in modeling these revenues and costs, and finding the right discount rate which is representative of a company's risk profile is why investment bankers get paid the way they do. However, understanding the basics of their strategy will help you make smarter decisions in your own portfolio. Based on their findings, bankers will come to a rating for a stock: either BUY, SELL or HOLD.

Let's take Apple Inc. (ticker: AAPL) as an example. Let's assume Apple is trading at $242/share still. The Goldman Sachs investment bank team will put a price target of $650/share on Apple shares and issue a BUY recommendation to their investors. What this means is that analysts at Goldman Sachs have forecasted Apple's revenue and costs and, when discounted back, realized this stock should be worth $650/share rather than the current $242. This puts an implied upside of about 169% ($650/$242 - 1).

It is important to know that you can find these types of analysts' reports online. While most full-service brokers offer these equity reports as part of their offerings, many can be found online on websites such as

Seeking Alpha. Another very good source of information is CNBC, where they update you with what Wall Street analysts are thinking about different stocks. These stock pick recommendations change on a quarterly basis and, as you will notice, they are based on many assumptions about the future of the company. In many cases, the analysts end up being wrong. Nevertheless, knowing how they value shares and what they think about each company's stock is a very valuable tool.

Boeing Co. (ticker: BA) was trading in the high $300 per share in late 2018. Almost 80% of Wall Street analysts had a BUY recommendation on the stock with high price targets. As I am writing this book in the early spring of 2020, Boeing stock is flirting at around $100 per share. Figure 9.15 below displays the drop in price of Boeing stock for part of 2020. Almost all of the analysts were wrong about the company and there is a significant chance that Boeing will be bailed out by the government. The moral of this short story is that in some cases, even people who are investing as their professional career, make wrong bets and end up far off the mark.

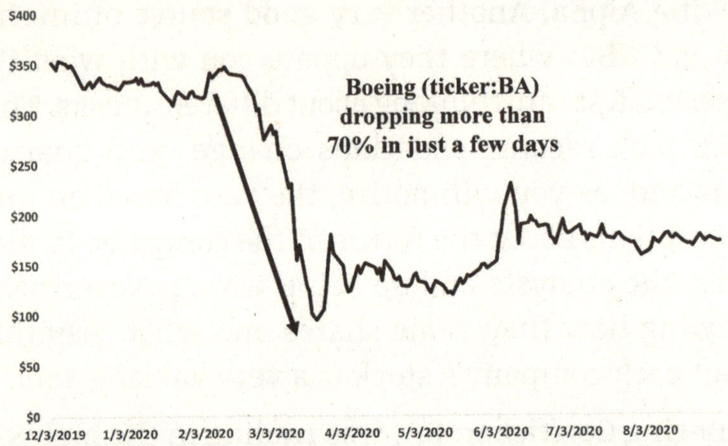

Figure 9.15: The stock of Boeing Co. (ticker: BA) selling off due to negative news.

RELATIVE VALUATION

One of the most widely used methods that analysts on Wall Street value companies by is comparing them with similar businesses. Not surprisingly, it's called the relative (or comparable) method. If you are a fan of ABC's hit show, *Shark Tank*, you have probably heard Kevin O'Leary say something like, "Your valuation is crazy," or "Companies like yours go for 5 to 6 times their earnings." Kevin O'Leary, along with many others, use multiples to value companies in order to discern whether or not they are overvalued or underpriced. There are literally tons of multiples out there that you can use to value stocks in order to learn whether or not they are good buys, but for the sake of simplicity I will only cover a very key one in this chapter. Before getting too technical however, I want to break down what multiples mean and how we use them.

The first step to value a company using multiples is to find the right comparable. There are 11 sectors in the stock market and within each sector there are companies that are very similar to one another in terms of business and potential customers. In the world of finance, we call these companies comparable (or comps).

Figure 9.16 below shows the 11 sectors of the stock market and a few examples of companies in each sector. These sectors are based on the Global Industry Classification Standard, which I will discuss further in the next chapter. While this "Standard" is meant to "standardize" how companies are classified in the financial markets, some organizations do differ from the "Standard"! For example, the sectors referenced as "Consumer Defensive" and "Consumer Cyclical" below are also called, respectively, "Consumer Staples" and "Consumer Discretionary".

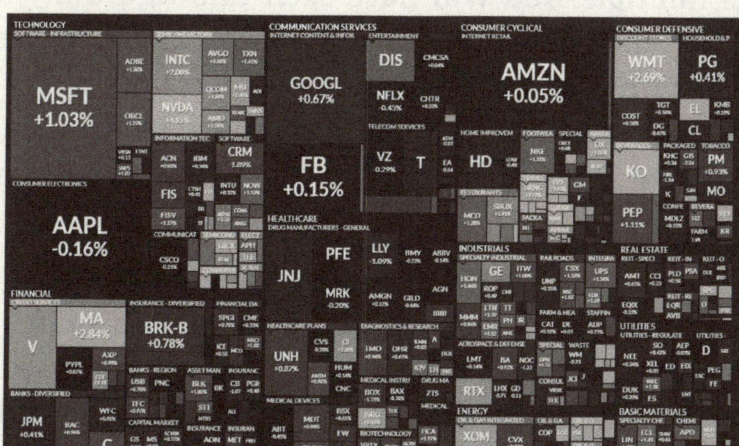

Figure 9.16: The 11 sectors of the stock market and a few examples of companies in each sector.

As an example, any company that is dependent on consumer spending power would fall into the "Consumer Cyclical" (also known as the "Consumer Discretionary") Sector. Nike Inc. (ticker: NKE), Lululemon Athletica Inc. (ticker: LULU), and Under Armour Inc. (tickers: UA and UAA) all fall into this sector and are considered a good set of comparables.

Now let's look at the most common multiple which is used widely on Wall Street to value companies.

P/E RATIO: HOLY GRAIL OF VALUATION

A very important multiple is the price over earnings multiple, which is also known as either the price-to-earnings ratio (P/E ratio), the price multiple, or the earnings multiple. You will have seen this figure in your iPhone Stocks app, on Yahoo Finance, and elsewhere, and it is by far one of the most important ratios in finance. The P/E ratio values a company by measuring its current share price relative to its earnings per share (EPS).

The P/E ratio is used by investors and analysts to determine the relative value of a company's shares in an apples-to-apples comparison. It can also be used to compare a company against its own historical record or to compare aggregate markets against one another or over time.

The P/E ratio is one of the most widely used stock analysis tools that investors and analysts rely on for determining stock valuation. In addition to showing whether a company's stock price is overvalued or under-valued, the P/E ratio can reveal how a stock's valuation compares to its industry group or to a benchmark like the S&P 500 index. Over the past 100 years, the average P/E ratio of the S&P 500 has been around 15. In the last few years however, as the market has been growing due to more relaxed monetary policies, the average P/E ratio is closer to 21. As a rule of thumb, sectors with a P/E ratio of under 20 are considered value and sectors with a P/E ratio higher than 20 are considered growth. Figure 9.17 below is a chart tracking the historic average P/E ratio of the S&P 500 index.

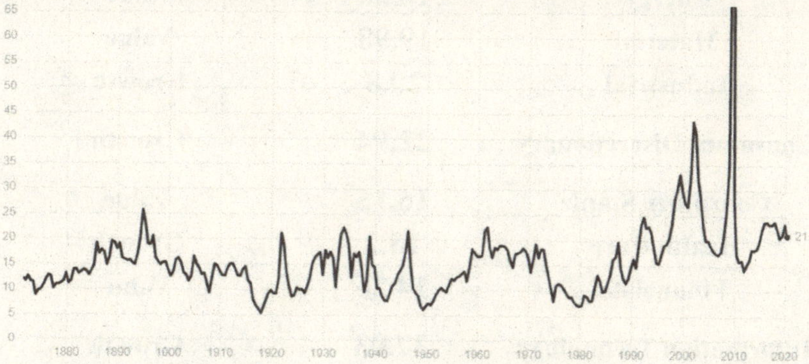

Figure 9.17: Average P/E ratio of the S&P 500 index dating back to the latter 1800s.

In essence, the P/E ratio indicates the dollar amount an investor can expect to invest in a company in order to receive one dollar of that company's earnings. If, for instance, a company was currently trading at a P/E ratio multiple of 20, it would mean that an investor is willing to pay $20 for $1 of current earnings.

Each sector has its own average P/E ratio which is the standard for that industry. Figure 9.18 below provides a summary of these. You can compare the P/E ratio of the stock you are considering against its sector average P/E ratio in order to see if you may be about to purchase an undervalued stock or if you may be about to overpay for the company. Nevertheless, remember, there will be cases when a company will have a higher P/E ratio than its peers, but it will still be a good buy because it is growing far faster than its peers. In those situations, you may very well be willing to overpay for it.

Sector	Average P/E	Type
Energy	16.20	Value
Material	19.98	Value
Industrial	20.8	Growth
Consumer Discretionary	22.94	Growth
Consumer Staple	16.15	Value
Health Care	18.2	Growth
Financials	14.26	Value
Information Technology	37.93	Growth
Communication Services	16.89	Value
Utilities	28.23	Value
Real Estate	19.07	Value

Figure 9.18: Sectors and their average P/E ratios. You can use this table as a guide to find good buys in each sector.

In addition to the P/E multiple, there are many other multiples that are used to value companies. Two common ones are EV (enterprise value)/EBIT (earnings before interest and taxes) and EV/EBITDA (earnings before interest, taxes, depreciation and amortization). I purposefully did not discuss these other multiples as they are beyond the scope of this book. However, there are plenty of online resources that discuss them in detail. These two particular multiples could be used for companies that are not yet profitable, and hence do not have a P/E ratio.

HOW TO ACTUALLY PICK STOCK

Over the last several pages, I have shown you how to read financial statements and what to look for when selecting good stocks to invest in. Despite all of this, you might still feel like there is a lack of strategies or an overall blueprint to follow in order to select the best possible stocks. I have summarized below the majority of the material we reviewed together in this chapter. This Figure 9.19 is an easy-to-read table which you can refer to when making investment decisions. While there is "no one size fits all" for investing, this table can make your decision making much more streamlined. Do not look at this table as the bible for investing though, but more as a step-by-step guide to de-risk your selections and pick the right stock from the many options out there.

I have divided stocks into the main buckets of growth or value. This is the same method I have used throughout the book. I then review, one by one, each indicator and a rule of thumb you could use to ensure the decision you are making is sound and that you are being financially responsible.

Indicator	Value	Growth
Dividend yield	Must be bigger than 1.5%	Must be between 0-2%, if they are redistributing cash, it might be at the price of their growth
Gross margin	Must be bigger than 45%	Must be bigger than 45%
Net margin	Must be bigger than 10%	They could be unprofitable, as long as they have a strong cash balance
Revenue growth	Between 2% to 6%	Must be at least 6% year over year
Interest coverage ratio	At least twice	At least twice
Current ratio	1.5 or more	1.5 or more
Capital structure	No more than 65% debt	No more than 65% debt
Share buybacks	At least twice in the last 5 years	No buybacks
Beta	Reasonable range between 1-1.3	Normal to have growth stocks with high beta. However, avoid higher than 1.8.

Figure 9.19: Key indicators discussed thus far in this chapter. Use this table as your guide for picking the best stocks for investment.

The first row in the above table refers to a company's dividend yield. If you are selecting a value stock, make certain that the company is paying out in dividends more than 1.5% of their share price. My logic for this recommendation is that if the company is making billions in profits, they can afford to have their dividends match the rate being offered by your local bank for money being invested in their savings accounts. At the end of the day, as a shareholder, you are bearing risk and must be compensated for it. In addition, be cautious of companies which pay a dividend yield that is higher than 10%. These companies are often financially distressed and will very likely either soon be cutting out the offering of dividends altogether or significantly reducing them.

On the other hand, if you are investing in growth stocks, you want to avoid companies that have a dividend yield higher than 2%. These companies are growing fast and should reinvest every penny back to their business in order to fuel revenue growth. If a growth company is paying more than 2% in a dividend yield, they are doing you, a shareholder, a disservice.

The next row in this table refers to a company's gross margin. Regardless of the bucket (growth or value), the company you are investing in must have a gross margin of more than 45%. This number might differ some from sector to sector, but a rule of thumb is that in order for a firm to have enough money to fund its operations, it must have a minimum of 45% in gross margin.

Value companies must have a net margin of more than than 10%. This is often called the bottom line rule in finance as you want a company to keep more than 6% of its sales as retained earnings. On the other hand, growth stocks can afford to be unprofitable and lose money on a yearly basis. As an example, I am a shareholder in Shopify Inc. (ticker: SHOP) despite them losing money in the last 5 years. I monitor my position by looking at their cash balance and revenue growth. In my example, Shopify has a more than $2 billion cash balance which can fund its operations for the next three years with minimal sales. I also ensured that the company is growing at a sufficiently fast pace to make up for its lack of profitability.

The next row in this table refers to a company's revenue growth. Value companies must grow each year by at least the same rate that the U.S. GDP does (which is somewhere from 2% to 6%). Growth stocks on the other hand must grow at a year-over-year rate of at least 6%. You should avoid companies with declining sales.

For the interest coverage ratio row in the above Figure 9.19, regardless of whether it is a growth or value stock, you want any company in your portfolio to be able to cover the interest owing on its debt at least twice from the cash it earns through its operations.

For the current ratio row in the above table, regardless of whether the company falls in the growth or value bucket, a company's current assets divided by its current liabilities should result in a quotient that is not less than 1.5.

The next row in Figure 9.19 is regarding a company's capital structure. Value stocks can afford having more debt on their balance sheet but please be cautious of companies that are in a growth stage and yet have debt equivalent to more than 65% of their capital structure.

With reference to the penultimate row in the above table, share buyback really is a must for a value stock. My rule of thumb for the inclusion of a value company in any of my own clients' portfolios is to have had at least two buybacks in the previous five years. Share buybacks signal to the investor that management believes that their shares are underpriced.

And lastly, in the final row of Figure 9.19, is the reference to beta. I cannot emphasize enough that you must avoid companies with beta higher than 1.8.

I want to end this chapter in a similar fashion to how I ended chapter 7. None of the strategies and criteria I introduced here are set in stone. You could find a stock with a much higher P/E than its peers, and despite overpaying for it, watch it outperform all of those peers. You could invest in a company with declining profit due to research and development expenses and have it outperform the whole market in a few years due to an innovative product launch.

Similar to trading, many successful investors develop an investing methodology for themselves and follow that. As an example, Bill Ackman, the legendary fund manager at Pershing Square Capital Management, only invests in companies with sustainable cash flows. Warren

Buffett, on the other hand, only invests in companies with a business model he understands. You will not find a single successful fund manager without a clear investment philosophy.

Work on developing your investing philosophy rather than memorizing a table. The reason behind every parameter I introduced in this chapter was in order to give you the necessary tools to make informed decisions. In the end, it is your responsibility to use this toolkit and invest your money wisely.

CHAPTER 10

HOW TO CONSTRUCT A WELL-DIVERSIFIED INVESTMENT PORTFOLIO

"Diversification is not putting all your eggs in one basket."

In the last chapter, we learned about techniques many analysts use to identify stocks to invest in. We reviewed what to look for in a company's income statement, balance sheet and cash flow statement, as well as how to calculate certain key ratios. The last chapter should help you pick the right stocks. But, it is important to note, selecting the right stocks is not all that there is to investing. In times of market downturns and recessions, such as the one we are in right now as I am writing this book in the spring of 2020, every single stock goes down regardless of its sector or how undervalued it was when you bought it. So, what can you do? How can you protect yourself against a recession? Well, the aim of this chapter is to teach you just that. The message behind this chapter is simple: do not put all your eggs into one basket.

"Diversification". You probably have heard of it many times. It is the buzz word amongst people who invest. But the truth is, except for professional hedge fund managers, a good number of people go about doing this in the wrong way. Buying Apple Inc. (ticker: AAPL) stocks and Microsoft Corporation (ticker: MSFT) stocks does not mean that you are diversifying. There are certain rules to this that money managers use to ensure their investments are protected against potential downturns.

This chapter in my opinion is one of the most important ones in the investing section of my book. I will go over concepts that have been proven over time to be the most effective in protecting your money.

UNDERSTANDING CORRELATION: KEY TO DIVERSIFICATION

The first step in building the right portfolio is to understand the meaning of correlation. While you do not need to be a statistician in order to become a world-class investor, a basic knowledge of statistics is necessary in order to build the right portfolio.

Correlation, in the finance and investment industries, is a statistic that measures the degree to which two securities move in relation to each other. Correlations are used in advanced portfolio management, computed as the correlation coefficient, which has a value that must fall between -1.0 and +1.0.

Let's break this concept down with an example. Higher weather temperatures tend to correlate with higher ice cream sales. This is an example of a positive correlation. As the temperature goes up, so will the sale of ice cream. If there was a betting game to predict when ice cream sales will be at their highest, we would all be millionaires. Although correlations in finance are a bit harder to guess, we will discuss some of the key ones in what follows.

An example of a negative correlation is that when a student skips more classes, their grades will decrease. One factor goes down as the other factor goes up. Another example is that as the weather gets colder, more electric heaters will be purchased. As more employees are laid off, the level of satisfaction among the remaining employees will decrease. The examples are endless.

A perfect positive correlation means that the correlation coefficient is exactly 1. This implies that as one security moves, either up or down, the other security moves in lockstep, in the same direction. A perfect negative correlation means that two assets are moving in opposite directions but at the exact same pace or rate. A zero correlation implies no relationship at all.

Why are we discussing correlation? You may have very likely guessed it by now! In optimal situations, you want some of the asset classes in your investment portfolio to correlate negatively with one another so that you can always be protecting your downside. (In case you don't recall, as I explained in Chapter 1, stocks, currency, real estate, fixed income investments, cash, infrastructure and commodities are some of the different "asset classes".)

During the 2008 crisis, a well-balanced portfolio would have lost 20% of its value as opposed to a portfolio only invested in the S&P 500. A portfolio with only stocks from the S&P 500 basket would have lost 56% of its value. Hopefully you now understand the importance of correlation much more! Imagine you were about to retire and you had $100,000 invested in the market. Not practicing correlation would have cost you half of your retirement savings.

Now that we have hammered down the correlation concept, let's look at some good portfolio making strategies.

WHAT DOES HEDGING REALLY MEAN?

You probably have heard the phrase "hedging" many times. Hedge fund managers may seem like mysterious people who know how to make money and time their forays in and out of the markets with exceptional precision and skill. The truth is, the concept of hedging is not very complicated.

A hedge is an investment that protects your finances from a risky situation. Hedging is done to minimize or offset the chance that your assets will lose value. It also limits your loss to a known amount if the asset does lose value. It's similar to home insurance. You pay a fixed amount each month. If a fire wipes out all of the value of your home, your only loss is the already known deductible.

Another example is when an airline company like United Airlines Holdings Inc. (ticker: UAL) wants to protect itself against the rising price of fuel. They usually enter into a futures contract in what is called a "hedging strategy" in order to minimize their losses if the price of fuel goes up.

The truth is that there are many hedging strategies, and some of them involve using complicated financial instruments such as derivatives, but practicing what I will refer to as a "true diversification" could protect your portfolio immensely during a time of crisis.

A simple way to practice diversification is to have multiple asset classes in your portfolio in such a fashion that when one asset class falls, another rises, and thus limits the potential losses.

11 SECTORS: THE GOOD, THE BAD, AND THE UGLY

In order to start picking stocks or other asset classes, you first need to understand the 11 sectors of the market and their relationship to one another.

Sectors are typically considered to be a broad classification. Within each sector, numerous subsectors and industries can also be further delineated. As mentioned in the previous chapter, the Global Industry Classification Standard, also known as GICS, is the primary financial industry standard for defining sector classifications.

GICS was developed by index providers MSCI and Standard and Poor's (now known as S&P Global Ratings). Its hierarchy begins with 11 sectors which can be further delineated to 24 industry groups, 68 industries, and 157 sub-industries.

The 11 broad GICS sectors commonly used for sector breakdown reporting are as follows (with examples given for each):

1. Energy: Drilling companies, energy conglomerates
2. Materials: Specialty chemical companies, paper products manufacturers, steel manufacturers
3. Industrials: Trucking industry, commercial printing companies
4. Consumer Discretionary: Hotels, clothing manufacturers
5. Consumer Staples: Grocery stores, food producers, beverage manufacturers
6. Health Care: Pharmaceuticals, biotech
7. Financials: Banks, investment banks, insurance companies
8. Information Technology: Software developers, semiconductor manufacturers

9. Communication Services: Cellular service providers, fiber optics manufacturers
10. Utilities: Electric and gas utility companies
11. Real Estate: Real Estate Investment Trusts (REITs) except for Mortgage REITs

It is important to understand the relationship between each sector before setting up your portfolio.

As an example, the stock of companies found in the Utilities Sector are usually considered to be "recession-proof". Why? Quite simply, no matter the state of the economy, you need to pay your hydro and water bills. During the times when the market crashes, these stocks usually hold their value or drop far less than other stocks. You do want to have certain Real Estate Sector and Utilities Sector stocks in your portfolio to protect you during a recession. As an example, during the 2020 market crash, these two sectors dropped, but far less than the Financials Sector did. (8% drop as opposed to a 13% drop). Figure 10.1 below is a graphic presentation of how various sectors perform in comparison to how the economy cycles.

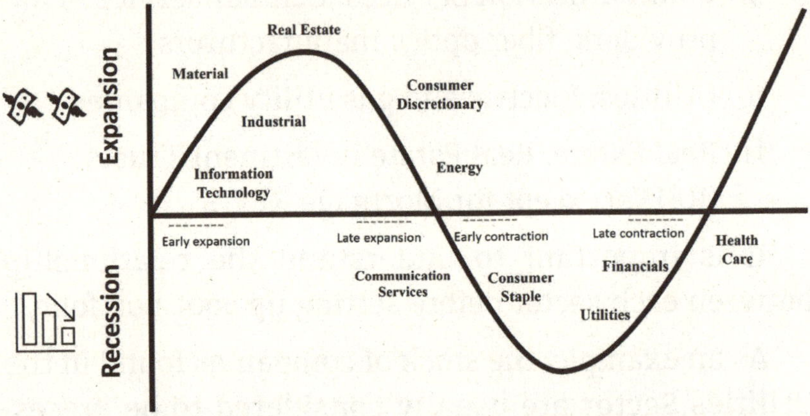

Figure 10.1: Each sector's performance in comparison to how the economy cycles. Sectors perform differently depending on the stages of the economic cycle.

I personally categorize these eleven sectors into two main buckets: growth and value. The growth bucket is characterized by companies with above average valuations and growth rates, while the value bucket is characterized by companies with below average valuations in comparison to the overall market. As a rule of thumb, growth stocks have P/E ratios of over 20, while value stocks have P/E ratios of under 20. Figure 10.2 below categorizes sectors based on whether they fall under the growth or value bucket.

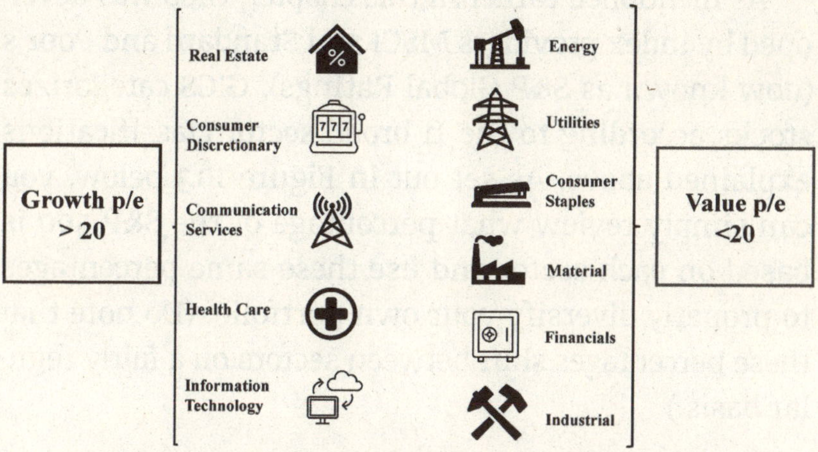

Figure 10.2: Sectors categorized based on growth or value. This should be used purely as a guide. There are cases where a stock may fall under the value bucket but is considered to be a growth stock (and vice versa).

Not everyone has a large sum of money available which they can use to purchase a few stocks from each sector, and that is why an ETF comes into play. For a fraction of the price of purchasing a few stocks from each sector, you can purchase an ETF that follows each sector.

Studies have demonstrated that you can eliminate the vast majority of individual stock risk with as few as 30 stocks if the selection is properly diversified. You can't capture the vast majority of the performance characteristics of an index as large as the S&P 500 by owning only 30 technology stocks; however, you can capture the vast majority of that index's performance if you choose 30 stocks that are representative of the index as a whole.

As mentioned earlier in this chapter, GICS was developed by index providers MSCI and Standard and Poor's (now known as S&P Global Ratings). GICS categorizes stocks according to the 11 broad sector classifications explained above. As set out in Figure 10.3 below, you can simply review what percentage of the S&P 500 is based on each sector and use these same percentages to properly diversify your own portfolio. (Do note that these percentages shift between sectors on a fairly regular basis.)

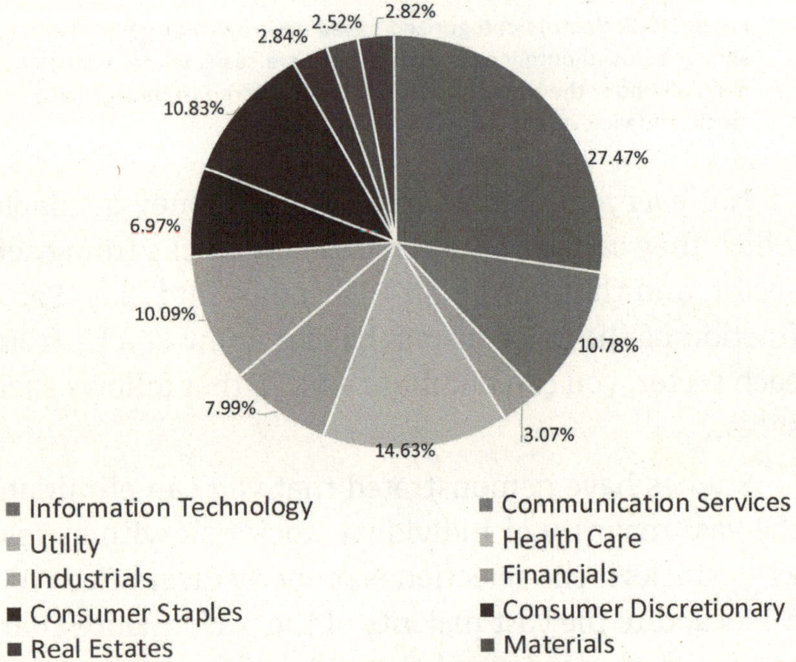

Figure 10.3: Breakdown of the S&P 500 based on sector (as of 2020)

For example, let's assume that you are planning to own 30 stocks. If the Financials Sector comprises 10% of the S&P index at the time that you are putting together your portfolio, you will want to own three stocks from this sector (approximately 10% of your 30 stocks). If the Utilities Sector represents 3% of the index, you will want to own one utilities stock (approximately 3% of your 30 stocks), and so on.

WHAT ARE SAFE HAVEN ASSET CLASSES?

So far we have established the differences between each of the 11 sectors in the market and how to diversify your portfolio using different stocks from different sectors. There is more involved though in diversifying than just simply picking stocks from different sectors.

In this section, I will introduce you to two other asset classes that are extremely helpful in creating your well-hedged portfolio: fixed income and commodities.

The meaning of the fixed income asset class is relatively self-explanatory. These are assets that will provide you with fixed payments throughout their life. For example, imagine you lend $100 for an agreed upon term of eight weeks to a very trustworthy friend named Alex. As part of offering him the cash, you request $1 every week, and the full $100 back in the 8th week. Alex agrees, and so you lend him $100 today, and eight weeks from now you will have received in total $108 back from him. This is an example of a fixed income asset where what is referred to as the balloon payment is $100 and the weekly payment of $1 is what is called the coupon payment. Since Alex is trustworthy, the chance of him not returning your money is very low. These type of fixed income products are called Treasury bonds (backed by government) or triple A rating bonds.

Fixed income investments are not always safe however. Let's imagine your other friend, Joe, is known for not returning borrowed money and you are having difficulty trusting him with your \$100. This time, instead of asking for a \$1 weekly payment, you request a \$10 weekly payment, in order to be compensated for the risk you are taking. (We won't consider any usury laws in this example!) This is an example of a subprime fixed income investment where you are receiving a higher return, but there is also a higher risk. Some corporate bonds are like Joe. They are perhaps issued by distressed companies flirting with bankruptcy. As part of lending money to them (buying their corporate bonds), you are risking your principal investment. These investments, called junk bonds, are investments with a lower than triple B rating.

In the 2008 crash, many of the mortgage-backed securities which were deemed to be investment worthy, were actually filled with risky junk bonds.

It is important however that your portfolio does have some high quality investment grade fixed income product in it. For starters, I recommend owning Treasury bonds or other fixed income assets that are backed by the government with a low to zero level of default. There are two main reasons why I recommend fixed income securities.

Firstly, government bonds usually have a negative correlation with the stock market. What this means is that during a time of crisis, when the market loses its value, the price of government bonds goes up. The logic behind this is that investors are always looking for the most returns for their money, so when the market crashes, large amounts of money move toward bonds, thus raising their prices. It's basically a supply and demand equation. This is why you want at least 20% of your portfolio to be in fixed income products.

The second reason is that fixed income instruments usually provide the investor with a fixed cash flow. You always want to have a consistent cash flow as part of your investment. This could be achieved partially through fixed income products and partially with dividend-paying stocks and ETFs. It is just like owning real estate that you do not personally use for yourself. In those cases, you want to be receiving monthly cash flow in the form of rent while the value of your property is increasing.

Now let's discuss the second category of the safe havens, commodities, and in particular gold.

You probably have heard in one form or another about the true value of gold and its importance in the market system. Gold is definitely a commodity that holds some value intrinsically, unlike Bitcoin or other cryptocurrencies. (I am not for or against crypto, I am simply pointing to the fact that, intrinsically, they have no value.) Up until the early 1970s, the U.S. dollar was in fact backed by gold.

Gold, similar to Treasury bonds, has a negative correlation with the S&P 500. Historically, when the markets have lost significant value for extended periods of time, gold prices have risen. The explanation for this is simple. (I hope by now you can easily guess why this is the case, without any need to read the next sentence!! If yes, then this book has done its job.) During economic crashes, investors will put their money in places that have intrinsic value, "just in case" (too many) companies end up going bankrupt. This creates an inflow of cash toward gold, which leads to a rise in the price of gold.

There is no rule of thumb when it comes to portfolio construction. It all depends on your risk tolerance, when you are retiring, and when you want to cash out. And this is why you purchased this book, because there is no one single portfolio that can provide everyone with exactly what they need.

The general rule however is that the more fixed income products and commodities that you have in your portfolio, the safer your portfolio is. If you are a risk averse investor, you should perhaps aim to have 50% Treasury bonds and gold, and then 50% stocks, in your portfolio. If you are young and are able to take on considerable risk, perhaps you should aim to have 80% of your funds in stocks and only 20% in Treasury bonds and gold.

Once the portfolio is created based on your risk profile, it is important to revisit your investments and rebalance your portfolio on a monthly or quarterly basis. A canny investor keeps an eye on the relative weights of assets, sectors, and asset classes in their portfolio. Say, for example, a portfolio was designed to be made up of 50% stocks and 50% bonds. Over time, one or two of the stocks soar in price, resulting in a 70% to 30% mix. That investor may very likely sell some of the high-performing stock, lock in some profit, and return the portfolio to a 50-50 balance.

AN EXAMPLE OF THE PORTFOLIO OF ONE OF MY CLIENTS

All of the techniques and strategies that I have taught you so far are used by professional asset managers around the world. These are well-known and well-practiced methods that have yielded results for many, many years. In order to show you that I am truly practicing what I am preaching to you, I have included, with permission, as Figure 10.4 below, a screenshot of the portfolio of one of my clients. I have been managing this particular portfolio since late 2019. Although the amount here is over one million dollars, the principle remains the same.

As you can see, I have broken down the assets into two main segments: capital preservation and capital appreciation. Capital preservation assets are fixed income assets and assets that are more resistant toward the market going down. I am holding Canadian fixed income products (investment grade corporate bonds and safe mortgage-backed securities). I have also allocated small amounts in non-Canadian corporate bonds which offer higher yields for my client. I am further holding over $300,000 in cash! Yes, cash is a position, especially during these uncertain times. You probably have heard of the saying, "*Cash is King*". Let me tell you, it especially resonates during times of economic uncertainty.

The second segment is capital appreciation assets. These are assets that have higher growth potential and therefore are riskier. I am investing over $170,000 of my client's money in Canadian equity. These are mostly blue-chip Canadian stocks trading on the Toronto Stock Exchange. Because I am Canadian and work with many Canadian clients, I spend time on a daily basis reviewing Canadian stocks, and have, dare I say, developed a solid working knowledge of the Canadian markets. South of our border, I am investing over $200,000 of my client's money in the U.S. equity market. U.S. stocks in most cases offer more aggressive returns and higher dividend yields than Canadian stocks do.

I am also investing around 8% of my client's money in non-North American equity markets. I have allocated certain parts of the portfolio to the Asia Pacific, European and Middle Eastern markets. You may not be aware that the Asia Pacific region has been growing at a much faster rate than the U.S. has in the past few years, and that has provided a great upside opportunity for investors. To put this in perspective, the U.S. GDP has recently been growing (pre-pandemic) at around 2% to 6% a year, while in the Asia Pacific region as a whole (China and Hong Kong, Philippines, Vietnam, etc.) it has been growing at around 6% annually.

This diversification has allowed me to protect my client's money through the 2020 COVID-19 downturn. My client's portfolio is down year to date only 3% (at the time of writing), as opposed to the S&P 500 being down over 13%. YES, with proper diversification, I have been able to save more than **$100,000** for my client.

While this entire portfolio construction process might look complicated to you, I know that by studying this part of the book, you can learn all of the skills necessary to create a portfolio as resilient as the one I did for my client.

All information on this screen is presented on a CAD, trade date basis

Asset Allocation

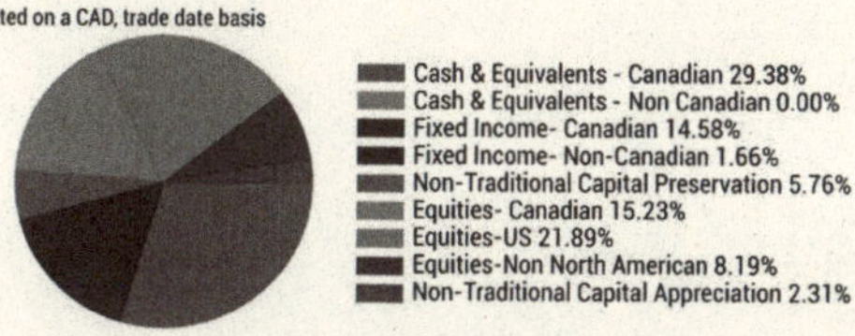

Asset Class	$ Market Value Including Accured Income	%Total Assets	$ Estimated Annual Income	$ Estimated Annual Income
Total Assets	1,098,432.46	100.00%	24,928.33	2.27%
Capital Preservation	564,349.00	51.38%	12,028.97	2.13%
Cash & Equivalents - Canadian	322,707.94	29.38%	4,646.99	1.44%
Cash & Equivalents - Non Canadian	33.11	0.00%	0.00	0.00%
Fixed Income - Canadian	160,143.18	14.58%	4,264.37	2.66%
Fixed Income - Non Canadian	18,191.53	1.66%	868.84	4.78%
Non-Traditional Capital Preservation	63,273.24	5.76%	2,248.77	3.55%
Capital Preservation	534,083.46	48.62%	12,899.36	2.42%
Equities - Canadian	178,314.04	16.23%	6,542.27	3.67%
Equities - U.S.	240,435.74	21.89%	3,835.93	1.60%
Equities - Non North American	89,969.40	8.19%	2,521.16	2.80%
Non-Traditional Capital Appreciation	25,364.28	2.31%	0.00	0.00%

Figure 10.4: A snapshot of my client's portfolio. This is a good example of proper diversification and capital allocation.

CHAPTER 11

INVESTING "TO DOS" AND "NOT TO DOS"

TRY TO FOLLOW THE ADVICE OF PROS

There are literally endless resources available online regarding hot stock picks. In some cases, they are right, and in some cases (more often than not) they are dead wrong. I remember not too many years ago when cannabis stocks were very hot. Everyone was talking about them! I was getting my hair cut one day when my barber, Pedro (the outcome of this story is not pleasant and so I have used a fake name to protect my friend's identity), told me how he had invested $10,000 of his savings into a pot stock called Aurora Cannabis Inc. (ticker: ACB). I asked him, "Man, have you looked at their balance sheet? What is their P/E ratio multiple? Are they underpriced relative to their peers?" (By the way, these are all questions that you should be able to answer now.) He said pot stocks are the future and he will double his investment by the following year. Sadly, Aurora's stock tanked. Figure 11.1 below is Aurora's price chart from the autumn of 2019 to the spring of 2020.

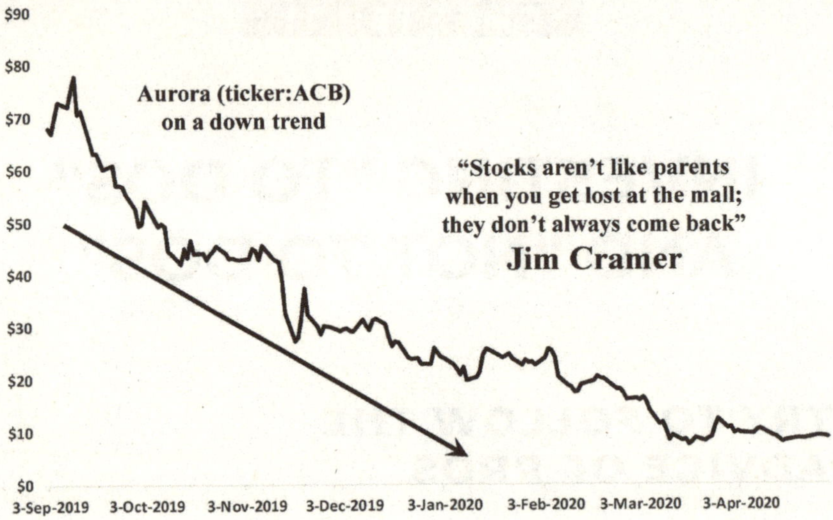

Figure 11.1: Aurora Cannabis Inc. (ticker: ACB) price chart for autumn 2019 to spring 2020.

Truth is, if you hear your barber, uncle or aunt talking about a stock, it is probably not a good idea to invest in it. I believe you should look to investment professionals and try to understand the reasoning behind their holdings and portfolios. As an example, you can know what Warren Buffett is investing in by reading his annual letter.

You can access his annual letters by going to this link and downloading the letter for the most recent year (as well as past years if you are so inclined): *berkshirehathaway.com/letters/letters.html*

If you scroll down through the letter, you will see a list of every stock that Buffett owns. As you will note, these are mostly well-known brands with strong balance sheets which at the time of purchase were considered undervalued. Buffett's investment strategy is simple yet effective. He invests in businesses he understands and he makes sure the companies he selects have pricing power. He puts it this way:

> *"If you've got the power to raise prices without losing business to a competitor, you've got a very good business. And if you have to have a prayer session before raising the price by 10 percent, then you've got a terrible business."*

Aside from Warren Buffett, you could follow the stock sales and purchases of any number of well-known investors. Mark Cuban, for example, revealed during the COVID-19 market crash in 2020 that he had purchased shares in Twitter Inc. (ticker: TWTR) and Live Nation Entertainment, Inc. (ticker: LYV). In addition, you could also read major investment banks' ratings regarding the stocks they cover. Point being, do not take advice from your barber, rather seek advice from professional investors.

BE CAUTIOUS WITH MESSAGING BOARDS

As Andrew mentioned in his day trading chapters of this book, becoming part of a community is very important when starting your career as a day trader. The same goes for swing trading and investing. It is a great idea to be part of a community where you can discuss trade ideas with one another and review each other's strategies. After all, we humans are a social species and work better when we collaborate. While I encourage you to be part of a community, I want to warn you about mirroring people's trades. Be cautious of other people making decisions for you and ensure you are making use all of the necessary tools you have learned in this book before entering into a trade. I have many stories of close friends of mine who have bought stocks or engaged in a trade just because of what they had heard from other people. Whether it is a "hot" stock like weed or Bitcoin was in their day, or a long-established and reliable entity, be cautious, and make the final decision to invest based on your own analytical thinking and the research you have conducted. Do not buy a stock just because everyone else in the community is telling you to do so.

DO NOT TRUST THE ANALYSTS AS MUCH

Over the course of this book, I have mentioned many resources that you can use to help you in your stock picking decision making. You could also review analysts' expectations and their ratings. You could get your hands on equity research reports published on different companies. CNBC has many excellent shows where there are tips given on how to find the right stocks. I even recommend watching Jim Cramer's show, *Mad Money*, for certain investing ideas. But despite the plethora of resources, you have to be the one who does the thinking. You cannot merely rely on the analysts of Wall Street.

Analysts can sell a BUY recommendation to anyone with money (and you can only shop around sell recommendations to people who actually hold the stock already), hence the number of buy recommendations far outweigh the number of sell recommendations. So, if you issue an opinion to buy a stock, you can shop that opinion to literally anyone with money. But, if you issue a sell recommendation, your target audience shrinks dramatically.

Moreover, as a group, analysts are often wrong about the timing of buys and sells. In 2005, Zacks Investment Research conducted a survey to find out whether buy-recommended stocks outperform sell-recommended stocks. You may guess that the demarcation between these two extremes is wide enough that this question doesn't need to be asked, but you'd be wrong. In a 2005 article entitled, "Analysts Keep Misfiring with 'Sell' Ratings", *The Wall Street Journal* found that stocks with a large proportion of sell ratings (that is, with more sell ratings than buy or hold ratings) performed better than stocks with no sell ratings and only buy or hold ratings.

The moral of this story: ensure you do your research before relying on any of the so-called "experts" out there.

DO NOT GO BOTTOM FISHING

Whether you are investing or trading, it is always tempting to buy a stock in a downward trend because you feel like you are getting a good deal. Some may call it "timing the market", but I like to call it "bottom fishing". In almost all cases, it is impossible to catch the bottom and enter the trade at that point. Security prices do not fall in a straight line. They often bounce back a few percentage points, by attracting new buyers, but eventually end up going even lower. At times, the stock of a company will go down but never bounce back. It is important to note, however, that on rare occasions, where you have done your homework, and know the underlying business fundamentals are solid, you could increase your position once the stock price goes down. Similar to a pair of expensive shoes at the mall, a sale price tag is not always a bad sign.

HAVE SOME DIVIDEND-PAYING STOCKS OR ETFS IN YOUR PORTFOLIO

Earlier, in the second chapter, I quoted Kevin O'Leary and why he only invests in companies that pay dividends. No portfolio would be complete without a dividend steady cash flow. In this section, I will introduce you to some of my favorite dividend-paying stocks and ETFs to help you get your portfolio off the ground.

Warren Buffett bought stock in The Coca-Cola Company (ticker: KO) in 1988. His effective dividend yield today on those original shares is over 60%. In other words, he now receives more in KO dividends every 1.7 years than the grand total that he paid for his original shares. KO is a special kind of dividend stock. It is a "Dividend Aristocrat", one of an elite group of companies that have raised their dividends every year for the past 25 years. Other Dividend Aristocrats include McDonald's Corporation (ticker: MCD) and Johnson & Johnson (ticker: JNJ). Chevron Corporation (ticker: CVX) is one of my favorites. It is an energy conglomerate that has a steady cash flow and a dividend yield of 6%. Being a conglomerate allows it to easily maneuver through the times when oil prices are falling.

There's an easy way to own a piece of every Dividend Aristocrat: just buy shares of ProShares S&P 500 Dividend Aristocrats ETF (ticker: NOBL). It trades just like a stock, and you can purchase it using any brokerage account.

As an example, if you are near retirement, or if you are looking for a steady cash flow, you could try investing in ETFs that pay you a dividend. The Vanguard Group offers some of the best dividend-paying ETFs in the market, and they all come with a very low expense ratio.

The Vanguard Dividend Appreciation ETF (ticker: VIG) tracks the performance of the Nasdaq US Dividend Achievers Select index. The focus of the fund is in tracking stocks of companies that have a history of growing their dividends year-over-year. The expense ratio of this ETF is at 0.06 percent (as at May 29, 2020). The current annual dividend yield for the fund is 1.81 percent and dividends are paid out every quarter. As of June 30, 2020, the fund comprises 214 stocks and the total net assets are more than $51 billion.

The Vanguard High Dividend Yield ETF (ticker: VYM) tracks the performance of the FTSE High Dividend Yield index. It offers a convenient way for investors to include international stock exposure in their portfolios while enjoying above-average dividend yields. The expense ratio for this fund is at 0.06 percent (as of February 27, 2020). The current annual dividend yield for the fund sits at 3.26 percent and pays out every quarter. This is double what you would get from government backed securities such as GICs or Treasury bills. Investing in this fund offers equity sector diversification with the largest percentages invested in stocks in the Financials, Health Care and Consumer Goods Sectors (Vanguard uses a somewhat different classification system than the Global Industry Classification Standard discussed in Chapters 9 and 10).

The SPDR S&P Dividend ETF (ticker: SDY) tracks the performance of the S&P High Yield Dividend Aristocrats index. It focuses on companies that have a track record of increasing their dividends every year for at least the past 20 years. The stocks are weighted by yield. The SDY exchange-traded fund has an expense ratio similar to VYM at 0.35 percent. Dividends are distributed quarterly, and the current annual dividend yield is 2.47

percent. It consists of 118 holdings (as at June 30, 2020) with the fund's total net assets sitting at nearly $18.3 million.

I began this section of the book with the recommendation that if you are near retirement, or if you are looking for a steady cash flow, you could try investing in ETFs that pay you a dividend. As you can see, there is more than one option available (and there are many more options than just these three ETFs that I have highlighted). In constructing your investment portfolio, there will always be many credible options to choose from. Depending on your risk tolerance and investment goals, you may find one option to be more appealing than another. I do not want to make your investment decisions for you, but I do want to give you the necessary tools to make the right decisions based on your goals and risk profile.

It is instrumental to the success of your portfolio though that it contain dividend-paying stocks or ETFs. I hope that the stories I have referenced regarding Kevin O'Leary and Warren Buffett will inspire you.

CHECK A COMPANY'S CREDIT RATING

There are two ways for a company to raise capital: through equity or through debt. They can either issue and sell new shares, and thus dilute the holdings of existing shareholders, or they can raise debt and, of course, thus pay interest. A company's debt gets sold as corporate bonds in the bond market. Many of the companies I have mentioned throughout this book have issued corporate bonds. To comply with government regulations, rating agencies give ratings to bonds based on their riskiness. Set out below as Figure 11.2 is the rating metrics:

Moody's	S&P	Definition	Notes
Aaa	AAA	Highest rating	Investment grade
Aa	AA	Very high quality	
A	A	High Quality	
Baa	BBB	Minimum investment grade	
Ba	BB	Low grade	Below investment grade
B	B	Speculative	
Caa	CCC	Substantial risk	
Ca	CC	Poor quality	
C	D	Imminent default	

Figure 11.2: The standard credit ratings given to bonds issued by companies for selling off their debt. Your goal is to only include investment grade bonds in your long-term investment portfolio.

These ratings are based on a company's ability to pay off its debt. Remember that looking at a company's debt rating should be in combination with all of the other techniques I taught you in Chapter 9. It cannot be your deciding factor. The reason for that is, as I wrote not too many pages earlier, before the crash of 2008, many mortgage-backed securities had investment grade ratings but were basically "junk". Although you must sign up with either rating agency first, you can find corporate bond ratings on the websites for S&P Global Ratings (*spglobal.com/ratings/en/index*) and Moody's (moodys.com).

BE PATIENT

When you are investing in the stock market, patience is key. It is very important to understand the history of the market and know that short-term volatility should not impact your decision making. During the crash of 2020, I had many panicked clients and friends calling me for advice. While there is no cookie-cutter answer to help everyone out during such a difficult time, my answer always included a comment about the need for patience. The situation is a bit different though if you are nearing retirement and require immediate liquidity. Looking at the data for the last 100 years, you can observe that markets have almost always bounced back after a down year, with the only exception being 1973 and 1974, when the markets dropped in value for two consecutive years. Never forget that the markets are a future-looking mechanism and often recover faster than the economy itself. If you have done your research and have selected your stocks accordingly, be patient, and expect the market to recover.

CONCLUSION

Congratulations! You have made it to the final chapter. By now you should have a clear understanding of the stock market and what it takes for a modern trader and/or investor to be successful in it. Whether you read this book so that you can sound smart at a cocktail party, or you want to manage the fortune you inherited, or you desire to carefully grow your savings account as you prepare for retirement, you should now have all of the foundational information necessary to begin taking the next steps. By no means though is this book meant to stand on its own and be a comprehensive handbook that makes any further education unnecessary. Success in the financial markets is a methodical *evolution* and not a fast-paced *revolution*.

One of the main goals I had while writing this book was to make a clear distinction between trading and investing. This is the most important lesson you can learn from reading my book. I have seen too many hopeful people enter the stock market but then become confused about what exactly it is that they want out of it. Before entering the market, you should define your timeline and methodology. Similar to a contact sport such as football, before you enter the field you should know your line up and the plays you will implement. One of the most dangerous mistakes beginners make is not defining who they are and why they are in the market. Many so-called "investors" get scared and sell their position at a loss in a market sell off, when they should have had a longer term horizon and not been distracted by sudden market movements. Similarly, many so-called "traders" do not take profit in a rally because they fall in love with their position and end up giving all of their gains back to the market.

So, before opening a brokerage account, ask yourself: Are you opening an account to be a trader? To be an investor? Or to be both? The answers to these very important questions are critical. Knowing the answers will save you many hassles in the beginning and will save you considerable money in the long term.

In addition, you must define your goals and your timeline. You must also be transparent with yourself. Before you enter the stock market, you need to be able to manage your expectations or you will lose money. If you are looking for a get-rich-quick scheme where you will become financially independent after a few months of investing or trading, you quite frankly wasted your time reading this book. I have never met anyone who became rich overnight. In light of the 2020 COVID-19 pandemic and social distancing guidelines, I would like to reiterate what was presented earlier. You must, you really must stay away from anyone who tells you that the stock market is a get-rich-quick scheme. Remember the figure that Andrew used in chapter 5?

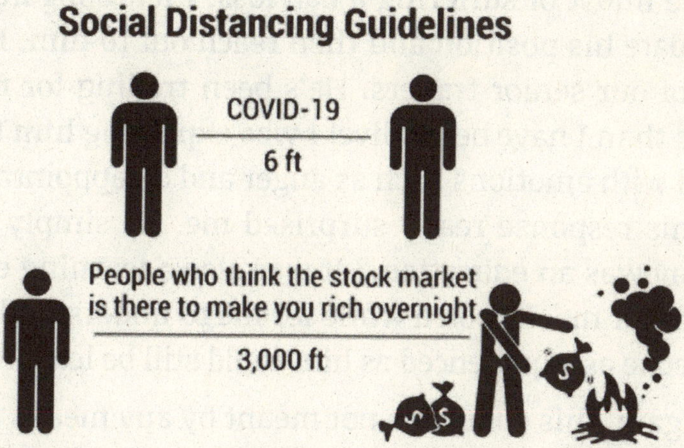

Figure 5.1: Images of a social distancing guideline related to COVID-19 (to protect your health), and a social distancing guideline related to those who want to make you rich overnight via the stock market (to protect your wealth). (For my non-American friends, 6 feet is about 1.8 meters, and 3,000 feet is about 900 meters.)

Andrew compares trading to starting a new career. I love this analogy because it perfectly captures the difficulties inherent in this field. As Andrew has written elsewhere, have you ever met a doctor who went to medical school and graduated after only a few months? Would you expect to become a qualified engineer after taking only one class? No, of course not. Thus, approach entering the market with the same caution and expectations. There is so much to learn. You must treat every day as a learning opportunity.

At Peak Capital Trading, I look over all of our traders' accounts and ensure they are within the risk parameters set by the firm and its investors. I still remember the day when one of our more experienced traders was in the midst of suffering a bad loss. I felt obligated to liquidate his position and then reach out to him. He is one of our senior traders. He's been trading for more years than I have been alive! I was expecting him to be filled with emotions such as anger and disappointment, but his response really surprised me. He simply said, "Today was an education." It was also a learning experience for me. It took a while for me to understand that someone as experienced as him could still be learning.

Again, this volume is not meant by any means to be a stand-alone book. I am a firm believer in the maxim that learning is a journey and not a destination. I spent five years at university studying finance and the markets. Once I started working, I realized that what we discussed at school only covered a small part of the overall picture. If there is one thing that I know for sure is that there will never be a day that I am confident that I know everything about the market.

I am humbled by the market every day. I spent most of my career being a Tesla denier and not recommending it to my clients nor owning any of its shares in my own portfolio. The run that Tesla Inc. (ticker: TSLA) had in 2019-2020 humbled me and made me realize that despite how much I thought I knew about the market, I could still be wrong.

There is no one book that can teach you everything. You might agree with some of the strategies taught in this book and disagree with others. Andrew and I certainly do not see eye to eye on every single strategy. Andrew has mentioned in his previous books, for example, how he does not believe in strategies such as Head and Shoulders and Cup and Handle. In contrast, I often make use of these patterns in order to decide on my entries for a position. There is no one correct way about going about stock market, but for sure there is one wrong way and that is not getting started.

The market is your opportunity to acquire a piece of the world's largest economy and get ahead in life. My only wish is that this book breaks the stigma and fear surrounding the market and gives you the confidence to get started. As you commence your journey of becoming a savvy participant in the market, I trust (and hope!) that you are prepared to be continuously learning and improving.

Be patient. Patience and discipline are not always popular or fashionable in investing and trading, but a patient, disciplined approach is the superior one. Remember, similar to starting any new career, the goal in the beginning is to simply learn. Just like the saying goes, you need to crawl before you can walk. Be patient with the processes and manage your risk accordingly. I myself am inspired by this comment from the actor, Will Smith:

> *"You don't set out to build a wall. You don't say, 'I'm going to build the biggest, baddest, greatest wall that's ever been built.' You don't start there. You say, 'I'm going to lay this brick as perfectly as a brick can be laid.' You do that every single day. And soon you have a wall."*

Your small actions every single day will have a compounding effect and, when repeated, can lead to something truly magnificent. If you tackle the market in the same manner, I have no doubt in my mind that you will become successful. Don't set out to be the next Warren Buffett, but instead aim to grow by learning something new every day. This book is only one of the bricks you need to build your wall of success in the stock market. Is your mortar ready?

If you have read this book and now feel overwhelmed and wonder whether it's possible to be an investor or a trader, please, do not feel discouraged. This book can still be beneficial if a bank or other professional firm manages your money. You have taken a huge new step toward understanding the stock market and improving your own financial literacy. At the minimum, you now have the necessary knowledge to engage in an intellectual talk with your financial planner. You now understand the importance of opportunity cost, and differing returns, and risk profile, and you can ensure that your financial planner is making the right decisions for you and your family. Make sure to use what you have learned in this book so that you can ask the right questions and have your money invested in products that are best for you. As I mentioned earlier, many banks do not have a fiduciary duty toward you, and they will sell you investment products that have the highest margins for them instead of the highest returns for you.

Last but not least, if you enjoyed reading this book and found it useful, I would very much appreciate your taking a few minutes to write a review on Amazon's website. The success of a book like this is based on honest reviews, and I will consider your comments in making revisions. Your review on Amazon will also help other people to make informed decisions about this book. My goal is to update the book regularly and implement your feedback in upcoming editions.

As a thank you, please send me an email and I will send you some supplemental presentation material that I have created to go along with this book. I can also add you to the mailing list for our biweekly newsletter, where we discuss markets, investment opportunities, and potential risks that every market participant needs to know.

I am well compensated in my work and do not view this book as a money-making venture. I purposefully priced this book at the lowest price allowed on Amazon so that it can be as affordable as possible. I am a firm believer that education should be free, as it is the only equalizer in the path to prosperity and eradicating poverty. If it was not for my own relatively inexpensive education at a Canadian university, I would have never been able to be where I am at today.

If you have any feedback, suggestions, or simply want to connect with me, feel free to send me an email at *ardi@peakcapitaltrading.com*. I enjoy getting to know my readers and sharing any advice I might have to help them with their journey.

Thank you, and happy trading! And investing!

GLOSSARY

A

ALPHA STOCK: a Stock in Play, a stock that is moving independently of both the overall market and its sector, the market is not able to control it, these are the stocks day traders look for.

ASK: the price sellers are demanding in order to sell their stock, it's always higher than the bid price.

AVERAGE DAILY VOLUME: the average number of shares traded each day in a particular stock, I don't trade stocks with an average daily volume of less than 500,000 shares, as a day trader you need sufficient liquidity to be able to get in and out of the stock without difficulty.

AVERAGE RELATIVE VOLUME: how much of the stock is trading compared to its normal volume, I don't trade in stocks with an average relative volume of less than 1.5, which means the stock is trading at least 1.5 times its normal daily volume.

AVERAGING DOWN: adding more shares to your losing position in order to lower the average cost of your position, with the hope of selling it at break-even in the next rally in your favor.

B

BEAR: a seller or short seller of stock, if you hear the market is bear it means the entire stock market is losing value because the sellers or short sellers are selling their stocks, in other words, the sellers are in control.

BEARISH CANDLESTICK: a candlestick with a big filled body demonstrating that the open was at a high and the close was at a low, it tells you that the sellers are in control of the price and it is not a good time to buy.

BEAR MARKET: When different indices in the market drop more than 20% in value.

BETA: In simple words, beta is riskiness of a stock, in compare to overall market. It is a mathematical regression of the stock weekly, monthly or daily return, regressed over the return of the overall market.

BID: the price people are willing to pay to purchase a stock at a particular time, it's always lower than the ask price.

BID-ASK SPREAD: the difference between what people are willing to pay to purchase a particular stock and what other people are demanding in order to sell that stock at any given moment, it can change throughout the trading day.

BOTTOMING: this is an expression used when the stock, or a specific market index, break their losing streak, and start rebounding. Many day and swing traders try to guess when a stock bottoms to take the reversal trade in the opposite side to maximize their profits.

BROKER: the company who buys and sells stocks for you at the Exchange.

BULL: a buyer of stock, if you hear the market is bull it means the entire stock market is gaining value because the buyers are purchasing stocks, in other words, the buyers are in control.

BULL FLAG: a type of candlestick pattern that resembles a flag on a pole, you will see several large candles going up (like a pole) and a series of small candles moving sideways (like a flag).

BULLISH CANDLESTICK: a candlestick with a large body toward the upside, it tells you that the buyers are in control of the price and will likely keep pushing the price up, Figure 6.1 includes an image of a bullish candlestick.

BUYING LONG: buying a stock in the hope that its price will go higher.

BUYING POWER: the capital (money) in your account with your broker plus the leverage they provide you, for example, if your broker gives you a leverage of 4:1 and you have $25,000 in your account, you can actually trade up to $100,000.

C

CANDLESTICK: a very common way to chart the price of stocks, it allows you to easily see the opening price, the highest price in a given time period, the lowest price in that time period and the closing price value for each time period you wish to display, some people prefer using other methods of charting, I quite like candlesticks because they are an easy-to-decipher picture of the price action, you can easily compare the relationship between the open and close as well as the high and the low price.

CAPITAL STRUCTURE: this ratio shows how much of a company is financed by equity and how much of it is financed by debt.

Capital Structure=(Long Term Debt)/(Long Term Debt+Share Holder's Equity)

CASH FLOW FROM OPERATION: This is the cash the company generates from its operation. This is the cash it has, after it pays all of its suppliers and other related costs.

CHATROOM: a community of traders, many of which can be found on the Internet.

CHOPPY PRICE ACTION: stocks trading with very high frequency and small movements of price, day traders avoid stocks with choppy price action, they are being controlled by the institutional traders of Wall Street.

CLOSE: the last hour the stock market is open, 3 p.m. to 4 p.m. New York time, the daily closing prices tend to reflect the opinion of Wall Street traders on the value of stocks.

COMMISSION-FREE BROKER: a relatively new type of broker which does not charge a commission for each trade you make, they are not suitable for day trading as they generally do not provide the fast execution of trades that day traders need, with that said, they have revolutionized the trading industry by forcing established players to either abolish or significantly reduce their commissions.

CONSOLIDATION PERIOD: this happens when the traders who bought stocks at a lower price are selling and taking their profits while at the same time the price of the stock is not sharply decreasing because buyers are still entering into trades and the sellers are not yet in control of the price.

CORRELATION: Correlation, in the finance and investment industries, is a statistic that measures the degree to which two securities move in relation to each other. As a rule of thumb, remember that bonds and fixed incomes have a negative correlation (smart way of saying relationship) with one another.

CURRENT RATIO: this is a very important ratio that shows solvency of a business and its ability to cover its short-term obligation. The formula is as follows:

Current Ratio=(Total Current Asset)/(Total Current Liability)

D

DAY TRADING: the serious business of trading stocks that are moving in a relatively predictable manner, all of your trading is done during one trading day, you do not hold any stocks overnight, any stocks you purchase during the day must be sold by the end of the trading day.

DISCOUNTED CASHFLOW MODEL: this a model most of the investment banks in the Wall Street used to value companies. This model forecast revenues and costs of the business into the future (usually 5 to 10 years), and then discount it back using an appropriate discount rate. Understanding the basis of this model can help you in reading other analysts reports.

DIVERSIFICATION: Choosing different stocks, bonds, and assets to protect your portfolio from downturn in one specific sector or asset class. For example, having government bond to protect your portfolio from potential downturn in the stock market.

DIVIDEND ARISTOCRAT: elite group of companies that have raised their dividends every year for the past 25 years.

DIVIDEND YIELD: Dividend per share divided by the share price. As an example, if a company's share is trading at $10, and is paying $1 per share in annual dividend, its dividend yield is 10%.

DOJI: an important candlestick pattern that comes in various shapes or forms but are all characterized by having either no body or a very small body, a Doji indicates indecision and means that a fight is underway between the buyers and the sellers.

E

ENTRY POINT: when you recognize a pattern developing on your charts, your entry point is where you enter the trade.

E.T.F: Exchange Traded Fund is a basket of investment that usually tracks an underlying index. As an example, SPY, tracks the S&P500 index, DIA tracks the Dow Jones Industrial Average and so on.

EXCHANGE-TRADED FUND/ETF: an investment fund traded on the Exchange and composed of assets such as stocks or bonds.

EXIT POINT: as you plan your trade, you decide your entry point, where you will enter the trade, and where you will exit the trade.

F

FIXED INCOME OR BONDS: These are assets that will provide you with fixed payments throughout their life.

FLOAT: the number of shares in a particular company available for trading, for example, in June 2020, Apple Inc. had 4.33 billion shares available.

FOREX: the global Foreign Exchange Market where traders trade currencies.

FUNDAMENTAL ANALYSIS: is a method of analyzing a company using macroeconomics and financial factors.

FUNDAMENTAL CATALYST: positive or negative news associated with a stock such as an FDA approval or disapproval, a restructuring, a merger or an acquisition, something significant that will impact its price during the trading day.

G

GAPPERS WATCHLIST: before the market opens, you can tell which stocks are gapping up or down in price, you then search for the fundamental catalysts that explain these price swings, and you build a list of stocks that you will monitor that day for specific day trading opportunities.

GROSS PROFIT MARGIN: Gross margin is a company's gross profit (gross (total) revenue minus cost of goods sold (cost of revenue)) divided by its gross (total) revenue.

GROWTH STOCK: A category of stocks that are growing at a higher rate, do not pay dividend or do share buy backs. They are strictly focused on growth.

H

HEDGING: A hedge is an investment that protects your finances from a risky situation. Hedging is done to minimize or offset the chance that your assets will lose value.

HIGH FREQUENCY TRADING/HFT: the type of trading the computer programmers on Wall Street work away at, creating algorithms and secret formulas to try to manipulate the market.

HIGH RELATIVE VOLUME: stocks that are trading at a volume above their average and above their sector, they are acting independently of their sector and the overall market.

I

ILLIQUID STOCK: a stock that does not have sufficient volume traded during the day, these stocks are hard to sell and buy without a significant slippage in price.

INDECISION CANDLESTICK: a type of candlestick that has similarly sized high wicks and low wicks that are usually larger than the body, they can also be called spinning tops or Dojis and they indicate that the buyers and sellers have equal power and are fighting between themselves, it's important to recognize an indecision candlestick because it may very well indicate a pending price change.

INDICATOR: an indicator is a mathematical calculation based on a stock's price or volume or both, you do not want your charts too cluttered with too many different indicators, keep your charts clean so you can process the information quickly and make decisions very quickly.

INSTITUTIONAL TRADER: the Wall Street investment banks, mutual and hedge fund companies and such, day traders stay away from the stocks that institutional traders are manipulating and dominating (I'll politely call that 'trading' too!).

INTEREST COVERAGE RATIO: The ratio that shows if the company can pay the interest owing on its debt from the cash it earns from its operations.

Interest Coverage Ratio=(Operating Income)/(Interest Expense)

INTRADAY: trading all within the same day, between 9:30 a.m. and 4 p.m. New York time.

INVESTING: investing is the science of taking your money, placing it in an asset class, and hoping to grow it in the short term or the long term. Investing should not be mistaken with trading.

INVESTMENT PHILOSOPHY: This is the methodology each investor defines for him or herself before entering the market. Are you a value investor, growth investor or both?

L

LAGGING INDICATOR: these are indicators that provide you with information on the activity taking place on a stock after the trade happens.

LEADING INDICATOR: a feature of Nasdaq Level 2, it provides you with information on the activity taking place on a stock before the trade happens.

LEVEL 2: Nasdaq TotalView Level 2 data feed, provides you with the leading indicators and information on the activity taking place on a stock before the trade happens as well as important insight into a stock's price action, what type of traders are buying or selling the stock and where the stock is likely to head in the near term.

LEVERAGE: the margin your broker provides you on the money in your account, most brokers provide a leverage of between 3:1 and 6:1, a leverage of 4:1, for example, means if you have $25,000 in your account, you have $100,000 of buying power available to trade with.

LIMIT ORDER: an instruction you give to your broker to buy or sell a specific stock at or better than a set price specified by you, there is a chance the limit order will never be filled if the price moves too quickly after you send your instructions.

LIQUIDITY: successful day traders need liquidity, there must be both a sufficient volume of stock being traded in a particular company and a sufficient number of orders being sent to the Exchanges for filling to ensure you can easily get in and out of a trade, you want plenty of buyers and plenty of sellers all eyeing the same stock.

LONG: an abbreviated form of "buying long", you buy stock in the hope that it will increase in price, to be "*long 100 shares AAPL*" for example is to have bought 100 shares of Apple Inc. in anticipation of their price increasing.

LOW FLOAT STOCK: a stock with a low supply of shares which means that a large demand for shares will easily move the stock's price.

M

MARGIN: the leverage your broker gives you to trade with, for example, if your leverage is 4:1 and you have $25,000 in your account, your margin to trade with is $100,000, margin is like a double-edged sword, it allows you to buy more but it also exposes you to more risk.

MARGIN CALL: a serious warning from your broker that you must avoid getting, your broker will issue you a margin call if you are using leverage and losing money, it means your loss is equal to the original amount of money in your account, you must either add more money to your account or your broker will freeze it.

MARKET CAP/MARKET CAPITALIZATION: a company's market cap is the total dollar value of its outstanding share.

MARKET MAKER: a broker-dealer that offers shares for sale or purchase on the Exchange, the firm holds a certain number of shares of a particular stock in order to facilitate the trading of that stock at the Exchange.

MARKET ORDER: an instruction you give to your broker to immediately buy or sell a specific stock at whatever the current price is at that very moment, I'll emphasize the phrase "whatever the current price is", the price might be to your benefit, it very well might not be though if it has suddenly changed in the time since you gave your instructions to your broker.

MEGA CAP STOCK: a company with a large market capitalization. Few examples are Apple, Amazon and Microsoft.

MICRO-CAP STOCK: a company with a small market capitalization.

MOVING AVERAGE/MA: a widely used indicator in trading that smooths the price of a stock by averaging its past prices, the two basic and most commonly used MAs are the Simple Moving Average (SMA) and the Exponential Moving Average (EMA).

N

NET EQUITY CURVE: your profit and loss after deducting your broker's commissions and fees.

NET PROFIT MARGIN: company's net income divided by its gross (total) revenue.

O

OPEN: the first thirty to sixty minutes the stock market is open, from 9:30 a.m. up to 10:30 a.m. New York time.

OPENING RANGE: when the market opens, Stocks in Play will often experience what I call violent price action, heavy trading will impact the price of the stock and you should be able to determine what direction the price is heading toward and whether the buyers or sellers are winning.

OPTIONS: a different type of trading, it's trading in contracts that give a person a right, but not a duty or requirement, to buy or sell a stock at a certain price by a specific date.

OVER-THE-COUNTER (OTC) MARKET: most day traders do not trade in the OTC market, it's a specific market used to trade in such items as currencies, bonds and interest rates.

P

PENNY STOCK: the shares of small companies that can trade at very low prices, the prices can be very easily manipulated and follow no pattern or rule whatsoever, fraud is rampant in penny stock trading, day traders do not trade penny stocks.

POSITION SIZING: refers to how large of a position you can take per trade, it's a technique and skill that new traders must develop.

PRICE ACTION: the movement in price of a stock, I prefer using candlesticks to chart the price action of a stock, capturing its highs and lows and the relationship between the open and close.

PRICE TO SALE RATIO: This ratio is calculated by dividing a company's market capitalization by its total sales in a given year. Like the P/E ratio, the P/S ratio is also widely reported.

PROFIT TARGET: as a trader, you should have a daily profit target and once you reach it, don't be greedy and risk it, you can turn off your computer and enjoy the rest of your day, in addition, for each trade you set up, you should have a specific profit target that your strategy is based upon.

PROFIT-TO-LOSS RATIO: the key to successful day trading is finding stocks that have excellent profit-to-loss ratios, these are the stocks with a low-risk entry and a high reward potential, for example, a 3:1 ratio means you will risk $100 but have the potential to earn $300, a 2:1 ratio is the minimum I will ever trade, also called risk/reward ratio or win:lose ratio.

R

REAL TIME MARKET DATA: to be a successful day trader, you need access to real time market data (that you usually must pay for), without any delay, as you will be making decisions and entering and exiting trades literally in minutes, swing traders on the other hand, who enter and exit trades within days or weeks, need only have access to end-of-day data, and that data is available for free on the Internet.

RETAIL TRADER: individual traders who do not work for a firm do not manage other people's money.

RISK MANAGEMENT: one of the most important skills that a successful trader must master, you must find low-risk trading setups with a high reward potential, each trading day you are managing your risk.

RISK/REWARD RATIO: the key to successful trading is finding trading setups that have excellent risk/reward ratios, these are the trading opportunities with a low-risk entry and a high reward potential, for example, a 3:1 ratio means you will risk $100 but have the potential to earn $300.

S

SCANNER: the software you program with various criteria to find specific stocks.

SHORT: an abbreviated form of "short selling", you borrow shares from your broker, sell them, and hope that the price goes even lower so you can buy them back at a lower price, return the shares to your broker and keep the profit for yourself, to say "*I am short AAPL*" for example means you have borrowed and then sold shares in Apple Inc. and are hoping their price goes even lower.

SHORT INTEREST: the quantity of shares in a stock that have been sold short but not yet covered, it is usually reported at the end of the day.

SHORT SELLING: you borrow shares from your broker and sell them, and then hope the price goes even lower so you can buy them back at the lower price, return the shares to your broker and keep the profit for yourself.

SHORT SELLING RESTRICTION/SSR: a restriction placed on a stock when it is down 10% or more from the previous day's closing price, regulators and the Exchanges place restrictions on the short selling of a stock when its price is dropping, when a stock is in SSR mode, you are still allowed to sell short the stock, but you can only short when the price is going higher, not lower, intraday.

SHORT SQUEEZE: occurs when the short sellers panic and are scrambling to return their borrowed shares to their brokers, their actions cause prices to increase quickly and dangerously, you want to avoid being stuck short in a short squeeze, what you do want to do is ride the squeeze when the price quickly reverses.

SIMPLE MOVING AVERAGE/SMA: a form of moving average that is calculated by adding up the closing price of a stock for a number of time periods and then dividing that figure by the actual number of time periods.

SIZE: the "size" column on your Level 2 will indicate how many standard lots of shares (100 shares = 1 standard lot) are being offered for sale or purchase, a "4" for example means 400 shares.

SMALL CAP STOCK: a stock with a low supply of shares which means that a large demand for shares will easily move the stock's price, the stock's price is very volatile and can move fast, most small cap stocks are under $10, some day traders love small cap stocks but do note that they can be really risky, they can also be called low float stocks or micro-cap stocks.

SOCIAL DISTANCING: for traders, social distancing means staying very far away from anyone who thinks the stock market is a get-rich-quick scheme, in light of the 2020 COVID-19 pandemic and social distancing guidelines, protect your wealth by staying away from anyone who think stocks are designed to help you get rich overnight.

STANDARD LOT: 100 shares, the "size" column on your Level 2 will indicate how many standard lots of shares are being offered for sale or purchase, a "4" for example means 400 shares.

STOCK IN PLAY: this is what you as a trader are looking for, a Stock in Play is a stock that offers excellent risk/reward opportunities, it will move higher or lower in price during the course of the trading day and it will move in a way that is predictable, stocks with fundamental catalysts (some positive or negative news associated with them such as an FDA approval or disapproval, a restructuring, a merger or an acquisition) are often Stocks in Play.

STOP LOSS: the price level when you must accept a loss and get out of the trade.

SUPPORT OR RESISTANCE LEVEL: this is the level that the price of a specific stock usually does not go higher than (resistance level) or lower than (support level), stocks often bounce and change the direction of their price when they reach a support or resistance level.

SWING TRADING: the serious business of trading stocks that you hold for a period of time, generally from one day to a few weeks, swing trading is a completely different business than day trading is which are both different from investing.

T

TECHNICAL ANALYSIS: is a method of identify entry points based on charts and indicators.

TICKER: short abbreviations of usually one to five letters that represent the stock at the Exchange, all stocks have ticker symbols, Apple Inc.'s ticker for example is AAPL.

TRADE PLAN/TRADING PLAN: the plan you develop before you actually enter a trade.

TRADING PLATFORM: a software that traders use for sending orders to the Exchange, brokers will offer you a trading platform that is sometimes for free but often for a fee, platforms are either web-based or as a software that needs to be installed on your computer.

V

VALUE STOCK: Stocks that are well established and are at the maturity age of their life cycle.

VOLUME WEIGHTED AVERAGE PRICE/VWAP: VWAP is a moving average that takes into account the volume of the shares being traded at any given price, while other moving averages are calculated based only on the price of the stock on the chart, VWAP considers the number of shares in the stock being traded at each price, VWAP lets you know if the buyers or the sellers are in control of the price action.

W

WARRANT: a tool used to purchase shares in the future at a set price.

WATCHLIST: before the market opens, you can tell which stocks are gapping up or down in price, you then search for the fundamental catalysts that explain these price swings, and you build a list of stocks that you will monitor that day for specific day trading opportunities.